PREFACE

This is a work of love. It stems from the many
decades of both effort and affection that we as social
anthropologists have invested in Jews in the Middle
East. Our combined years in this field of scholarship
are now around forty. Our major concerns have been in
uncovering the nature of ongoing present-day life and
culture of Middle Eastern Jews, mainly in Israel, but
also in some parts of the Diaspora, the United States
and Mexico. On this subject, each of us has over the
years published many ethnographic studies. Both of
us, however, have also entertained a strong interest
in Jewish social history and an early part of our
training was in that area, Deshen at the Hebrew University in Jerusalem and Zenner at the Jewish Theological
Seminary in New York. Many of our ethnographic writings, over the years, have touched on points of history,
and have relied on the work of social historians.
Sometimes, we actually engaged in primary source research, and currently, one of us is engaged in a major
project entailing research on rabbinic responsa. In
the present volume, we have let that old flirtation of
ours out of the closet.

We have gathered here studies that describe the
life and culture of Jews in the traditional Middle East,
which no more exist. These are studies that we found
useful when teaching undergraduate courses on the
Middle East and on traditional Jews. While some of the
articles included are fairly recent, some are not, and
the latter particularly have, over the years, proved
themselves to be very useful in teaching. We have now
let our interests in, and attraction to, matters
Jewish and Middle Eastern, express themselves in the
noncontemporary materials offered in this volume. We
aim to present well-informed reconstructions of traditional communities, as well as a synthesis of what
anthropologists and historians know about these
societies. The best sources are scattered in a variety
of often inaccessible journals, while some were presented at meetings, and never published. Many years
ago, on one of Deshen's visits to the United States,
we first discussed the need for such a collection of
studies, and over the years the project evolved slowly,
at our leisurely and infrequent meetings.

Our experiences have made us aware of elements
which Middle Eastern Jews share with each other and
with European Jews, as well as of the differences
between Middle Easterners and Europeans, and variations within the Middle East itself. The chapters of
this volume are of two basic varieties. Our introductory chapter and the two by Katz and Sharot present
synthetic overviews of Middle Eastern Jewry and link
studies of these communities with general perspectives
in Middle Eastern and Judaic Studies, as well as in
comparative social science. The remainder of the book
consists of specific case-studies. Most of these concentrate on one aspect of Jewish communal life in a
particular area. Insofar as the literature allows,
we have tried to provide coverage on the internal
affairs of Jewish communities, as well as on relations
between Jews and their non-Jewish neighbors.

We are thankful for the help and cooperation that
many friends have extended to us, primarily the people
of various Middle Eastern Jewish communities whom we
studied over the years. We are also thankful to the
contributors who granted us permission to reproduce,
and in some cases translate their work. Several essays
were translated from the Hebrew by Debbie Golde and
Shlomo Deshen. Robert Carmack and Moshe Shokeid read
a draft of the introductory essay and offered some
valuable suggestions. James Lyons and Helen Hudson of
UPA counseled us on editorial matters. We also acknowledge the help of Joann Somich, Betty Kruger, David
Simms, Karyn Kay, Hadassah Raab and especially of
Harriet Spector who typed the final version. Deshen
acknowledges gratefully the assistance extended to him
by the Bar-Ilan University Research Authority. Finally,
we are thankful to several generations of students of
Deshen at Bar-Ilan and at Tel-Aviv Universities, and
of Zenner at the State University of New York at Albany,
who jointly with us explored the usefulness of these
and many other articles.

                    Shlomo Deshen and Walter P. Zenner

JEWISH SOCIETIES IN THE MIDDLE EAST

Community, Culture and Authority

Edited by
Shlomo Deshen
Walter P. Zenner

UNIVERSITY
PRESS OF
AMERICA

Copyright © 1982 by

University Press of America, Inc.

P.O. Box 19101, Washington, D.C. 20036

Library of Congress Cataloging in Publication Data
Main entry under title:

Jewish societies in the Middle East.

Bibliography: p.
1. Jews--Arab countries--Addresses, essays, lectures.
2. Arab countries--Ethnic relations--Addresses, essays,
lectures. I. Deshen, Shlomo A. II. Zenner, Walter P.
DS135.A68J44 1982   306'.0899240174927   80-6285
ISBN 0-8191-2578-4
ISBN 0-8191-2579-2 (pbk.

CONTENTS

Preface   iii

CHAPTER 1   INTRODUCTION: THE HISTORICAL
              ETHNOLOGY OF MIDDLE EASTERN JEWS   1
              Walter P. Zenner and Shlomo Deshen

CHAPTER 2   TRADITIONAL SOCIETY AND MODERN
              SOCIETY   35
              Jacob Katz

CHAPTER 3   JUDAISM IN "PRE-MODERN" SOCIETIES   49
              Stephen Sharot

CHAPTER 4   PATRONAGE AND PROTECTION: THE
              STATUS OF JEWS IN PRECOLONIAL
              MOROCCO   85
              Allan R. Meyers

CHAPTER 5   JEWISH EXISTENCE IN A BERBER
              ENVIRONMENT   105
              Moshe Shokeid

CHAPTER 6   THE SOCIAL STRUCTURE OF SOUTHERN
              TUNISIAN JEWRY IN THE EARLY 20TH
              CENTURY   123
              Shlomo Deshen

CHAPTER 7   FROM SHAIKH TO MAZKIR: STRUCTURAL
              CONTINUITY AND ORGANIZATIONAL
              CHANGE IN A TRIPOLITANIAN JEWISH
              COMMUNITY   137
              Harvey Goldberg

CHAPTER 8   JEWS IN LATE OTTOMAN SYRIA:
              EXTERNAL RELATIONS   155
              Walter P. Zenner

v

CONTENTS (Cont'd.)

CHAPTER 9   JEWS IN LATE OTTOMAN SYRIA:
             COMMUNITY, FAMILY AND RELIGION   187
             Walter P. Zenner

CHAPTER 10   THE SOCIAL STRUCTURE OF JEWISH
             EDUCATION IN YEMEN   211
             Shlomo Dov Goitein

CHAPTER 11   THE AUTHORITY OF THE COMMUNITY
             OF SAN'AA IN YEMENITE JEWRY   235
             Yosef Tobi

CHAPTER 12   ASPECTS OF THE SOCIAL LIFE OF
             KURDISH JEWS   251
             Dina Feitelson

CHAPTER 13   FAMILY CONFLICT AND COOPERATION
             IN FOLKSONGS OF KURDISH JEWS   273
             Donna Shai

CHAPTER 14   PRESTIGE AND PIETY IN THE IRANIAN
             SYNAGOGUE   285
             Laurence D. Loeb

CHAPTER 15   THE DOWRY AS CAPITAL ACCUMULATION
             AMONG THE SEPHARDIC JEWS OF
             ISTANBUL, TURKEY   299
             Mark Glazer

             Recommended Readings   311

             Notes on the Editors   321

CHAPTER 1

INTRODUCTION

THE HISTORICAL ETHNOLOGY OF MIDDLE EASTERN JEWRY

W. P. ZENNER and S. DESHEN

An American Jewish soldier was in China
during the Second World War. He walked
into a building one Saturday. Lo and behold,
he saw a small group of Chinese men, chanting
prayers in Hebrew and reading from a scroll.
To his amazement, he realized that they were
Jews. After the service, he went up to the
cantor and told him that he, too, was a Jew.
The cantor looked at him in astonishment and
finally said in broken English: "Funny, you
no look Jewish."

While not true for China in recent times, this
anecdote could, with minor variations, be applied to
the experience of American Jewish tourists in Iran
or Morocco and elsewhere in the non-Western Jewish
world. While the physiognomy of the congregants,
their spoken language, their musical traditions, and
their ways of pronouncing Hebrew may be unfamiliar,
the fact that one is in a synagogue, worshipping with
essentially the same text, is obvious. Clearly,
traditional Jewry is a coat of many colors. Jewish
life, society and culture were different in Morocco
from what they were in Lithuania, in Iraq from
Tunisia, in Galicia from Tripolitania.

Presently, in America, however, and indeed elsewhere also, this is not always generally realized.
All too often, one encounters persons who, while con-
concerned with matters of Jewry and Jewish culture,
conceive that subject in a totally ethnocentric
European-oriented frame. The prevailing conception is
one in which the Eastern European shtetl community is
naturally assumed as a prototype and model of
traditional Jewry on the eve of 19th century modernization and later destruction. In this view
traditional Jewry is seen in a simplified way as congruent to shtetl society. Jewish communities which
differ from that model are deemed to require either
justification or improvement, but they are not perceived for what they are, simply traditional manifestations of Jewry.

1

Moreover, the Eastern European shtetl, as popular-
ized in modern literature, art and theatre, conveys a
romantic picture that is not well-grounded in sober,
historically informed knowledge. The popular prevailing view of traditional Jewry is thus not only
flawed ethnologically, but also historically. The
work of modern historians of Jewry eventually will
diffuse, make its mark, and the popular conception
of the European background of most American Jews will,
as a result, become more sophisticated. On the
ethnological side, however, a great deal more research
needs to be done because the basic work is very meager.
Very few scholars have described in depth the institutions, culture, and life of Jews in the vast belt
between Morocco and India in the period preceding
the incorporation of these countries into the modern
world system, in the 19th and 20th centuries. In
this volume, we propose to bring together some of the
most insightful studies of those communities, both
previously published and unpublished. We aim to contribute toward greater knowledge and understanding in
the area of comparative Jewish ethnology. We have
chosen selections on the following basis: (a) they
contain descriptions of significant social institutions
such as the economy, religion, education, or deal with
important relationships, such as Jewish-Gentile, or
inter-class relations. (b) They are descriptive, with
an orientation to a broad picture of the society and
not merely a collection of disjointed data of a purely
folkloristic or ethnographic nature. (c) They deal
with the penultimate "pre-modern" period. (d) They
are grounded in historically well-informed research.

These points require some elaboration. Histories
of Jews in Muslim lands deal in depth only with
medieval Muslim Spain, and most recently with medieval
Egypt, what is becoming known as Genizah society.
After the 13th century, the historical study of non-
European Jewry is spasmodic. There is a brief treatment of Jews in the 16th century Ottoman empire
(especially Turkey and Palestine) through the reign
of Suleiman the Magnificent. For the late 17th century
we have studies of the background and circumstances of
Sabbatean messianic movements. Therefore, little is
known of Middle Eastern Jewry in historiography except
for the international uproar surrounding the blood
libel against and the arrest of the Damascus Jewish
communal leaders in 1840. While we know that such
countries as Iraq, Tunisia and Morocco contained in

recent centuries a large proportion of the Jewish
people, and that communities such as Fez, Aleppo,
Tunis, and Baghdad were major centers of Jewish culture, our detailed knowledge of these Jewries remains
limited.

In recent decades, sustained interest in our subject has begun to develop. This mainly results from
the immigration of the bulk of Middle Eastern Jewry
to Israel. These people and their cultures have thus
become more exposed to Western Jews and have aroused
both their curiosity and sustained scientific interest.
This interest also is rooted in some of the ongoing
social problems of Israel in the course of immigration
absorption and nation-building. The problems of
absorption have prompted studies of the recent background and culture of the immigrants, many by scholars
whose academic background was applied anthropology
and sociology.

At the time of the mass immigration, for instance,
there was a debate in Israel as to which policy was
best suited to integrate the new immigrants from
Africa and Asia with those from Europe. Some favored
dispersion of immigrants into mixed settlements,
while others suggested settling them into homogeneous
villages and neighborhoods as sounder in the long run.
The village of Tripolitanian immigrants described
in Chapter 7 by Goldberg is an example of the latter
variety. In Israel one hears such villages described
as islands of underdevelopment. Such communities, it
is sometimes argued, should have been dispersed
immediately. Such arguments, however, do not take
into consideration that alternative policies are not
bereft of problems. In fact, heterogeneous immigrant
communities in Israel and elsewhere have given rise
to serious problems of conflict, apathy, and alienation. The study by Goldberg which is reprinted here,
in fact, demonstrates the positive side of homogeneity,
namely the contentment arising from cultural and social
continuity and stability as opposed to the social upheavals apparent in other immigrant villages. Much of
the research represented in this volume was directed
towards the solution of social problems in Israel,
including some of that by Feitelson, Goitein, Deshen
and Shokeid. At a more profound level, the new
interest in non-Western Jewry is probably also rooted
in the holocaust background of modern Judaic studies.
There may operate a feeling that, after the uprooting

3

of European Jewry, a wide-ranging exploration of
sources of Jewish vitality is called for, and those
traditional Jewries that survived physically intact
to the present arouse special interest.

Most of the authors whose selections we chose
are social scientists, particularly social anthropologists. In most cases, they initially undertook
the investigation of the recent past of their
communities in order to interpret the present situations of Jews from these communities better.
Several investigators studied the communities first
in Israel (Feitelson, Zenner, Goldberg, Deshen,
Goitein, Shai), while a few actually did their field
work in the country of origin (Meyers, Glazer, Loeb).
In some cases, research involved a variety of mater-
ials--historical documents, secondary sources,
supplemented by oral testimonies and the use of the
present situation as a clue to the past. Not all
those using this eclectic approach are anthropologists,
however. Goitein, an Orientalist, in his research
on both the Yemenite Jews and the "Geniza" people,
used a similar approach. A close reading of Goitein's
A Mediterranean Society, (about the society reconstructed through documents from the Cairo Geniza),
will reveal that he used his experiences among Yemenites and other Middle Eastern Jews in Israel, as well
as drawing parallels with American Jewry (1969, 1971).
Our work is thus part of a general effort which,
despite its underdeveloped state, has already borne
some fruit. Some of the best known among these are
the writings of Patai (1971), Hirschberg (1974),
H. J. Cohen (1973), Chouraqui (1968), Stillman (1979),
and also many of the Middle Eastern entries in the
Encyclopaedia Judaica. But we differ from these
workers in our social anthropological perspective.
We are interested in particular details and events
only insofar as these can be integrated into general
presentations. This leads us to discussion on
higher levels of abstraction than ordinarily engaged
in by historians, and thus of course, also to the
problems inherent in historical reconstruction.

Locating "the societies" of which we speak, in
time and space, is often problematic. Sources may
come from more than one community, and localities may
differ from each other. Sources may also refer to
more than one period. In dealing with sources, one
must translate the language of the document into the

language of the social scientist. A document such as a legal inquiry and responsum has problems of its own; it often deals with legal cases which are unique and unusual, yet the social scientist may be tempted to see it as more typical than it is. Use of other materials, such as folklore, oral testimonies, moralistic literature, and travellers' accounts have similar difficulties. Historical reconstruction based on oral reports is a methodologically debatable practice among both historians and anthropologists. Some have argued that such reports express primarily the contemporary conditions of the informants and do not reliably reflect past situations. Others however, view oral reports as valuable sources of information when controlled and used critically through parallel data of other types, primarily written sources and participation-observation. Anthropologists may infer aspects of the culture of the past by observations in the present. For instance, we may see the way in which Iranian Jews compete for honor in their synagogue as a retention of their traditional social life. When such inferences are drawn, as in the chapters by Goldberg, Loeb and Glazer, it is done with the full knowledge that the present context differs in many particulars from the situation fifty or a hundred years ago and that our inference is to be examined with more direct documentation.

Some of the theoretical concerns of social anthropology thus inform the selection of materials that constitute the bulk of this volume, as then do the generalizations we tentatively attempt to draw in this introduction from the historical data. We operate with two sets of concepts, one sociological and one ethnographic. On the sociological plane, we aim to illuminate spheres of social activity, such as political action, economic action, religion and culture, action relative to kinship and to socialization. We are interested in relating our work to general conceptualizations of cultural development. Therefore, we use general models, such as those of Katz and Sharot as well as others discussed in this book, in relation to specific communities. These constructs, however, should be seen as hypotheses to be tested, not as established facts.

Culture Areas of Middle Eastern Jews

In this introduction, we attempt to draw a composite portrait of Jewish culture in the Middle East, that huge "cultural continent" which stretches from Morocco to Afghanistan and which has been dominated by Islam since the seventh and eighth centuries (Patai 1962). Before we proceed, it is important to remember that the Middle East, however it is defined, is a mosaic of many cultures, language groups, and environments. It can be seen as containing a variety of culture areas, and the Jews in the various regions are often very different from each other.

While the concept of "culture area" in social anthropology is problematic, the delineation of such areas provides us with a convenient handle for illustrating the internal diversity of Jewish societies in the Middle East. We will paint the culture areas in broad strokes, stressing the ethnic and linguistic mix, the political map of the pre-modern period, and selected characteristics of the Jewish populations. One area is Morocco, the westernmost part of what is called the Maghreb or "Arab West." This area shares with the eastern Maghreb (Algeria, Tunisia, Tripolitania) an ethnic mix of Arabic- and Berber-speaking peoples. Morocco has maintained a distinct political existence as a separate kingdom for centuries, while the eastern Maghreb fell under the rule, albeit loose at times, of the Ottoman empire. Spain, Portugal, Italy, and France all played important roles in these two areas of northern Africa. While most Jews spoke Maghrebine Arabic, there were important enclaves of Spanish and Italian Jews. As will be noted below, the Jewish communities of these two areas developed different patterns of community leadership and religion. To the east of the Maghreb lies the Fertile Crescent region, including Egypt, Palestine, Syria, and Iraq. In this area, Arabic-speaking Jews and Christians co-existed as minorities alongside the Muslim Arabs (who also were divided by sect). This region, too, was dominated by the Ottoman empire from the 16th century until its dissolution at the end of the First World War. "Turkish Jewry" constitutes a distinctive cultural enclave, marked by the dominance of Jews speaking Ladino (or Judezmo), a language stemming from Spanish and written for a long time in Hebrew characters. The area includes western parts of Anatolia, Greece, Bulgaria, and parts of Yugoslavia.

Here the Jews lived in a polyglot society with Turks,
Greeks, Slavs, Armenians, and others.

Yemen in the southern part of the Arabian peninsula, Kurdistan to the north of the Fertile Crescent,
and "Persia," comprising the Jewries of Iran, Afghanistan, and the Uzbek and Tajik areas of what is now
Soviet Central Asia, constitute still other culture-
areas, numbering seven altogether. These culture
areas comprise the bulk of the Middle Eastern Jewries,
though smaller groupings which are not contained within them can be considered as separate areas or enclaves (e.g. the Jews of Georgia in the Caucasus, the
Egyptian Karaites).

The differences between the culture areas can be
illustrated by briefly comparing the Jews of Kurdistan with those of Yemen. Kurdistan has been one of
the most heterogeneous environments of the Middle
East, comprising various ancient Christian, Muslim,
and other religious sects, besides the Jews. While
the Indo-European Kurdish language is spoken by the
group which gives the area its name, one can also find
Aramaic-speaking Jews and Christians in Kurdistan, as
well as Turks, Arabs, Persians, and Armenians. Each
of these various groups have retained traditional
lifestyles of their own. From the accounts of Kurdish
Jews, we hear of considerable social interaction
between Jews and Gentiles. The communities were small
and people wandered far to make a living. The Jews
of the region did not maintain as closed a cultural
or communal life as was found among the Jews of Yemen.
Internal Jewish communal institutions in Kurdistan
were few and often weakly developed, and Jews of the
region were not noted for their learning. Synagogues
were described as having activities mainly on the
Sabbaths and festivals. The constricted development
of Kurdish Jewish institutions, from the viewpoint of
the Great Tradition, is extreme in terms of Jewish
ethnography (see the chapters by Feitelson and Shai).
It is possible that the "weak" religious institutions
can be explained by the measure of tolerance nurtured
in the peoples of Kurdistan. Consequently, religious
and social pressures on the Jews were not severe and
they were not driven to develop their own defensive
institutions.

Yemenite Jewry stands in sharp contrast to that
of Kurdistan. Yemen appears to have been a much more

closed society than the former. In Yemen, stratifi-
cation was rigid and it is often described as a
virtual caste system. Principles of social and
religious exclusiveness operated among the Jews, just
as it did among their Muslim neighbors. The government of traditional Yemen also put pressure on the
Jews, such as laws which forcibly converted orphaned
children to Islam. The development of many symbols of
Jewish distinctiveness was stimulated by the challenges of the political environment (see the chapters
by Goitein and Tobi, below). While also in the Yemen
formal communal institutions were not highly developed,
the family took on additional roles there. The
educational system, as described by Goitein, Chapter
10, is imbedded in family institutions and fathers
took special care to make sure that their sons were
learned in the Jewish tradition. Yemenite Jewry has
often been characterized as one in which there was a
passionate and virtually uniform attachment to the
Jewish literary tradition.

Let us now summarize the main features of the
major spheres of the social activities of Middle
Eastern Jews mentioned earlier. We start with the
pervasive area of culture and religion.

(a) Jewish Tradition, Literacy and Religion

While we are concerned in this volume with those
features of Jewry that distinguish Middle Eastern
Jewries in particular, it is important to bear in
mind, as Katz (Chapter 2) argues, one major background datum. The Jews of the Middle East constitute
traditional societies, and their major cultural
tradition is common to that of Jews elsewhere, in
Christian environments and in India. It is a characteristic of traditional Jewry, and of traditional
societies generally, not to admit to the fact of
change, to be virtually unaware of it. So that while
Jews everywhere mutated their culture and religion
along with the vicissitudes of their varying existential
situations, they always deemed their particular variant of Judaism to be authentic and legitimate. The
realization that things do actually change, and, more,
the claim that change is legitimate, is by and large
foreign to traditional Jewry. This conception of
cultural reality enabled gradual changes to occur
painlessly, but at the same time, it also stymied
radical breaks with the past. Jewry in traditional

8

times maintained a basic unity that crossed the boundaries of gentile politics and cultures. As late as
the 18th century, we find in Morocco scholars with
European surnames signed together with local dignitaries on legal decisions (and suffixing to their
names the acronym S.T.[1] typical of Middle Eastern
scholarly practice). This attests to the channels of
communication that traditional culture afforded as
late as on the eve of the European Enlightenment,
when national political boundaries began to affect
Jewish culture and consequently to block such
communication.

Until the late 18th century Judaism everywhere
had a basic uniformity. As a socio-religious phenomenon, it was characterized by a precarious balance
between this- and other-wordliness. On the side of
basic spiritual life, there was also a valuation,
albeit qualified and delimited, of achievement in
material matters and in secular scholarship. In
Europe, by the late 19th century, as a result of two
major Jewish religious movements in Eastern Europe,
Hasidism and Musar, this has changed, and the balance
tilted in favor of spirituality and other-wordliness.
On the other hand, powerful forces for secularization
acted for far-reaching disengagement with the whole
world of tradition.

But the Middle East was spared such developments
for over a century or more. Traditional Torah learning remained a requisite practice for self-respect in
many communities and honor and esteem awaited ranking
scholars. Only in the late 19th century were the
effects of European modernization and secularization
beginning to be felt in Middle Eastern Jewry (specifically in Iran, in the Balkans and in Algeria). While
the events in themselves were not entirely different
in Europe and in the Middle East, there was a time lag
between their occurrence. In many Muslim countries,
traditional Jewry remained viable well into the present century, and in some regions, it remained so until
the time of mass emigration in the contemporary period.
In this book, we are concerned mainly with the traditional past, and if one wishes to allude to European
parallels, only those taken from traditional times
are salient.

Also in traditional times, Judaism changed, and
there were differences between various branches of

9

Jewry. These differences were relatively considerable between the major branches of Jewry living in Christian and Muslim societies respectively, and less so within communities of the major divisions. Jews altogether were reluctant to acculturate to their non-Jewish neighbors. There were, however, differences in this attitude. As Sharot (Chapter 3) points out, in Islamic lands, the cultural milieu was comparatively close to that out of which Judaism had developed, while in Europe this was less so. In the Muslim Middle East, Jews were more inclined to acculturation than in Christian Europe. This datum is linked with a fundamental difference between Christianity and Islam. The institutions of Christianity developed first as those of a minority religion, not as the state religion, and later, when it became a state religion, it retained a well-differentiated structure of its own. Particularly, in the West the church became a power center separate from that of the various polities which were forming during the Middle Ages. Thus a clear institutional separation of church and state, even when the two co-operated, came into being. In Islam, no such distinction was made, and overlapping institutions persisted in the more traditional Islamic states virtually into our days. The overlap between sacred and secular which typified Islam, as well as the view that Scripture contained the devine law, were also Jewish. The differentiation of the church from ongoing social concerns often caused medieval Christianity to adopt an aggressive religious stance, whereas the requirements of Islam tended typically to be diluted by the practical requirements of sovereigns. These differences, and the many other more obvious and concrete ones that Sharot outlines, had ramifications in the variety of Jewish expression under Christianity and Islam.

There also are important parallel differences between the intellectual styles of Christendom and Islam on the one hand, and European and Middle Eastern Jewries on the other, which are less well understood. Christianity already in its early phases, could be distinguished from Judaism and Islam by its application of a highly sophisticated casuistry to theological questions (such as the nature of the Trinity and the divine and human essences of Christ). The concern with having a well-defined creed commanding the adherence of all Christians was involved in this process. While medieval Islam and Judaism had a phase of similar concern with doctrine, it was short-lived and no comparable body of dogma or theology grew up within these religions.

Judaism and Islam did, of course, develop sophisticated bodies of legal interpretation. Still, the highly casuistic argumentative style of legal reasoning is more characteristic of medieval European Jewry than of its Middle Eastern counterpart. This style is a distinctive part of the intellectual style of East European Jews and their descendants, perhaps even of those who are secularized (Ben-Sasson 1959:22-23, 171, 191; Zborowski and Herzog 1952:88-104), and one can speculate about its relationship to scholasticism. While the intellectual styles of Middle Eastern Jews have hardly been studied, Goitein's study of Yemeni education gives us some insight into that community (below). More work needs to be done on other communities, comparable to Eickelman's recent study of Muslim academies in Morocco (1978). MAGIC

Another important dichotomy between European and Middle Eastern forms of Judaism lies in the areas of popular religion and mysticism. In Europe, powerful moves to rid Judaism of magical and mystical elements appeared beginning in the 18th century. The Kabbalah came into disrepute in many circles and few rabbis did such things as give amulets for healing. Such a division generally did not occur among Middle Eastern Jews until the period of their mass immigrations to Israel. Among Middle Easter Jews, the hakham or rabbi remained legal authority, scholar and pastoral leader. The roles were not divided. While non-believers and scorners appeared in modernizing communities like Istanbul, Algiers, and Baghdad, many continued to make pilgrimages to the reputed tombs of ancients (such as the two sons of Jacob, said to be buried in Lebanon, or Esther and Mordecai in Iran, and the many tombs of more recent dignitaries in Morocco). Some rabbis in Israel continue to write talismans which protect against "frights" and other diseases.

The various religions of Middle Eastern people are embedded in literate traditions but must appeal to a populace which is either barely literate or illiterate. Among Middle Eastern Jews, certainly since the 17th century (after the decline of Muslim medieval culture), much of the tradition was transmitted orally, rather than through learned texts. European Jews on the other hand, were more dependent on literary texts.

11

In sociological terms, the culture of Middle Eastern
Jews was relatively undifferentiated from other
social institutions. To a considerable degree it was
vested in certain individuals, who, in fulfilling
given social roles, imparted it to their communities.
To a far lesser extent did Middle Eastern Jews
apprehend learned texts, accessible to one and all
for study, as depositories of culture. Typically,
the hagiography of Moroccan rabbis included statements
to the effect that the saintly rabbi, so wise and
learned, solved the most complex problems of ritual
and law without having to have recourse to books.
This kind of praise would have been completely out
of character in other Jewish communities bred more
strongly in the literary tradition. Among Tunisian
Jews, for instance, a parallel hagiography runs something like that: The saintly rabbi, despite the profundity of his wisdom, was so modest and careful, that
he would not resolve the simplest problem without
first having recourse to books. Generally, however,
Middle Eastern Jewry tended toward the Moroccan model,
and European Jewry was parallel to the Tunisiam.
While ideally Jewish boys all over the Middle East
went to school, in some regions the degree of functional literacy achieved was low, such as in Kurdistan or
among the lower classes of Syria and many parts of
North Africa (cf. Feitelson, Chapter 12; Zenner,
below). In other areas, such as Yemen and Southern
Tunisia, a higher level of Hebrew scholarship was
generally achieved (Goitein, Chapter 10; Deshen,
Chapter 6).

The Hebrew word in Scripture and other holy books
had a sanctity and power all its own, whether or not
the reader understood the meaning of the word, and
thus literacy was ritualized (see Deshen, 1975). The
talisman, with its permutations of the divine name and
other sacred words, was an example of this. Another
was the recitation of prayers by those who are illiterate, the reading and study of the Zohar, a highly
mystical text, most of it incomprehensible to the
uninitiated in Kabbalah (Stahl 1979), and the high
respect, close to adoration, known in the synagogue
to the Torah scroll as an artifact.

A common denominator of all traditional Jewish
communities is the illiteracy of women. While girls
and women in their child-rearing years did not go to
the synagogue frequently, women did resort to

hakhamim for their needs. They went to them for
advice, for amulets and talismans to guard against
disease or the evil eye or to protect them against
barreness. Older women were more likely than younger
women to go to the synagogue and make pilgrimages to
the various shrines. Whether one can read into the
participation in the popular religion, especially the
pilgrimages to saints' tombs, a reaction to subordinate status on the part of women and lower-class
men, is a question for further study. The Moroccan
feminist, Fatima Mernissi (1977) argued this quote
cogently for Muslim women, but it needs to be examined
spearately for Jews throughout the Middle East.

The synagogue is the major institution of
traditional Jewry everywhere. Social scientists of
Judaism have understood that synagogues fill a major
role in Jewish societies. Not only are synagogues
vehicles for Jewish religion and other aspects of
Jewish culture, but they also fill important inte-
grative roles, such as encouraging the emergence of
leadership and internal social control. However,
until social scientists began to direct their interests into synagogues, insight did not run much beyond
these generalizations. This was true for studies of
Jews of European and Middle Eastern backgrounds
alike. Anthropological and sociological research on
synagogues of various kinds is just beginning, but
the studies conducted so far have enriched our knowledge as to the dynamics whereby the social functions
that we have mentioned are attained. Examples of
such studies are those on American Ashkenazi
"synagogue life" (Heilman 1976), on Moroccan synagogues
in Israel and Morocco (Shokeid 1971; Deshen in press),
on Israeli Tunisian immigrant synagogues (Deshen 1970;
1974) and on Persian synagogues by Loeb (below).
These studies focus on the intersection of the sacred
and the secular. Politicking, competition for status,
and expression of ethnicity are among the areas
covered. Such activities are found in synagogues
everywhere, although no full-scale comparison of how
they appear has been attempted. Loeb's attempt to
relate the "status juggling" in the Shirazi synagogues
which he observed to traditional Persian Jewish
etiquette should be reproduced elsewhere.

The modes of expressing religious sentiments
differ from area to area in terms of language, pro-
nunciation, musical expression and the various

emphases. Loeb (1976) has attempted to compare the
way in which the different sense are stimulated by
the synagogue rituals of Persian and Yemeni Jews,
including sight, hearing, touch and smell. While
this attempt is premature, one should note that
surrounding the rituals of different groups one does
find such differences. For instance, after some
Syrian Jewish Sabbath synagogue services in both the
U.S. and Israel, there are men who sprinkle each
worshipper's hands with rosewater. This will certainly give the worshipper a different association with
the Sabbath and the synagogue from a service where
this is not done. While such subtleties are ill-
understood, they show the persistent cultural distance
that has existed between different parts of the Middle
East and between the Jews of the Middle East and those
of Europe.

(b) The Economic Basis

The Jews of the Middle East and India, like other
Diaspora Jews, have generally lived as small minority
groups within other societies. Such minorities tend
to specialize in particular crafts or forms of trade,
and this is certainly characteristic of both the
Middle East and India. Parts of the Middle East
have in fact been characterized as having a human
"mosaic" on ethnic and religious lines. There is a
tendency for such small powerless groups to be drawn
into niches in the economy which are not desired by
either the elite or the masses. Positions in these
niches are often those which require unusually hard
work or involve activities that are unpleasant (such
as the work of dyers and tanners who acquire odors
in the course of their work), or activities that are,
for religious reasons (such as processing precious
metals under Islam), looked down upon. Various social
systems dictate a connection between occupation and
ascribed status, and in the Middle East there are
wide differences concerning the extent to which
economic roles are fixed and statuses ascribed to the
Jews.

Goitein (1971) contrasted the relatively fixed,
closed, caste-like character of Yemen in the 19th
century to the competitiveness and openness of
medieval Egyptian society, and Rosen (1972) described
19th and 20th century Morocco as a highly individual-
istic society. However, even where such individualism

is the case, there has been a tendency for Jews in any single area to be concentrated in a fairly limited set of occupations. Early in medieval times, Jews had begun their transformation into a minority which was not landed. The transformation in areas like Palestine and Babylonia (southern Iraq) took place under conditions which are not yet well understood. Goitein suggests that it may have been due to the policies of early Muslim rulers who taxed the non-Muslim peasantry in a discriminatory manner, thus encouraging either conversion to Islam or leaving the land (Goitein 1955a). In a few places, especially mountainous refuge areas, Jews have continued to be agriculturalists, as they had been in Palestine and Babylonia in ancient times. One hears of Jewish cultivation in this century (as a fulltime occupation) in Iraqi Kurdistan, and also some Yemeni Jews farmed, at least as a part time occupation (Feitelson, see below; Goitein, 1955b).

In more recent traditional times, most Middle Eastern Jews were engaged either in the crafts or in trade and commerce. The trades included work with textiles, metals, upholstery, and food preparation. This did not mean, however, that the Jews lived and worked solely in urban areas. Besides the cities, there were Jews in small market towns on the fringes of the Sahara, in the Atlas Mountains of Morocco, throughout the Kurdish areas of Turkey, Iraq and Iran, as well as the Caucasus and Yemen. Even many of the urban Jewish craftsmen, not to mention the peddlers, were itinerants who left their families in town and traveled for extended periods among isolated tribes.

The rural craftsmen and peddlers were "strangers" in Simmel's sense. They had regular relations with the tribesmen whom they served, and they occupied positions in the rural social structure that were reserved for those who were not of the tribe. The positions that Jews occupied, based on fixed relations with the gentiles with whom they interacted, afforded Jews protection from the hazards of life in societies that lacked well-developed formal organs to assure law and order. In many parts of the Middle East, Jewish traders and peddlers maintained variants of client-patron relationships with local potentates and thus assured themselves of minimal security to maintain their activities. These relationships were usually of a particular nature. They required the

15

Jew to offer his wares or services to a certain patron, and in return, the latter extended protection. The patron-client relationship of course froze the economic system and blocked the kind of developments feasible under a free economy. But there were differences of nuance in various parts of the region. In southern Morocco, for instance, Shokeid (Chapter 5) and others describe a system that was relatively closed. The patron-client tie seems to have been formalized and symbolized by a sacrificial act. The Jewish partner established such a tie only with one potentate at a time, and there are indications that such patron-client relationships were often hereditary. In Kurdistan the patron-client tie was even more stifling, and sometimes amounted to virtual serfdom for the Jewish partner (Ben-Yaakov 1961). In the Yemen, on the other hand, one gains the impression that the system was less constricting. Individual Jews established ties with several local dignitaries at one and the same time. Thus, presumably, they were also able to play off one potentate against the other and maintain themselves in relatively greater freedom.

Another facet of the Jews' position in Muslim societies was that they were outside of the hurly-burly of political conflict, including feuds. This role of the institutionalized stranger was one which was commonly suited to smiths, traders, and shamans in many Old World societies. This was an additional source of the protection that the Jew's role of stranger afforded him in Muslim societies (Simmel 1908; Hallpike 1971; Rosen 1972; Chouraqui 1968:131-3; Goldberg 1981). The paradox of the stranger role is that one may be a native of a place and still be a stranger to one's neighbors by virtue of caste and/or religion. The stranger often performs the role of trader, because of the contradiction between the reciprocity expected of kinsmen and the hard-headed-ness required of those dealing with money. Therefore, it is not surprising, for instance, that the Djerban Muslims of Southern Tunisia are grocers and other sorts of retail middlemen in Northern Tunisia, but the local, non-migrant, Jewish population of Djerba provides the local traders on that southern Tunisian isle (Stone 1974; Deshen Chapter 6; Foster 1974). Some Jewish villagers, as well as urbanites, were highly specialized in their occupations. One low-land Yemenite village was described by Goitein (1955b)

16

as a "weaver's village;" the Jewish community of
Habban (south Yemen) was one of itinerant silversmiths
(Loeb 1980), and most of the population of the Jewish
village of Hara Sghira on the Island of Djerba engaged
in the processing of wool (Deshen, Chapter 6).

In the large cities, the economic activities of
Jews were more diversified, but they still tended to
be concentrated in certain branches of the economy.
In Istanbul around 1900, for instance, there were
many Jews who were wholesale and retail traders,
porters, fishermen, boatmen, goldsmiths, jewelers,
and money changers. Also, there were several Jewish
banks, and several "large Jewish houses" were engaged
in the manufacture of novelty items, while cigarette-
cutting was a Jewish specialty. There were factories
for ready-made ware, owned by Viennese Jews, and one
Jew owned a glassworks. While most Jews were poor,
there were also wealthy merchants, manufacturers and
bankers (Broyde and Goldschmidt 1903). As the mention
of the banks and the stock exchanges indicates,
Istanbul is obviously a modernizing community. Nevertheless, such a variegated occupation structure could
also be found in other large Jewish communities in
traditional times, such as medieval Cairo and later
in Damascus, Salonica and Fez.

In their roles as economic middlemen, both as
artisans and as traders, the Jews were subject to the
vagaries of international commerce. The decline of
the caravan trade across the deserts and the severe
competition with European industry had an adverse
effect on many Middle Eastern Jewish communities.
Jewish merchants were often leaders in shipping Middle
Eastern commodities, such as Egyptian cotton and
Syrian silk, to Europe and importing European fabrics,
and Jewish peddlers often brought these European
manufactures into the rural areas of Syria, Turkey,
Kurdistan and elsewhere. The way in which the domination of the Euro-centered world economy affected the
Jews was thus complicated.

(c) The Political System: The Role of the State and
     Interethnic Relations

In the sociological study of "whole societies,"
the ecology and economy is often seen as the basis of
the political system. However, in the study of en-
capsulated, caste-like groups, such as minorities in

17

traditional societies, much of life is determined by the political and material domination of specific wielders of power outside the group.

Jews and Christians living in the Muslim world had a special status, that of dhimmis, members of protected minorities. Stated succinctly, Jews and Christians were tolerated and permitted to practice their religion and earn their livelihood as long as they recognized the authority of the Muslim state and kept a low profile. The maintenance of a low profile varied considerably from period to period. Among the restrictions which recur, one finds that non-Muslims were not permitted to build houses of worship or repair them or to be officials with authority over Muslims. Often we find positively humiliating regulations, such as those that obliged Jews to wear a distinctive garb and prohibited Jews from riding horses or crossing the path of Muslims. Under Shi'ite Islam, Jews were barred from the streets on rainy days (Loeb 1977). There were many places and times in which these regulations were not fully observed. Obviously new churches and synagogues were built from time to time and dhimmis did serve as officials, if not in the same kinds of positions as held by Muslims. Still, the special position of the dhimmi was a reality in the Muslim world (Goitein 1955a:62-88).

While historians and Orientalists have often written on the positions of Jews in the Muslim world in terms of their legal situation, there also is a practical side to this. Because of the Jews' occupational specialties, they often were useful to their Muslim neighbors and developed correct, sometimes cordial, everyday relationships with them. Such relationships were rooted in the marketplace, but they often had wider ramifications. There were towns where Jews and Muslims lived side by side, and Jewish itinerant craftmen and peddlers would stay overnight in the homes of Muslims. Some of this is indicated in the interpretation of proverbs. One type of proverb takes the theme "Eat at A's but sleep at B's." In one Lebanese Christian formulation, it is "Eat at a Druze's, but sleep at Christian's (home)." It is interpreted by Frayha (1953:Nos. 1174; 1175) in terms of the well-known hospitality of Druzes together, with mutual hostility between Druze and Christian, which make Christians fear for their lives in Druze homes.

Obviously the proverb is sufficiently ambiguous for it to bear alternative meanings even there. In Iraq, it took the form for Jews: "Eat at a Muslim, but sleep at a Christian." There it meant that Muslim dietary laws are closer to those of the Jews than are Christian dietary practices. If one should die, however, Muslims might bury a circumcised Jew in a Muslim cemetery, while Christians would make sure that the body was transferred to a Jewish grave (Hayim J. Cohen, personal communication). While this version implies tension, it refers to mundane interpersonal relationships of the different religious groups. Some of the areas in which Jews and their non-Jewish neighbors interacted included magic and personal counseling. Wise men of all religions were consulted when needed, both for personal and communal matters. Visits were made to shrines of saints of all groups. In times of drought and plague, all religions prayed and held processions to alleviate the decree which had been imposed from on High (Goldberg 1981; Feitelson, Chapter 12; Zenner, Chapter 8).

In tribal areas, which were not under the control of the central government, there was often unrest. The Jews, like other non-combatants, were outside much of this contention, but they did obtain in many places the protection of powerful individuals. In some places, such as Kurdistan and Tripolitania, there is mention of a Jewish serfdom to the feudal lords. This appears to be a variation of the protection which such a powerful individual granted his Jewish clients in return for their services. This meant that an attack on these protected Jews was an attack on the patron himself, who often could and would retaliate. The shielding of Jewish clients continued into the period of the Arab-Israeli struggle. In Tedif al-Yahud, a village near Aleppo (Syria), a local headman protected the synagogue and shrine of Ezra the Scribe in 1947, at a time when the synagogues of Aleppo were attacked in a riot (Zenner, Chapter 8). Goldberg (1977) described a similar incident in Tripolitania in 1945 after the UN Resolution favoring the establishment of a Jewish state.

In the towns and centers of government, those Jews who were directly in contact with high officials were the clients, and in most cases, this meant those Jews who were wealthy and often powerful within the community. There are also instances where Jews became retainers of the powerful for short periods of time, only to fall with great rapidity, sometimes provoking an anti-Jewish riot in their wake. One such individual was Barukh ben Shmuel, a Russian-born emissary from Safed who became a physician and advisor to an Imam of Yemen in the 1830's until he was killed by the Imam in 1834. Women also might become clients of those in power, as in the case of Jamimah who became a favorite of the governor of Oran in Algeria and a leader of the French faction there in the early 19th century. When her patron fell, Jamimah and her sons were killed (Chouraqui 1968: 115-6). The favored Jews often became symbols to the Muslims of illegitimate <u>dhimmi</u> influence and power, and they easily became targets of hostility (see Boure 1946 for Morocco). A sarcastic medieval Arabic poem from Egypt which was repeated in later periods and in other places expresses this sentiment:

> "Today the Jews have reached the
> summit of their hopes and have be-
> come aristocrats. Power and riches
> have they and from among them are
> councillors and princes chosen.
> Egyptians, I advise you, become Jews,
> for the very sky has become Jewish."
> (Fischel 1969:88).

A balanced view of the treatment of the <u>dhimmi</u> in Islamic societies must take into account <u>the formal official status with its implied inequality, the interpersonal ties developed in everyday life, and the ambiguities of patron-client relations.</u> In addition, there is a whole variety of local variations. In North Yemen, there was a law which mandated that Jews orphaned prior to puberty must convert to Islam (Goitein 1955a:77-81). In nearby Habban (South Yemen), where the physical habitat was very harsh, Jewish folk traditions do not dwell on such features of history, but report of distress by the frequent famines (Loeb 1980). Elsewhere, as in 19th century Morocco and Syria, the murder of Jews, as often as not, was due to general exploitation, insecurity and brigandage in the countryside, rather than specific acts of Jew-hatred (Chouraqui 1968:54-5; Braver 1945-6).

The presence of Christians and of other minorities not part of the Islamic Sunni majority (such as Druzes, Alawais, and Shi'ites in predominantly Sunni Syria) added additional contours to the shape of Muslim-Jewish relations. Through the 19th century and until the rise of Jewish and Arab nationalism, Jews and Christians were often competitors for the favors both of Muslim patrons and of representatives of European powers, with the Jews appearing as less of a threat to Islam than the Christians (cf. Zenner, below; Feitelson, below). Druzes, on the other hand, although they did receive de facto recognition, were not an officially tolerated group in Sunni Islam. Druzes therefore preferred to have dhimmi neighbors to Sunnis, and one finds that most village Jews in southern Syria, Lebanon and northern Palestine in the 19th century lived in Druze areas, as did many Christians.

The interpretation of the facts of interethnic and inter-religious relations in the Middle East is often caught up in polemic. Since the 19th century, they have been used to embroider a myth of a Golden Age of Islamic tolerance (as opposed to Christian bigotry) or to embellish a "black legend" of Muslim fanaticism (as opposed to Christian love and Western liberalism). In the 19th century, the Golden Age myth was utilized by Protestant, Jewish and anti-clerical liberals as evidence of the benefits of a policy of religious toleration and liberal reform, while today it is a weapon in the armory of those who are pro-Arab. The "black legend," which was formerly manipulated by Western missionaries and their proteges, may now be used by supporters of Israel and the Lebanese Maronites. Unfortunately for those who like their histories plain and simple, there is no clear and straightforward generalization about Islamic treatment of minorities in all times and places.

(d) The Political System: Internal Community Organization

The internal organization of Jewish communities is the product of both external forces and of Jewish tradition. Those who adhere to traditional Judaism seek to reproduce a certain blueprint wherever they

21

live. The synagogue, the school for teaching Torah,
the rabbinic court, the provision of charity for the
poor, the regulation of kosher meat, maintenance of
the ritual bath and the Jewish cemetery - all these are
among the institutional roles, organizations and
expressions of this blueprint. The Jewish community,
whether officially or tacitly recognized, had considerable juridical autonomy in Muslim lands and
in other traditional societies. This went well beyond the areas of marriage, divorce and inheritance,
so recognized under Ottoman law in the 19th century.
The responsa and other legal writings of Middle
Eastern Jewish sages shows how far-reaching this
jurisdiction was in fact. All business law, certain
aspects of housing, as well as many areas of ritual
law, were considered by rabbinic courts; Jewish
authorities were able to impose fines, ostracise,
mete out corporal punishment, and, on rare occasions,
even carry out capital punishment indirectly through
the organs of the State. While Jews could turn to
Islamic courts, as they sometimes did, the web of
Jewish relationships involving family and economic
ties and socio-religious sanctions made this
difficult. The outside courts might also demand
expensive bribes and were often said by Jews to be
corrupt (Zenner, Chapters 8 and 9; Goitein 1971:2-3).

An autonomous Jewish community must have its own
system of finances, and Jewish communities accomplish-
ed this through direct and indirect taxation, such as
on the sale of kosher meat (Kedourie 1971). Gifts
for honors in the synagogue were another means of
contributing to the community (Loeb, below), and
people also endowed property for communal needs.
But the way in which most Middle Eastern communities
worked was less formal than the way in which traditional Jewish communities usually functioned in
Europe ever since late medieval times, until the
transformations of the late 18th century. Goitein
(1971:4-5) characterized the government of Jewish
communities in medieval Egypt and other Islamic-
Mediterranean lands as "a medieval religious democracy." He explicitly states that such "democracy"
lacked the formal legal framework of modern representative government, including procedures for
election, budget preparation, and legislation.
Instead, the government of Jewish communities entailed informal mechanisms by which the people
could make their will known to the leadership. One

22

"Relig. Democracy"

way in which this was done was through protests which might take place in the course of a synagogue service. The small size of the Jewish community in most places, even in large cities, made this possible, since most people knew each other and were aware of actions that were taken. There was also less need for legalistic procedures, because all believed that the society was "under the safe guidance of the Law of God".

While Goitein's use of the term "democracy" is probably an exaggeration even for his period and place, his usage of the term underlies the need to scrutinize our material carefully, so that we will look for ways in which the people participated in the public affairs of the Jewish community and in the manner of control that public opinion might have over local potentates, however autocratic they may seem. Goitein is certainly correct in having us look beyond formal procedures for such communal decisions as the selection of leaders, or the specificity of their roles. There were several principles for the selection of community leaders. Heredity and such personal attributes as wealth, learning, piety, and governmental connections were all considered. There were, of course, also many local variations; the situation of community leadership in Yemen is summarized by Goitein (1953). While the hereditary principle was followed there in selecting an individual for a communal post which his father had held, this principle was qualified by one's own personal attributes. Thus, candidates had to be learned by religious standards. There were no formal elections; representatives of the various extended families made the selection. When there was severe factional division, the Muslim authorities might intervene. The leaders of the community had both sacred and secular authority in Yemen. Especially in Sana'a, the capital of the Zeidi Imams, where they had extensive authority recognized by other Yemeni Jews. The community leadership at times included individuals, like members of the originally Egyptian al-Iraqi family, who were councillors to the Imam. Some leaders were also given the authority to collect the poll tax from the Jewish community (Tobi, below). This mixture of worldly and religious power is not that different from the kinds of authority held by rabbis and other Jewish community leaders in other parts of the Middle East. But in small communities in the Yemen, such as in villages or small market towns, there was no clear distinction between the headman of the community and the rabbi, and often the same individual occupied both posts. Alternatively there was probably no more than one rabbi who served in various ritual roles. In large communities, where there was a formal rabbinic court of three members, there was more variety and differentiation of roles.

Most of the Jews of Yemen were dispersed in many very small communities. These communities were characteristically homogeneous from the aspect of kin allegiances, so that community leadership tended to overlap the role of elder of the extended family. This homogeneity is congruent with the occupational homogeneity that we noted earlier in the small Yemenite communities. The Yemenite community organization, familistic and often ascriptive yet achievement-oriented, is only one of the types we encounter in the fascinating variety of detail that constitutes Middle Eastern internal Jewish politics. In Morocco, on the other hand, we encounter the phenomenon of the established aristocratic lineage which provides religious and secular leadership within the context of heterogeneous communities for many consecutive generations (Shokeid, Chapter 5). Moving to Southern Tunisia, we encounter yet another political system: communities governed by relatively formalized ordinances that prevail over the power of local families (Deshen, Chapter 6).

The leaders of the local Jewish community in both smaller and larger localities had ties to local elite and to the wider world, both Jewish and non-Jewish. Goldberg demonstrates this in his description of the Gharyan shaykh (in Tripolitania) who is a relatively learned individual and who has ties with the gentile authorities, thus providing both spiritual and political leadership and useful connections (Chapter 7). Smaller communities, such as that described by Goldberg, often turned to the pretigious rabbinical courts of larger communities for authoritative decisions, and for material support and intervention with gentile authorities in case of need. This kind of connection is seen also in other ways. The Tuscan port of Leghorn, during the 18th and early 19th centuries, was both a major Mediterranean port and a major Hebrew scholarship center. Many volumes of responsa of rabbis throughout the Mediterranean area were printed there, and leaders of several Jewish

24

communities had familial ties with the Leghorn community. Economic power and sacred learning flowed
in and out of the same center. The Jewish communities of Palestine also had a special place in this
communications network although they were not major
centers of trade. European and Middle Eastern pilgrims went back and forth to the four "holy cities",
Jerusalem, Safed, Hebron, and Tiberias, even during
periods when there was much conflict in the area.
Official emissaries were sent by those communities
to obtain financial support, and they commonly provided learned advice to distant otherwise isolated
communities. The Palestinian emissaries thus helped
maintain contact between various parts of the Jewish
world.

A striking instance of the important organizational and religious role of the emissaries can
be seen in the case of the Bukharan community in
Central Asia. The Jewish community there underwent
a thorough reform and revival as a result of the
activity of one such emissary, Rabbi Joseph Maman,
at the end of the 18th century (Moshavi 1974:329-
331). Through their communications network and
through the patronage of the wealthier and more
powerful Jews in market towns and in large international entrepots, the Jews in small isolated
communities, whether in Kurdistan, in South Yemen,
or in the Atlas Mountains, were connected to a wider
community of Jews throughout the world.

(e)   The Family and Gender Roles

Below the level of the community, the family and
its extensions was the major source of Jewish identity.
The Jewish family in the Middle East and in India was
similar to that of surrounding Gentile family-types,
differing slightly in some specifically Jewish features and having some characteristics determined by
the social position of the Jews in particular
communities. Until recently, anthropologists characterized the family types of particular culture
areas in typological form. If we were to do this,
we would describe the Middle Eastern family in the
following terms: the Middle Eastern family is
patrilineal in that most property and titles are
generally inherited in the male line, from fathers
to sons; it is patriarchal in that authority is
vested in the oldest male, and virilocal, in that
the preferred residence is with or near the family

25

of the husband. Marriage with all four first cousins
is permitted with some preference for marriage with
a man's father's brother's daughter. Polygyny is
permitted, although often restricted. Divorce and
remarriage of those divorced is also permitted (cf.
Patai 1959; Murdock 1967). High value is placed
on the premarital virginity and chastity of women.

This summary, based primarily on Muslim Arab
and related groups, rides roughshod over some important variations within the area, although it does
present a model which is useful for formulating
hypotheses and for comparing one group with another.
It is certainly possible for Jews conforming to
Jewish law to have families along the lines indicated. Christian groups differ in that their
ecclesiastical law prohibits and/or greatly restricts
some attributes, particularly first cousin marriage,
polygyny, and second marriages for those divorced.
Much of this characterization, however, must be used
with care since some aspects of family life ought
best be studied empirically, rather than by using
normative models. Extended family residence,
whether virilocal or other, the prevalence of polygyny and divorce, and the practice of a preference
or right to marry one's father's brother's daughter
must be examined in reality. Certain studies have
done this. A study by geneticists, concerned
particularly with birth defects and related phenomena,
has tried to examine the marriage system of Middle
Eastern and European Jews living in Israel. Goldschmidt, Ronen and Ronen (1960) report higher rates
for uncle-niece, father's brother's daughter, and
other forms of first cousin marriage among Middle
Eastern Jews than for the European Jews. Much of
the data on the traditional, pre-Israeli situation
was obtained through questioning the subjects, women
who had given birth in Israeli hospitals. Also
several anthropologists have reconstructed the marriage and family systems of Jewish communities in
Islamic societies. For instance, Goldberg (1967)
studied father's brother's daughter marriage in a
community of Tripolitanians resettled in Israel,
and concluded that one must take-non-kin factors
into account in explaining differing ratios of marriage with first cousins and with other kin and
non-kin.

Despite our qualifications, it is still correct
to see the original characterization of the Middle

26

Eastern family as patriarchal, as capturing the
ideology, and to a certain extent also the reality,
of Middle Eastern Jews. Male authority is recognized.
Male heirs are desired, while female offspring are
not given equal weight. The birth of girls usually
was not celebrated (but there were exceptions, see
Deshen 1970:140-7), while the circumcision of male
infants was elaborately celebrated. Jews shared
some of their neighbors' norms regarding honor and
shame. "Honor and shame" in the Middle East and
the Mediterranean are closely tied to the chastity
of the women, on the one hand, and the virility and
courage of the men, on the other. Consequently a
family takes pride from the proof that their brides
are virgins upon marriage. Elaborate steps must
therefore be taken to keep young men and women apart.
In many places, such as Bukhara, the bloody sheet
testifying to the virginity of the bride was publicly
displayed, or at least examined by female relatives
of both bride and groom (Moshavi 1974). But the
minority status of the Jews made it difficult at
times for them to defend their "honor". In fact,
honor has two aspects -- one is a kind of pugnacity,
the other is the defense of the chastity of one's
womenfolk. The lack of "resort to arms", in defend-
ing the virtue of Jewish women against majority group
males made maintenance of honor more difficult.[2]

The status of dhimmi and the fact of being outside the field of political contention no doubt contributed to the vulnerability of Jewish women to
seduction, abduction and rape by Muslims. In
Kurdistan there are stories about the seduction and
rape of young women (Feitelson, below; Shai, below).
Jewish poverty and, in some areas, outcaste status
contributed to a situation in which women worked outside the home, again increasing their vulnerability.
In Damascus, there were Jewish dancing girls in the
late 19th century, while some Jewish women were
prostitutes in Iran (Cohen 1973:158-9; Loeb 1977).
All this is linked with the occasional Muslim prohibition of Jewish women from covering their faces
as, of course, positively required of Muslim women,
thus contributing to the degrading view of Jewish
sex roles by Muslims. It, of course, fixed in with
a view of women as passionate creatures common in
the area.

27

Also in this area of social life there are
differences within Middle Eastern Jewry, not all
Jewish groups were equal. When Zenner worked in
Jerusalem in the 1960's, Baghdadi and Halebi Jews
were stereotyped as being pusillanimous, while Urfali
and Kurdistani Jews from more tribal areas in the
Fertile Crescent had a reputation for boldness and
courage. In Iran, where there were Jewish men and
boys who were entertainers and prostitutes, the view
that Jews lacked honor was particularly marked.
Altogether family and gender roles are one of the
least studied topics in Middle Eastern Jewish
ethnology, and the lacunae are numerous. The
selections in this volume help us to understand
certain aspects of this subject. Feitelson (Chapter
12) and Shai (Chapter 13) deal extensively with
family life including marital relations, child-
rearing, and sex roles. Goitein, in his study of
education and socialization in Yemen, describes the
high degree of responsibility that families took for
the formal literary education of their sons and the
interwoven nature of socialization of the young and
of economic activities. Goitein also shows that
childhood and youth were less discrete as phases of
life and social spheres than they are in the modern
West.[3] Glazer (Chapter 15) shows the social functions
of the dowry among the Jews of Istanbul, while Zenner
(Chapter 9) describes aspects of family tensions as
they appear in the legal responsa of Syrian Jews.

Modernization

We have, in this chapter, summarized some of the
main findings in the historical ethnology of Middle
Eastern Jewry. We have limited ourselves, both in
the following selection of materials and in the foregoing discussion, to what we loosely labeled as
traditional times; when traditional times started and
when they ended are highly complex socio-historical
questions which we did not choose to tackle here.
Suffice it to say that the point of beginning lies
somewhere in the early Middle Ages when the normative
rabbinical tradition   crystallized and came to predominate, after its victory over the Karaite protest.
In any case, the question is not of immediate concern
to us, because we concentrate on the 18th and 19th
centuries as indicated at the beginning of the chapter.
The end point is, in our case, more problematical.
One can view the end of traditional times in terms of

increasing interdependence with the West: when
European powers penetrated the Muslim Orient,
traditional times ended. Contact with Europe, how-
even, is age-old, so this is far from a clear-cut
solution.

Pending more detailed research on the subject,
we conceive the end of traditional times in the
Jewish Orient as linked to the transformation of
traditional educational institutions, education
functioning as a catalyzing factor for change in
many areas of society. The development is, of
course, intimately linked with the highly accelerated
penetration of Western imperialist influences during
the 19th century. As part of these events, the
political and economic dependency of Middle Eastern
Jews on European powers and European Jewish communities increased. Except for isolated areas like
Yemen and Kurdistan, the major Jewish communities
became involved with such organizations as the French
Alliance Israelite Universelle, which sought to
defend Jews throughout Eastern Europe and the Middle
East from persecution, and also endeavored to provide
education and other social services which would enable Jews to become self-supporting in a modern
Western way. Later, other Jewish organizations of
various origins, German, British, American, and
Israeli, made similar efforts to aid Middle Eastern
Jewry. Like other Western do-gooders, these Jewish
"missionaries" achieved ambiguous results. They
furthered the alienation of Middle Eastern Jews from
both their non-Jewish neighbors and from their own
indigenous traditions, and they prepared them for
work in the Westernized sectors of the local and
international economies (Netzer 1974). Middle Eastern
Jews were encouraged to look to outside agencies for
education and for political protection. The same
pattern was repeated with other Middle Eastern
minorities and was a factor contributing to their
basic insecurity in the era of nationalism which
followed, although it was by no means the only factor
(cf. Joseph 1961; Naby 1977; Sanjian 1965). It
made these Jewish communities weaker in their response
to cultural modernization. But on the other hand,
outside intervention often also provided material and
cultural support, and was sometimes instrumental in
the physical safety of people.

If one follows this approach, one might set a
zero point for the beginning of significant moderni-

zation and Europeanization with the establishment of Jewish schools along modern European lines in major Middle Eastern cities during the late 19th century. This period is not a precise zero point[4] because, in some communities, Jewish children may already have been going to the schools of Christian missions. By the late 19th century Jews were already long involved in the world market and worked for the occupying European powers, nevertheless the establishment of Alliance schools marked a crucial turning point for the Jewish communities. The Alliance school in Edirne (Turkey) was established in 1867, in Aleppo (Syria), 1869, and in Istanbul, 1875. Fez got an Alliance school in 1883 and Teheran in 1898, and so on. Those communities, which had modern schools by 1900, obviously turned an important historical corner.

In the chapters of this volume we are concerned with Middle Eastern Jewish societies on the eve of these events. Indeed, our understanding of these societies is still imperfect, but scholars working in the field have now formulated some models and hypotheses, and that is a promising beginning. The historical ethnology of Middle Eastern Jewry has progressed to the stage where significant questions can be raised.

NOTES

[1] The meaning of the acronym is a little unclear. The concensus of scholarly opinion is that it stands for the Aramaic seifa tav, a good end. Jews in the Middle East used to terminate their letters with these words as an auspicious omen. The acronym certainly does not stand for sephardi tahor, a pure Sephardi, as it sometimes popularly claimed.

[2] The vulnerability of women of minorities and of low status families was not limited to Jews. In 19th century Palestine, Christians and Druzes were also in this position, cf. Zenner (1972a, 1972b).

[3] Aries (1962) has argued that the present Western conception of childhood is in itself a modern development.

[4]Anthropologists in describing culture contact and change often posit a "zero point," before which there was no change from the traditional setting and after which change is rapid. The conquest of Mexico by Cortez is a classic example of such a "zero point." In an area like the Middle East, establishing such an event as a zero point is somewhat arbitrary.

REFERENCES

Aries, Philippe
1962   Centuries of Childhood. London: Jonathan
                    Cape.
Ben Sasson, Haim Hillel
1959   Hagut veHanhagah. Jerusalem: Bialik
                    Institute.
Ben-Ya'akov, Abraham
1961   The Jewish Communities of Kurdistan.
                    Jerusalem: Ben-Zvi Institute.
Braver, Abraham Jacob
1945/6   The Jews of Damascus after the Blood Libel
                    of 1840. Zion 10:83-108 (Hebrew).
Broyde, I., and R. Gottheil
1903   Constantinople. Jewish Encyclopedia IV:
                    241-2.
Chouraqui, Andre
1968   Between East and West: A History of the
                    Jews in North Africa. Philadelphia:
                    Jewish Publication Society.
Cohen, Hayim J.
1973   The Jews of the Middle East: 1860-1972.
                    Jerusalem: Israel Universities Press.
Deshen, Shlomo A.
1970   Immigrant Voters in Israel: Parties and
                    Congregations in a Local Election Campaign.
                    Manchester: Manchester University Press.
1975   Ritualization of Literacy: The Works of
                    Tunisian Scholars in Israel. American
                    Ethnologist 2:251-259.
in press   Individuals and the Community: Social Life
                    in 18th-19th Century Moroccan Jewry.
                    Tel Aviv: Tel Aviv University (Hebrew).
Deshen, Shlomo A., and Moshe Shokeid
1974   The Predicament of Homecoming: Cultural
                    and Social Life of North African Immigrants
                    in Israel. Ithaca, N.Y.: Cornell University
                    Press.

31

Eickelman, Dale
1978   The Art of Memory: Islamic Education and
      Its Social Reproduction. Comparative
      Studies in Society and History 20:485-516.

Fischel, Walter
1969   Jews in the Economic and Political Life of
      Medieval Islam. New York: Ktav. (Reprint
      with new material; orig. ed. London, 1937).

Foster, Brian
1974   Ethnicity and Commerce. American Ethno-
      logist 1:437-448.

Frayha, A.
1953   Modern Lebanese Proverbs. Beirut: American
      University of Beirut.

Goitein, Shlomo D.
1953   On the Communal Life of Jews in Yemen.
      M. Kaplan Jubilee Volume. New York: Jewish
      Theological Seminary. Hebrew Section
      pp. 43-61.

1955a   Portrait of a Yemenite Weavers Village.
      Jewish Social Studies 16:3-26.

1955b   Jews and Arabs. N.Y.: Schocken.

1969   A Mediterranean Society. Vol. I.
      Berkeley and Los Angeles: University of
      California Press.

1971   A Mediterranean Society. Vol. II. Berkeley
      and Los Angeles: University of California
      Press.

Goldberg, Harvey
1967   FBD Marriage and Demography among Tripolitan-
      ian Jews in Israel. Southwestern Journal of
      Anthropology 23:176-191.

1977   Rites and Riots: The Tripolitanian Pogrom
      of 1945. Plural Societies 8:35-56.

1981   Modecai's Story. Philadelphia: Institute
      for the Study of Human Issues.

Goldschmidt, E., A. Ronen, and I. Ronen
1960   Changing Marriage Systems in the Jewish
      Communities of Israel. Annals of Human
      Genetics 24:191-204.

Hallpike, C. R.
1971   Some Problems in Cross-Cultural Comparison.
      In The Translation of Culture (T. Beidelman,
      ed.). London: Tavistock.

Heilman, Samuel
1976   Synagogue Life. Chicago: University of
      Chicago Press.

Hirschberg, Hayim Z.
1974   A History of the Jews in North Africa.
               Leiden: Brill.
Joseph, John
1961   The Nestorians and Their Muslim Neighbors.
               Princeton: Princeton University Press.
Kedourie, Elie
1971   Jews of Baghdad in 1910. Middle Eastern
               Studies 7:355-61.
Loeb, Laurence D.
1976   Sense Stimulation and Ritual Response: A
               Classification of the Religious Symbolism
               Behavior of the Persian and Yemenite Jews.
               In The Realm of the Extra-Human: Agents
               and Audiences. A. Bharati, ed., The Hague:
               Mouton, pp. 167-177.

1977   Outcaste: Jewish Life in Southern Iran.
               London: Gordon and Breach.

1980   Jewish Life in Habban: A Tentative
               Reconstruction. In Studies in Jewish Folk-
               lore, F. Talmage, ed., Cambridge, Massa-
               chusetts: Association for Jewish Studies,
               pp. 201-219.
Mernissi, Fatima
1977   Women, Saints and Sanctuaries. Signs 3:101-
               112.
Moshavi, Barukh
1974   Customs and Folklore Among 19th Century
               Bukharian Jews in Central Asia. (Ph.D.
               Diss., Yeshiva University). Ann Arbor:
               University Microfilms, Order No. 74-23, 553.
Murdock, George P.
1967   Ethnographic Atlas. Ethnology: 6:2:7.
Naby, Eden
1977   The Assyrians of Iran: Reunification of a
               'Millet'. International Journal of Middle
               Eastern Studies 8:237-249.
Netzer, Amnon
1974   The Jews of Persia and the Alliance in the
               Late 19th Century: Some Aspects. Paper
               delivered at the International Conference on
               Jewish Communities in Muslim Lands. Jerusalem:
               Institute of Asian and African Studies and
               the Ben Zvi Institute.
Noy, Dov
1974   Jewish-Gentile Relationships as Reflected in
               the Folktales of the Jews of Kurdistan.
               International Conference on Jewish Communi-
               ties in Muslim Lands. Jerusalem.

Patai, Raphael
1959   Sex and Marriage in the Bible and the Middle
                        East. New York: Doubleday.

1962   From Golden River to Golden Road. Philadel-
                        phia: University of Pennsylvania Press.

1971   Tents of Jacob. Englewood Cliffs, N.J.:
                        Prentice-Hall.
Rosen, Laurence
1968   A Moroccan-Jewish Community During the Middle
                        East Crisis. American Scholar 37:435-51.

1972   Muslim-Jewish Relations in a Muslim City.
                        International Journal of Middle Eastern
                        Studies 3:435-449.
Sanjian, Avedis
1965   Armenian Communities in Syria Under
                        Ottoman Dominion. Cambridge, Massachusetts:
                        Harvard University Press.
Shokeid, Moshe
1971   The Dual Heritage: Immigrants From the Atlas
                        Mountains in an Israeli Village. Manchester
                        University Press.
Simmel, Georg
1908   The Stranger. In Soziologie. Leipsig:
                        Drucker u. Humbolt.
Stahl, Abraham
1979   Ritualist Reading Among Oriental Jews.
                        Anthropological Quarterly 52:45-120.
Stillman, Norman
1979   The Jews of Arab Lands: A History and Source-
                        book. Philadelphia: Jewish Publication
                        Society.
Stone, Russel
1974   Religious Ethnic and the Spirit of Capital-
                        ism in Tunisia. International Journal of
                        Middle Eastern Studies 5:260-273.
Zborowski, Mark, and E. Herzog
1952   Life is with People. New York: International
                        Universities Press.
Zenner, Walter P.
1972a   Some Aspects of Ethnic Stereotype Content in
                        the Galilee: A Trial Formulation. Middle
                        Eastern Studies 8:405-416.

1972b   Aqiili Agha: The Strongman in the Ethnic
                        Relations of the Ottoman Galilee. Comparative
                        Studies in Society and History 14:169-188.

CHAPTER 2

TRADITIONAL SOCIETY AND MODERN SOCIETY

JACOB KATZ

To the observer of the contemporary scene
in the U.S. and in Israel, it sometimes
appears as if great social and cultural differences separate such Jewries as those of
Yemen and Hungary, and those of Morocco and
Poland. The aim of this chapter by Jacob Katz
is to give the reader a fundamental historical
and sociological perspective in this matter.
Jacob Katz, Professor Emeritus of social history
at the Hebrew University of Jerusalem, and one
of the leading Judaic scholars of our time,
traces the general characteristics of Jewish
traditionalism in various spheres of social life,
particularly in the area of education. These
characteristics are generally common to all pre-
modern Jews. They vary only in matters of relative detail from one pre-modern type of Jewish
community to the next. As against this, the
great differences between Jewish communities,
that strike one's attention in modern times, stem
from processes of modernization which operated
in radically different ways in various Jewish
communities. Katz formulated this thesis in the
1950s, in terms customary among sociologists, for
the benefit of Israeli educators. The paper was
influential, at that time, in helping to counteract prejudices among officials who were not familiar with the cultures of the new immigrants.
Despite the passing of time, Katz's thesis is still
fresh and worth studying, for prejudices of all
kinds are still very much alive. Moreover, cultural
and sub-ethnic consciousness among Middle Eastern
Jews, in Israel and to a certain extent also in the

SOURCE: Translation of "Traditional and Modern Societies." Megamot Vol. X:4:304-311 (1960). By permission of Henrietta Szold Institute: The National
Institute for Research in the Behavioral Sciences,
Jerusalem. © Copyright 1960.

U.S., is on the rise. This sometimes causes differences to be emphasized to an extent beyond acceptable historical and sociological proportions. The chapter serves to develop a reasonable and balanced position on a crucial issue of Jewish diversity.

A great deal has been said about the cultural differences between various ethnic groups in Israel, and doubtless such differences do exist. The issue I would like to raise is whether these differences ought to be considered as elements that separate specific ethnic groups or rather ought to be considered as all-encompassing differences between two types of society, the traditional type and the modern type. Professor Goitein[1] has compared the Jewish-Yemenite educational system with the educational system of the Talmudic period. Goitein was able to interpret Talmudic sources by virtue of the comparison with what he actually saw at work in Yemenite Jewish society. Vice versa, he was also able to understand much of what he found in Yemenite society on the basis of the comparison with the original sources of traditional Jewry. Goitein concluded that the differences between the variety of traditional Jewish societies are minor and should be seen in the context of a fundamental principle that is common to all of them. In all traditional societies, man's aspiration lies in seeking religious justification for his existence. This stands in contrast to modern man whose main aspirations lie in other fields, that of financial success, standard of living, and so forth.

I do not discuss this distinction here, but merely state that I shall proceed on the assumption that traditional society is an all-encompassing type, within which there is a variety of historical manifestations. I shall use the sociological concept "traditional society" to designate societies that, although not primitive, are not societies of the type in which we live today. The key-term for comprehension of the concept "traditional society" is "tradition." Rather than founding their existence and aspirations on values and on knowledge yet to be discovered and developed, people in traditional societies assume that all the practical and theoretical knowledge that they require has been inherited by them from their forefathers, and that it is man's duty to act in accordance with the ancient customs. Furthermore, there is the added

36

assumption, that there is no essential difference between the various spheres of human activity, in the
sense that all activities require justification in
terms of religion. This assumption of people in traditional societies does not, however, imply, that
traditional society undergoes no changes. There can
in fact be no society that does not change. Karl Mann-
heim long ago suggested that we attempt to imagine a
society in which no children are ever born. Though
such a society would appear like any other, it would,
in actual fact, be lacking one of the most important
elements of social dynamics, the coming and going of
the generations. All societies in actuality are
based on generational turnover, and this perforce en-
tails social change. Historical sources, in particular
those that deal with the history of education, indicate
that also in traditional societies people complained
that times were changing and that the younger generation
was not faithful to customs of the fathers. It appears
that a certain amount of friction between generations
is inevitable everywhere and at all times. This
friction is a consequence of differences that distinguish each generation from its predecessor.

We know that traditional societies underwent
changes in such matters as technology and fashions of
dress. We also know that there was development on a
spiritual level. Thus there was a time in Yemen when
the Zohar was still unknown. Only later did the Zohar
penetrate the lives of the Jews of Yemen, and eventually
became a guiding religious source, directing thought,
emotion, religious experience and outlook. This is
also pertinent to the halakhic literature. The acceptance of the Shulhan Arukh by Yemenite Jews was a
definite change in the community. How can these facts
be resolved with the claim of traditional society that
it bases its present on the past? Evidently in using
the term "traditional society," we do not wish to
suggest that this is a society without change, but
rather, that it is a society that does not wish or
aspire to change. Indeed people in traditional society
attempt to resolve changes in the light of tradition
and tend to declare what is novel to be old. This
state of affairs stands in contrast to that in modern
society wherein the old is declared to be new, in order
to facilitate its acceptance. Traditional society,
though, in fact, undergoing changes, makes itself out
to be static, while modern society on the other hand,
aspires toward change. It is difficult for modern man
to attribute value to anything just by virtue of its

being inherited from the past. The fact that our forefathers acted in a particular way does not provide
modern man with the confidence that this indeed is the
correct manner. Man in modern society feels compelled
to justify his behavior on another level altogether,
on a rational, scientific or pseudo-scientific base,
that does not rest on the acceptance of values of the
past.

At this juncture lies the real distinction between
traditional and non-traditional society. Traditional
society seeks justification for its way of life from,
within the realm of tradition, and it tends to blur
distinctions between the different   spheres of activity,
and to adopt a single measure of legitimization vis-a-
vis one and all. In modern society, on the other hand,
the hold of tradition varies from sphere to sphere.
As regards technology, for instance, tradition is not
held to be valid at all. On the other hand, to the
extent that modern society does admit to religious
values, it does not deny that these are to be derived
from the traditional sources. Aside from the source
of individual emotions, religion even in modern society
is supported by institutions which cannot possibly be
renewed every generation or even periodically every
year. .As regards other spheres of life we find that
compromises are made. Thus for instance, in the sphere
of education, while efforts are made to train students
to understand their present and to be prepared for the
future, some subjects of study are based on traditional
principles, and religious education is not the only
such subject. The study of language and literature,
for instance, is based on what has been absorbed from
the past, and there is no attempt to make daily inno-
vations. Also in the area of education to behavior and
good manners, the past controls the present to a considerable extent. Also in the study of national history
the past determines ongoing life. The opposite, however, is the case in the study of the natural sciences,
where there is barely any study of their history, but
rather an attempt to teach the latest scientific accom-
plishments (to the extent that these can be conveyed to
the young generation).

These essential distinctions between areas of life
in modern society do not hold for traditional society.
At this point we come to the central issue. In traditional soceity, at least theoretically, there is no
distinction between different spheres of activity.

38

When we say that traditional Jewish society is religious, we mean that the religious world-view penetrates into areas which we would not regard as associated with religion. Certain customs concerning dress, language, and manners are accepted only by virtue of their being in accordance with tradition, while the tradition itself is validated on the basis of religious beliefs. There were, however, always differences of opinion as to the degree of the validity of tradition, and it is possible to distinguish between two attitudes. On the one hand there is traditionalism based on direct acceptance of the tradition conveyed through social channels. Every traditional Jewish community, whether located in Yemen, Iraq, or in Ashkenazic Europe, accepted the rabbinic Jewish tradition, that had been passed down through the generations by means of a written compilation. On the other hand, each Jewish culture area had its own specific local traditions, which were conveyed through the generations by unmediated personal contact, rather than through the impersonal and formal literature. Here the child meets the tradition, not by studying books in which it receives its theoretical formulation, but by the very fact of his being born and brought up within traditional society. The sense of value attributed to the tradition is not founded on theoretical justifications provided by men of ideas; rather, the person is absorbed into traditional society by the very fact of his education. The conceptual world is molded by the unmediated impressions created on the child which convey a satisfying and safe world. Thus, the link between the child of the society and the tradition is created.

The fundamental education in traditional society is based on the study and absorption of formal knowledge from books and written sources, but the essence of the power of the tradition is created through the unmediated contact with the surroundings. This straightforward attitude toward the personal and local tradition sometimes acquired theoretical justification; there were those who claimed that the legitimization of customs lay in the very fact of their practice throughout the generations. There was, however, another outlook according to which only those customs, that can be justified by reference to the traditional literature, are binding. Both attitudes towards custom regarded themselves, and rightly so, as traditional, but the one referred to traditional written sources for legitimization, while the other was satisfied with the very fact of practice of the customs for their legitimization.

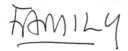

It now seems to me, that the Jewish communities of
the Middle East are particularly associated to the
latter type, where justification for tradition lies in
its very existence and practice and in the personal
link of the individual to his society.

As I stated earlier, all spheres of life in traditional society, such as family life, practices of
government and law-maintenance, the educational system
and religious activities, are governed by a similar
world-view. Let us begin with the family. The Jewish
family has an ancient tradition. In the same way that
Goitein succeeded in carrying out a comparison between
the Yemenite education system and that of the period of
the Talmud, it should not be difficult to compare the
traditional Jewish family (of which there are still
remnants), and the Jewish family during the period of
the Talmud, even though the differences are considerable. The Jewish family of the 17th century in Poland
is similar to the Yemenite family of both the past and
the present day. In both, religion-based tradition
legitimizes internal family relations, including the
relationship between husband and wife and relation
between the generations. The father, who regards himself as having the right to determine the fate of his
children in their studies, in their choice of profession and of marriage-partner, is supported by the firm
belief that tradition legitimizes his actions. The
same holds for the control of the wife by the husband;
although sources in halakha and homiletics suggest an
idealized image of harmony and consideration in this
area (and indeed something of that has remained in
every Jewish home), much of the behavior within the
family, does not coincide with the ideal. Again, the
justification for actual behavior lies in the stamp of
custom through the generations.

Let us turn to the area of education. In traditional Jewish societies education has one major function:
to convey traditional values from generation to generation. Here the great difference between traditional
and modern societies can be seen best. Education in
modern society aspires to provide the child with knowledge that will stand him in good stead from a practical
point of view, and to develop his inner capabilities,
so that he will be able to come to a happy combination
between his personal needs and the benefit that he can
contribute to society. Traditional society knows no
such aims, and educators in Israel are faced with

problems that arise when immigrants who are accustomed
to a traditional educational system are confronted with
the demands of a modern educational system.

In traditional society, institutional education
is responsible for providing the child with knowledge
of Judaism. All other matters, such as preparation
for earning a living and training in the practical
aspects of daily life, are given over to other agencies.
The heder of Ashkenazi Jewry, which has its equivalents
in all other traditional Jewish societies, was never
an institution that provided technical or practical
training of any kind. The struggle that did take place
within traditional society, particularly in the Ashkenazi communities, as to the provision of practical
knowledge to the younger generation, did not focus on
the question as to whether these studies be permitted
or not, but rather as to which educational institutions,
public or semi-public, were to be charged with them.
It was admitted that a man must train himself for a
craft, trade or some occupation that would provide him
with a living, and children were permitted, at the
correct time, to be apprenticed to a craftsman, particularly if the community's economy was based on crafts.
Similarly, there was no opposition in traditional Jewish society to the study of useful subjects, such as
languages, mathematics and other subjects of general
knowledge, and there were always small groups that
engaged in these.[2] When traditional society was viable,
total and all-encompassing, at least parts of the communities were compelled to engage in matters that
deviated from the fostering of the tradition in its
restricted sense, such as certain occupations or
diplomatic activities. There was no opposition to
this, but the problem remained as to which community
agencies would bear the responsibility for preparing
people for these positions. The traditional institutions saw themselves as responsible for the teaching
of religious and cultural values, and they refused to
take on themselves the teaching of secular matters. A
similar situation exists to this day in the major
traditional institutions in Israel, talmudei torah and
yeshivot. Many of these schools, though not opposed
to practical studies and to general knowledge, do not
wish to become involved in their teaching and prefer
to rely on other bodies for these functions. If
yeshivot do engage in the teaching of these matters it
is with great reluctance. The great achievement to
which we are witness in today's religious educational

establishments, albeit in the non-extremist institutions, is the attempt to combine the two together.
The problem, however, has not been entirely solved:
one still has the feeling that one corner of the school
belongs to the traditional world, while other corners
emanate an entirely different atmosphere. At certain
hours of the day the child finds himself in the traditional heder, not very different from what it must have
looked a few hundred years ago, and at other moments,
in a modern school. For someone who is only familiar
with the traditional image of these institutions, this
is evidence of revolutionary measures, and it appears
as if the sacred and the profane have gotten mixed up
with each other, and as if the inner unity of the
sacred institutions has collapsed.

These remarks are also pertinent to the family
sphere. A person who has been brought up within the
framework of traditional society, and accepts the
almost unrestricted authority of the father, will find
it difficult to become accustomed to the sharing of
this authority with other agencies and persons such as
the mother and elder siblings of the younger generation.
This divided authority implies that the principles on
which he has based his existence hitherto are now being
fundamentally undermined. This is also true for other
areas of activity, such as the sphere of socializing
and unmediated contact between people. Traditional
society is never ascetic up to the point of denying
social pleasures. Social enjoyments exist everywhere,
and there are institutions that provide opportunities
for people to meet each other for no other reason than
to enjoy company. Jewish traditional society is no
exception to this, although there have been attempts
to impose restrictions on social amusements. The Gaon
of Vilna (in the late 18th century) advised his wife
to pray at home rather than at synagogue in order to
avoid idle chatter. He was ready for her to forego
the religious satisfaction attached to public prayer
in order to avoid contact with the profane. But the
attitude of the Gaon of Vilna was unusual; on the whole
traditional society does offer scope for social enjoyment as long as this takes place under the auspices of
the existing social institutions, whose legitimization
is rooted in tradition. Thus, for instance, it was
permitted to engage in leisure activities in the study-
house, in addition to the activities for which it was
created. Also, traditional wedding festivities were
sometimes extended over more than the seven days of
customary feasting, and included festivities before

the actual wedding ceremony, and sometimes even before and after betrothal. In other words, enjoyment for its own sake was forbidden; it had to be given justification from within the accepted traditional framework. The usage of the concept seudat mitzva, that is a festive meal of religious significance, was greatly extended over time. In the early halakhic sources the concept was very restricted, and festive meals that would to-day be classified as seudot mitzva were originally not considered as such. Over time the concept grew less restricted and the legal authorities exerted themselves to classify more and more social occasions under this heading. One gets the impression that they wished to be generous in permitting social gatherings, and thus to give these occasions a religious seal, in accordance with tradition.

This phenomenon, whereby people in traditional society were able to satisfy their needs for friendship and socializing in accordance with traditional require-ments, gave society much resilience and adaptability. Although there were always moralists who disapproved of recently-legitimized social gatherings and festiv-ities, it was nevertheless possible to live in tradi-tional society without perceiving of enjoyment as misconduct. It was considered wrong only if a man invited his friend to a festive gathering for no explicit reason. This close link between the sphere of social life and religious beliefs is just one illustration of the unity of different spheres of activity within traditional society. But what happens when such a society shakes itself free of tradition? Then sociability and enjoyment for their own sake become acceptable. Both young and old discover that they have the right to go out and enjoy themselves for no reason other than their own pleasure. We are wit-ness to such a process when young people, brought up in a traditional society, find themselves in modern society and discover the facilities available for enjoyment. But more important, these young people also discover that modern society sees no harm in the fact that a man, at the end of his working day, goes out and looks for relaxation in an activity for which there is no explicit religious or moral justification. This, in my opinion, is one of the outstanding examples of the gradual separation of institutions that were originally combined, which occurs in the transition from life under traditional conditions to modern conditions.

Further examples may be drawn from the fields of government and economics. The term "government" refers to arrangements determined by the ruling authorities, which are obeyed by those further down the social hierarchy. We do not need to explain the secret of government, why it is that those below obey those above; this is one of the basic sociological facts. Government is an institution for which every society provides its own particular form of legitimization. In a society founded on a secular-rational basis the tendency is to justify the organs of government by referring to necessity, namely that society cannot exist without some form of law-maintenance. In fact education towards good citizenship in modern societies seeks to ensure the identification of the younger generation with the authorities that direct the society. Traditional societies, on the other hand, work on a quite different basis. Those societies are usually much smaller than modern mass societies, therefore contact between the ruler and the ruled is more personal, direct and unmediated. The governor is often personally known to the public, and most crucially, his position in accordance with religious tradition, is believed to be blessed from above.

Government in modern society is founded on the rational concept of the decentralization of power (such as the principle that the executive body is answerable to the legislative body and both of these are answerable to the judiciary). The principles governing decentralization are so abstract that they cannot be deduced from simple observation of the workings of the government. Someone who has no notion of the functional significance of a Parliament, and who is witness to groups of people arguing vehemently, sometimes aggressively, is likely to be repelled by the apparent lack of meaning. On the other hand, such a person observing the President at a ceremony will become aware of the existence of the governing body, by virtue of the concrete manifestation, and he will be more likely to identify with it. Now traditional society combines the two elements: the governor is both the institution and its symbolic representative. Modern government, on the other hand, is based on the separation of its symbolic and the functional aspects. This is one reason why newcomers from traditional society have not easily adjusted to modern political functions. Though such people may identify with the symbolic aspects of government, their initial understanding of the inner workings of politics are limited.

44

Let us address ourselves to the economic issue.
Economics is surely a rational matter: man works in
order to earn a living and provide for his family.
Here, seemingly, tradition cannot have much say. But
in fact this is not the case. Modern economic activity assumes that man is rational, and rationality in
the sphere of economics implies optimal material
success by the easiest means feasible. Also in traditional society people aspire to material success,
though not necessarily by the easiest means possible.
Economic activity in traditional society is carried
out in accordance with custom. Thus for instance,
where it was accepted that a particular skill be passed
down through the generations, the individual was not
given the opportunity to choose his profession according to his own will. This contrasts with modern life
where the trend is to direct the individual to that
profession which will be best for the individual and
for the community. But that is unfamiliar to people
who were raised in traditional society.

Before concluding let me add a more general comment. Traditional Jewish society in the diaspora was
characterized by the fact that it was never a whole
society. Jewish society took on the form of a sect or
of a caste, not in the full sense of the term as used
by sociologists, but certainly in the sense of a
group that fulfilled roles within strict limitations,
some of them self-imposed and some of them imposed
from outside. In traditional society man was not able
to achieve much for his children, and the future,
though secure, promised very little variety. His steps
were guided by tradition; he could not and did not
have to make far-reaching decisions. Now one of the
great consequences of the establishment of the State
of Israel is the fact that Jewish society has become
whole, and is able to offer its citizens a wide
choice of professions, thus accommodating the needs
of both individual and society. However, people who
are unfamiliar with the modern outlook, and who are
accustomed to have their existence largely defined by
their circumstances, find this to be a situation in
which they lose control over their world. They often
do not comprehend the potential benefits inherent in
the new situation. Integration into the new society
requires that people from the traditional world cut
themselves off from much that has guided their way
in the past. Otherwise, that which is a potential
advantage in modern society remains a disadvantage
for them.[3]

45

Let us summarize. A society is classified as traditional, not because it has no future or no present. Society can only continue to exist by virtue of the past that molds its present, and each generation adds its particular contribution to the heritage of the past. Traditional society is thus compelled to adjust to changes that occur in its midst. In traditional society, however, the traditional frame of reference provides justification for changes. In modern society the situation is radically different, and little value is attributed to tradition. Though there are still hesitant attempts to establish links with the tradition, on the whole it is assumed that the activity of people in various areas of life is to be based on the inner rational of each particular activity. Thus, economic activity proceeds according to its own rules, and similarly in matters of government, education, family and leisure time. For those who come from traditional societies all this raises profound existential problems and inevitable clashes between the two worlds. These clashes are particularly evident in Israel, where the situation I have outlined is not the consequence of a historical process, but of the sudden transition through migration from one type of society to another.

NOTES

[1](See Goitein, Chapter 8. The comparison of Yemeni with Talmudic education is most fully documented in Goitein 1953. Also see Goitein 1980. The editors.)

[2]A frequent mistake is made in this connection, as if Jews in traditional times opposed secular education or vocational training. This mistaken conception stems from a view of 19th century European Jewish society, when traditional society was no longer total. At that time it already had a periphery of people who had abandoned the tradition and who, for the most part, were engaged in the representation of the community to external bodies. These people were also engaged in occupations which required a general education. Those who, on the other hand still adhered to traditional ways devoted themselves to study and were indeed more strictly orthodox than their ancestors had been in traditional times.

[3]The following is a concrete expression of this dilemma. A few years ago the salaries of new immigrants employed in a particular occupation were raised. The response of the workers was to reduce their number of working days from six to three weekly. (That was before the era of rapid inflation.) This reaction is puzzling: why earn less if you can earn more? Similar phenomena, however, occurred during the transition from traditional to modern society in Europe as shown in Max Weber's book on the development of modern society. The possibility of increased financial gain was responded to by less work, just enough to continue to preserve the old standard of living. Evidently traditional man is not always oriented to connect the means and the goal. Often he is primarily concerned to preserve the old, customary standard of living. Though this attitude is increasingly rare nowadays, the fact that it still occurs indicates the link between traditional attitudes and the problems of adjustment in the modern world.

REFERENCES

Goitein, S.D.
1953   Jewish Education in Yemen. In Between Past
            and Present (C. Frankenstein, ed.). Jeru-
            salem: Szold Institute, pp. 106-109.

_____
1980   Research Among Yemenites. In Studies in
            Jewish Folklore (F. Talmage, ed.), pp. 121-
            136.

CHAPTER 3

JUDAISM IN "PRE-MODERN" SOCIETIES

STEPHEN SHAROT

Steven Sharot, senior lecturer in sociology
at Ben Gurion University in Beersheva, stresses
the differences between the traditional Jewries,
in contrast to Katz's emphasis on their uniformity. Sharot compares four major Jewish
culture-areas: China, India, the Middle East,
and Christian Europe. The comparison deals with
the degree of socio-cultural openness (as
opposed to closure) which these Jewries exhi-
bited towards their respective Gentile environments. The Jews in India and China were the
most open to Gentile influence, while those in
pre-modern Europe were the least open, and Jews
under Islam stood between these two poles. The
differences are explained by characteristics of
the host-societies.

Dispersal and Isolation

After the Temple of Solomon was destroyed and
Judea captured by the Babylonians in 586 BCE (before
the Common Era), the major part of the Jewish
population was exiled from its homeland to Babylonia,
while some fled to Egypt. From that period only a
minority of the Jewish people continued to live in
what had been the kingdoms of Israel and Judah, and
in the following centuries, the Jews gradually settled
throughout the Near Eastern and Mediterranean empires.
On the destruction of the Second Temple in CE 70 and
the crushing of the Jewish revolt against the Romans,
the Jews became a truly exiled people. Their further
dispersion followed the political expansion and long-
range trading routes of first the Roman and then the
Arabic empires. From the area of the first diaspora,
the Middle Eastern and Mediterranean territories, the
Jews dispersed farther north and west into Europe and

SOURCE: Stephen Sharot: Judaism: A Sociology (Newton
Abbot: David & Charles, 1976) 5-36; 190-192.
© Copyright 1976 by Stephen Sharot. Reprinted by
permission of Stephen Sharot and David & Charles.

a smaller number settled farther south in the Sahara and farther east in the Caucasus, Turkistan, Afghanistan, India, and China.

With the decline of the empires and the contraction of world trade, the connection between many Jewish communities was severed. The Chinese Jewish communities, which were predominantly composed of Jewish traders who had settled in China from about the ninth century CE, were effectively isolated from other Jewish communities from about the twelfth century. The Jewish community in Kaifeng, which began in the eleventh or twelfth century and was the only community to survive until the nineteenth, had, by 1605, lost contact not only with Jews from the West but also with other Chinese Jews.[1]

Jewish communities in India also had little or no contact with other Jewish communities for a long period. The Cochin Jews, whose existence on the Malabar coast of India from the end of the tenth century is firmly established, became effectively isolated from other Jews from the thirteenth century. Jews from Spain and Portugal migrated to the Malabar coast and intermarried with the Cochin Jews from the early sixteenth century, but the isolation of the Cochin Jews was effectively broken only with Dutch rule in the second half of the seventeenth century. The origins and date of settlement of the Indian Jewish community, the Bene Israel, who resided in the villages of Konkan, are obscure, but their isolation from other Jewish communities lasted longer than that of the Cochin Jews. The Bene Israel probably lost contact with other Jewish communities, including other Indian Jewish communities, early in the second millennium, and sustained contact with other Jews began again only in the nineteenth century. However, there is evidence that the Bene Israel were known to Western Jews in the twelfth century and that contacts with Cochin Jews were frequent in the eighteenth century.[2]

There was also little contact between the majority of Jewish communities under Christendom and Islam up to the nineteenth century. In the fourteenth and fifteenth centuries, Jews from Spain and Italy migrated to North Africa where they culturally absorbed a number of North African Jewish communities, although in some cases the European Jews were culturally absorbed by the Oriental Jews. Other Jewish communities under Islam, such as those in the Grand Atlas of southern Morocco, the Algerian desert, Ethiopia, Yemen, Kurdistan, the Caucasus, and Afghanistan were isolated, not only from the Jews under Christendom, of which some were not even aware, but also from other communities under Islam. Both during the centuries before Islam, and in the first centuries of the Arabic political unification, communication between communities was precarious. From the tenth to the thirteenth centuries, mobility and connections between the communities were comparatively high, but these declined again with the break-up of the Arabic empire.[3] In the Middle and Far East, the isolation of many Jewish communities resulted in the development of religious practices which were not shared with other Jewish communities. In contrast, the European Jewish communities formed a vast network with many ties, and, although numerous local variations developed, there remained a basic unity in religious beliefs and practices.

The connections between the majority of Jewish communities considered here were broken only after the post-exilic characteristics of Judaism had evolved into stable and distinctive forms. The Babylonian Talmud had been codified about CE 500 and was accepted by most Jewish communities as authoritative over the Jerusalem Talmud. Babylonia had been the most important cultural centre of Jewry from at least the third century, and it was clearly the centre of the study of the Torah from the seventh to the eleventh centuries. During this period, Babylonian-Persian Jewry was highly centralised: the communities were already scattered, but they all recognised the geonim, the chief judicial leaders, of the Talmudic academies in Sura and Pumbedita as the legitimate religious authorities.[4] The Jews who migrated from Persia to areas as far east as India and China in the last centuries of the first millennium came, therefore, from the centre of Talmudic Judaism. From Persia the authority of the Babylonian Talmud came to be accepted by most Jews under Islam, and, in the last centuries of the first millennium, by the growing Jewish communities in Europe. Thus, at the time of the settlement of Jewish communities over many parts of the world and before their connections were broken, Judaism had become clearly identified with an ethnic group, the Talmud

51

was widely diffused, and other religions in the monotheistic tradition (Christianity and Islam) were
clearly distinguishable from Judaism.

It is clear that Jews were not initially disposed
to acculturate to the environmental non-Jewish
religio-cultures. Although, like all the major world
religions, Judaism had been syncretistic in its
formative stages, it had become a comparatively
distinctive religion with clearly defined boundaries
setting it off from other religions. Jews had come
to put a great emphasis on the maintenance of their
strict monotheistic beliefs, to protect them from the
'idolatrous' beliefs and practices of non-Jews. This
insular, as opposed to syncretic, attitude predisposed
them further to construct social barriers between
themselves and non-Jews. Adherence to Judaism
involved, therefore, both the construction of religio-
cultural barriers against other religions, and
voluntary segregation from non-Jewish groups. Hence,
an explanation of variations in levels of Jewish
acculturation requires an analysis of those aspects
of the religio-cultures and social structures of the
'host' societies which would either strengthen or
reduce the Jews' religious doctrinism and voluntary
segregation.

Levels of Acculturation

An obvious place to begin a comparison of levels
of acculturation among Jewish communities is the
Middle East; in contrast with Europe and the Far East,
the Jews had not transplanted their culture to an
alien environment, but were, from the outset, very
much a part of the indigenous culture. The expansion
of the Arabic empire facilitated the widespread
dispersion of Jews over the Middle East, but in many
areas, Jews were established long before the advent
of Islam. In its formative stages, Islam incorporated
many religious, legal, and moral conceptions from the
Jews, and even after the boundaries between Islam and
Judaism were clearly drawn, Jews and Muslims continued
to share many beliefs and practices.

Levels of Jewish assimilation and acculturation
to Islamic societies have varied greatly over
different areas and periods. Although following the
Islamic conquests, significant numbers of Jews were

totally assimilated, often by conversion, into the "host" population, the rate of assimilation was rarely high enough to reduce the overall numbers. In contrast to the Christians and Zoroastrians, who were unable to adjust to their newly acquired minority status, the number of Jews increased in the centuries after the Islamic conquests.[5] The Jews remained a distinct socio-cultural group under Islam, but they shared far more of the culture of their non-Jewish neighbours than the Jews in Europe. The influence of Judaism on early Islam had been considerable, but, after its crystallisation, Islam in turn had an influence on Middle Eastern Judaism. As in most cases, the subordinate minority was acculturating to the dominant majority, rather than the other way round.

In general, there was little that outwardly distinguished Jew and Muslim: they spoke the same language and wore the same clothes, despite occasional regulations seeking to differentiate Muslim and Jewish dress. It has often been said that the Middle Eastern Jews were "Arab in all but religion," but this oversimplifies and distorts the true situation. Religion pervaded Middle Eastern culture and a distinction between "religious" and "secular" areas of culture is often difficult to make. For example, adoption of the dominant language was bound to have implications for the minority's religion. By about CE 1000 the majority of Middle Eastern Jews had, like the rest of the population, adopted Arabic,[6] and this involved the adoption of Arabic ways of thinking and Arabic religious concepts. The Jews used Arabic for translating and teaching the Bible,as well as discussing Jewish law and ritual. Although the Muslim's emphasis on the study of the Arabic language also influenced the Jews to study Hebrew, the use of Arabic for both secular and religious purposes contrasts with the development of language barriers between Jews and Christians in Europe.[7]

Furthermore, if we take the term "religion" to mean not just the "orthodox" doctrines of Judaism and Islam but all the supernatural beliefs and practices found among the Middle Eastern population, then there was considerable overlap between the religion of Muslim and Jew. Much of the "popular" religion shared by Muslim and Jew was pre-Islamic. One central cult, especially important in North Africa,

53

which had many pre-Islamic elements but which was
brought into the framework of both Islam and Judaism
in the Middle East, was that of pilgrimage to the
tombs of saints. Both Muslims and Jews sought the
intercession and protection of the saints, offering
them candles and oil lamps and performing rituals
by their tombs. Family pilgrimages were made when
important family events occurred and collective
pilgrimages were made on the anniversary of the death
of the saint. In addition to certain saints worshipped by both Muslims and Jews, the two religious
groups shared many magical practices and beliefs
associated with witchcraft, sorcery, divination,
ecstatic prophecy, demons, the evil eye, the magical
significance of numbers, and the protective power of
amulets.[8] In many cases, the "popular" cults appear
to have attained a greater place in the total
religious system of Middle Eastern Jews than the
distinctive beliefs and practices of Judaism. The
trend from local religious diversity to Talmudic
uniformity, which had occurred under the Roman and
Persian empires and which was at first strengthened
under Islam, was reversed in the later Middle Ages
when local religious customs again assumed importance.
A European Jew who made a number of visits to North
African Jewish communities between 1906 and 1916
found widespread ignorance of Judaism but a great
variety of "popular" cults and magical practices. In
the interior of Morocco, he found that the religious
beliefs of the Jews had a polytheistic character
which approached fetishism.[9]

In addition to sharing much of the "popular"
religion of their neighbours, Jews were also influenced
by more "orthodox" Islamic practices. The short,
intense features of Muslim prayer impressed the Jews,
whose services displayed far more decorum than
European Jewish services. Like the Muslims, the Jews
practised polygamy, and the religious position of
Jewish women deteriorated in Islamic environments. In
the highlands of Yemen, where Islamic women did not
attend the mosque, Jewish women did not attend the
synagogue and were completely cut off from the
religious life of the men.[10]

Although most Middle Eastern Jewish communities
shared much of their culture with their Muslim
neighbours, their distinctiveness as religious
minorities varied greatly, even among those who had

little or no contact with other Jewish communities. For example, the Yemenite Jews had no contact with Jewish communities outside Yemen, but their religio-culture remained very distinct from that of their non-Jewish neighbours; they had evolved certain unique religious practices, but, like the Jews of Europe, prayer in the synagogue and study of the Talmud were central.[11] They provide a sharp contrast with other isolated communities which were highly acculturated, such as the Mountain Jews of the Caucasus (Tats), the Jews in Kurdistan, and many communities in the interior of North Africa.

There are few studies by trained observers of Middle Eastern Jewish communities before their dis-integration in the last few decades, but two studies, one of Jews in north-east Iraq and the other of Jews in the north-west Sahara of Algeria, provide interesting sources for comparison, especially since both communities had no significant contact with other Jewish communities.[12] In the former case, the Jews were highly acculturated to the environmental Kurdish culture: in addition to sharing values with respect to such areas as marriage, family, and honour, they also held common magical beliefs and worshipped at the same holy graves. The Jews observed the Sabbath, dietary regulations, and the purity laws, but they had virtually no knowledge of the Talmud, and religious learning was not important. In contrast, the Jewish community in Ghardaia in the north-west Sahara shared few religious practices with the neighbouring Muslims. They adhered rigidly to traditional Jewish values and practices; they prayed in the synagogue three times a day, and religious learning was highly valued in the community. Inte-grated with "orthodox" Jewish practices were local magico-religious practices whose historical origins were often lost, but only a few of them were held in common with Muslims. The customs peculiar to the Ghardaia Jews sometimes functioned to uphold traditional values; for example, at the age of five years every boy had to undergo an elaborate ceremonial initiation which served to dramatise the importance of religious learning for Jewish males.

The Jewish communities under Islam varied greatly in their levels of acculturation to the culture of the majority, but, on a continuum of religious accultur-ation, most of the Middle Eastern communities may be placed mid-way between the highly acculturated Jewish communities of the Far East (India and China) and the very strong sub-cultural distinctiveness of the pre-nineteenth century European Jewish communities. In the early Middle Ages, Jews migrated from the Middle Eastern centres and transplanted their religio-culture to 'alien' environments: the majority migrated to Europe and a much smaller number migrated farther east. The contrast between the development of Judaism in East and West is striking: in the West the Jews not only retained but reinforced their religio-cultural distinctiveness, while in the East the Jews adopted much of the local culture and religion into their own system.

The Jews of China provide one of the few docu-mented Jewish communities which were entirely absorbed, culturally and socially, by a 'host' society. There were probably a number of small Jewish communities in both inland and coastal Chinese towns by CE 1200, and a number of communities, some quite large, are known to have existed in coastal towns between the fourteenth and seventeenth centuries, but the community in Kaifeng was the only one to survive into the nineteenth century. By the end of the nineteenth century, the Jews of Kaifeng too had almost entirely disappeared through assimilation, but there is historical evidence of their substantial acculturation long before this.

There is no doubt that the first Jewish settlers in Kaifeng were Talmudic Jews; in 1850 they still had all the prayerbooks and scrolls required for daily and Sabbath services and for all the festivals and fasts. It appears, however, that Chinese influences entered the Jews' beliefs and practices at an early stage, and Western visitors in the seventeenth and eighteenth centuries found a highly acculturated community whose religion combined certain distinctively Jewish beliefs and practices with beliefs and practices from the environmental Confucian, Buddhist, and Taoist religions. The Jewish temple was still flourishing, and the Jews still practised a number of traditional Jewish commandments such as abstinence from pork, but the attenuation of their Judaism was observed in their poor Hebrew and ignorance of many Jewish rites and festivals. The influence of the non-Jewish religious environment was clearly visible in the architecture of their temple, the use of non-Jewish ritual objects, the observerance of Chinese seasonal festivals, ancestor worship, and absorption of Chinese rituals into the rites of passage, and the use of inscriptions written on stone tablets for the transmission of religious beliefs.   The inscriptions on both the stone tablets and temple archways were written in Chinese, used Chinese terms for God, contained quotations from Confucian writing, and proclaimed that the principles of Confucianism and the religion of the Chinese Jews were the same.[13]

Unlike the Chinese Jews, the Jews in India increased in number, but during their period of comparative isolation from other Jewish communities, their Judaism lost much of its distinctiveness; they adopted many Hindu customs, and they were assimilated into the caste system.   In the sixteenth and seventeenth centuries, European Jews migrated to India and established an orthodox form of Judaism among the Cochin Jews.   The Jews from Europe probably intermarried with the wealthiest families of the established Jewish community, but they came to form a White Jewish caste and completely distinguished themselves from the indigenous Black Jews.   A third caste, composed of the slave and servant converts of the White Jews, also emerged.

Little is known of the religion of the Cochin Jews before their contacts with Western Jews, but it is evident from the thirteenth century tombstones that even then they had an imperfect knowledge of Hebrew and the Bible.   There is more information of the pre-Westernised Judaism of the Bene Israel who, unlike the Cochin Jews, did not come into sustained contact with early European Jewish immigrants to India.   A more distinctive Judaism was introduced to the Bene Israel in the nineteenth century by Cochin Jews, Jewish immigrants from the Middle East, and, somewhat paradoxically, by Christian missionaries who translated the Bible into Marathi and taught Hebrew. But before the recent period of contact with non-Bene Israel Jews, the Judaism of the Bene Israel took highly acculturated forms.   The Bene Israel observed the Sabbath, some of the holy days, some dietary regulations, and circumcision, but knowledge of Hebrew had been lost, and they had adopted a number of religious beliefs and practices from their Hindu neighbours, especially from the higher castes - they objected to the remarriage of widows and they believed that the eating of beef was prohibited by the Jewish religion.

The Bene Israel held a comparatively low-caste position; in the villages of Konkan their traditional caste occupation was oil pressing, and in Bombay, where they concentrated in the nineteenth century, they became a caste of clerks. In addition, the Bene Israel were divided into two sub-castes: the Gora or 'White' Bene Israel, who claimed they were pure descendants of the first Jewish settlers in India, and the lower caste Kala or 'Black' Bene Israel.[14]

Although most Jewish communities under Islam retained a greater religio-cultural distinctiveness than the Jews of China and India, it is the Ashkenazi Jewish communities of medieval and early modern Europe that provide the strongest contrast with the Jewish communities of the East. The Ashkenazi came to put an enormous emphasis on the strict interpretation of religious law and the observance of religious ritual; a "wall" was built around the Torah to lessen the possibility of ritualistic mistakes. In the twelfth and thirteenth centuries, the Haside Ashkenaz ('pious men of Germany') established more rigid precepts against contact with Christian symbols and imposed upon themselves an even stricter ritualism than that required by the Talmud.[15] The cultural distinctiveness of the Jews was not limited to religious beliefs and practices but came to encompass such spheres as everyday language and clothes. Yiddish developed as the distinctive everyday language of the Jews, and in eastern Europe, from the seventeenth to the early twentieth centuries, Jewish appearance and clothes visibly set them apart from non-Jews: the men grew long beards and sidelocks and wore long black caftans and large hats. That special clothes came to signify the orthodox Jew illustrates the encompassing importance of Judaism to Jewish society in Europe. The religious law of the Talmud and its commentaries, codified in the Shulhan Arukh in the sixteenth century, regulated life in the traditional Jewish community, prescribing ritualistic observances and regulating social, business, and filial relationships, as well as dress, diet, and hygiene.

Jewish society in the medieval and early modern period was a traditional one in the sense that change was only accepted if it could be legitimised by values and practices handed down from the past. Legitimacy had to be found in the codes of religious law, and this gave enormous significance to religious scholarship. Men were regarded as superior to women since they were the main 'carriers' of the religion, bearing the major part of the "yoke of the Law." Women had only to learn enough to read their prayers and perform their special ritual activities, but it was the duty of every man to study, and a large proportion did devote part of the day or a certain day of the week to the study of the law. It was common for the wife of a scholar to manage both the home and a business while her husband devoted his time to study of the sacred texts.

At the chedarim (schools) boys first learned to read and write Hebrew and Yiddish. This was followed by the study of the Pentateuch when the boy began to understand, translate, comment, and interpret; and finally he progressed to the study of the Talmud. The aim of the cheder was to turn the more capable pupils into scholars who would study at the community-maintained yeshiva (advanced educational institution) from the age of twelve or thirteen. Only a minority studied at a yeshiva,but the teaching of the basic aspects of Judaism to the majority was a secondary function of the cheder compared with the primary function: the rearing of scholars. Since the hope of most fathers was to see their sons become yeshiva students, they regularly tested their sons and asked learned men to give an opinion on their sons' talents for study. Demands by the child for logical justification of religious rules and norms were welcomed by adults as an indication of the child's intellectual precocity. At the yeshivot, boys analysed the Talmud and its commentaries, compared the different interpretations and attempted to reconcile apparent contradictions in the sacred writings. Students did not achieve rabbinical status at the yeshivot; they had to study for a minimum of six years after marriage before they could receive the scholarly title which entitled them to rule on religious questions. These titles, which accorded the holders special privileges within the community, were awarded by the rabbis officiating in the community, and the status of the title depended on the scholarly status of the rabbi who awarded it.

The three major status attributes in the traditional Jewish community were learning, wealth, and lineage (the scholarship and wealth of ancestors and relatives). Since wealth was not always sufficient to achieve status in the community, many prominent merchants and bankers sought to obtain rabbinic standing. If a man could not achieve high scholarly status, the next best thing was to support his son-in-law while he studied. Marriage and dowries were arranged according to the bridegroom's religious scholarship.

There were no estates within the Jewish community and many gradations of wealth and learning. Wealth had a precarious basis because of the insecure conditions of Jewish life, and high status based on a scholarly lineage had to be validated by the individual's own scholarship. Educational opportunities were formally open to all males, but environmental factors made the opportunities more accessible to some. In eastern Europe, for example, a child born into a scholarly and wealthy family residing in a centre for rabbinical scholarship in Lithuania had an environment far more conducive to study than a child born into a non-scholarly poor family residing in a small village without a rabbi in the Ukraine. Thus, long rabbinical lineages developed. If a rabbi had no son, he generally obtained a scholarly son-in-law to carry on the rabbinical tradition in his family.

The status system was given expression and sanction in the synagogue. During public prayer the women were segregated in a special section or room above the synagogue hall from which, through special windows, they could hear and see the men at prayer. Scholars and wealthy men sat at the Eastern Wall towards which all faces were turned when prayers were said. Those seated farthest from the Eastern Wall had the lowest status. It was an honour to be called to the reading of the Torah, but certain passages were more honorific than others and these were given to the scholars. The rich displayed their wealth and reinforced their status by pledging large sums for charity when "called to the Torah" and by donating scrolls, curtains for the Ark and other ritual objects in the synagogue.16

Jews and Christians held many magical beliefs in common, but even in this sphere there were important differences between them. The invocation of demons and the distinction between white and black magic were of minor significance for the Jews compared with their importance in the Christian religio-culture.

Another difference was that magic did not have an anti-establishment function among the Jews; the more scholarly Jews emphasised the need for both adherence to the legalistic rabbinical classification of magic and knowledge of the mystical cabbalistic writings. Talmudical scholars were often the greatest miracle workers.[17] Thus, although there was some cultural overlap in magic between Christians and Jews, this was of limited significance, and in general the religio-cultural distinctiveness of the Ashkenazi Jews remained very marked in most parts of Europe up to the end of the eighteenth century.

In comparison with the Ashkenazi, the Sephardi Jews of the Iberian peninsula adopted a greater part of the dominant culture. Judaism was less encompassing in the socio-cultural system of the Sephardim, and from the thirteenth century onwards refernces to non-observance of the religious law by the Jews in Spain are common. The Ashkenazi observed a greater number of rituals, interpreted the religious law in a stricter fashion, and took greater heed of their rabbis.[18]

Environmental Culture and Social Structure

Any explanation of the different levels of acculturation among Jewish communities must take into consideration demographic distribution. The Jewish population in each single community was not, however, a significant independent variable: urban concentration did not guarantee, and rural distribution did not necessarily weaken, continuing socio-cultural distinctiveness. A few of the Chinese urban communities were fairly large at one time, but they disappeared, while Jewish communities in rural areas in India, the Middle East, and Europe increased in number. The largest urban communities were found in the Near Eastern and Mediterranean areas where many Jewish communities occupied entire quarters of the towns. In Europe most communities were not large; the number of Jewish families in a few commercial centres reached the hundreds but European Jewry was widely distributed in many towns and villages, especially in eastern Europe.

Far more significant than the number in each community was contact with other communities, and here

the greater density and communication of Jews within
Europe must be considered. In the High Middle Ages,
western and central Europe contained most of the
European Jews, but there was a movement east in the
latter part of the medieval period, and, in the early
modern period, the vast majority of European Jews
lived in eastern Europe. In the pre-modern societies,
mobility between communities was law, but the Jews
were more mobile than most, and, although often
infrequent and irregular, the network of contacts and
ties between the European communities supported
the knowledge of, and identification with, a "people"
which stretched far beyond the immediate community.
This was not the case for the Jews of the East and
some parts of the Middle East, many of whom knew
little or nothing of a Jewish people outside their
own immediate community.

Although the most acculturated communities are
to be found among those isolated for long periods
from the centres of Jewish settlement, there are also
examples of isolated communities which retained a very
high level of religio-cultural distinctiveness, and
the history of Western Jewry since the eighteenth
century has shown that large numbers, extensive
communication, and a sense of identity with a far-
ranging "people" do not prevent substantial acculturation. It is clear that small numbers and lack of
contact with other communities only made a community
particularly susceptible to an absorbent environment.
An explanation of variations in the level of Jewish
religious acculturation requires, therefore, an
analysis of those aspects of the religio-culture and
social structure of the "host" societies which would
affect the cultural and social barriers between
minority and majority.

In the cultural environments of the "pre-modern"
societies under discussion, religion was central and
played a very important part in the dominant groups'
orientations to religious minorities. The major
religions in China were both syncretistic and culturally pluralistic; they combined and reconciled
diverse beliefs and practices, and little or no
attempt was made to demand the exclusive allegiance
of worshippers. In accommodating non-Jewish practices
into their religion, the Chinese Jews were following
the general Chinese practice of observing sacraments
from a number of religious traditions - Buddhist,

Taoist, etc. - side by side.

Confucianism, the official Chinese state doctrine, was neither a state religion nor a church in the Western sense; the literati espoused a doctrinal orthodoxy and emphasised the necessity of performing certain rites, but there was little or no attempt to coerce others. The Chinese political elite permitted and encouraged religious syncretism if it was politically efficacious, and it tolerated diverse religions, as long as they were not hostile to the state. Max Weber wrote, "the most important and absolute limit to practical tolerance for the Confucian state consisted in the fundamental importance of the ancestor cult and this-worldly piety for the docility of the patrimonial subject."[19] There was little or no formal constraint on Chinese Jews to conform to non-Jewish beliefs and practices, as long as they recognised the ancestral cult and religious status of the Chinese emperor. In addition, neither religious nor nationalist notions predisposed the dominant group to separate the Jews from other Chinese. The concept of nationalism or of a nation did not arise in China since the empire was regarded as the universe, composed of concentric circles, becoming increasingly barbarous the farther they lay from the Chinese core.[20] Like the Muslims, with whom they were sometimes categorised, the Chinese Jews lived within the universe and were not, therefore, subject to any differential legal, political, economic or social treatment.

The important elements of the Chinese social structure, the extended family, clan, and political rule by a centralised bureaucracy, did not dispose the Jews to enter a peculiar structural niche in the society. The original Jewish settlers in Kaifeng were probably specialists in manufacturing, dyeing, or pattern printing of cotton fabrics, but economic diversity among native Kaifeng Jews is illustrated by a 1512 inscription which mentions degree-holders, civil and military officials, farmers, artisans, traders, and shopkeepers. In the fifteenth, sixteenth, and seventeenth centuries, a number of Jews attained high political and military posts, and others were successful as physicians and scholars.[21]

The majority of Kaifeng Jews were members of the small Chinese merchant-artisan class which occupied

63

a social position between the mass peasant base and the literati, but from the beginning of the fourteenth century, Kaifeng Jews entered the scholar-official class in increasing numbers and some held important positions. In contrast to the free towns in Europe, Chinese towns were seats of the mandarinate, and the ambition of most merchant families in the towns was to break into the scholar-official class.[22] The literati was not a completely closed class, and in the large, wealthy, imperial city of Kaifeng, Jews, as much as others, could take advantage of the limited opportunities for mobility. Song Nai Rhee has argued that the civil service system transformed Jewish intellectuals into Confucian literati, a transformation which affected their total philosophical and religious perspective. Some members of the Jewish community, who were more conscious of their religious distinctiveness, disapproved of the Confucianisation of the Jewish intellectuals, but as members of the Chinese elite, the Jewish scholar-officials were bound to have an important influence on the whole community. In addition, participation in the civil service contributed towards intermarriage and assimilation; the Jewish literati had to leave Kaifeng since, like all other civil servants, they were prohibited from holding official positions in the place of their birth.[23] It may be hypothesised, therefore, that the substantial acculturation and assimilation of the Chinese Jews was related both to the Chinese cultural orientations (religious syncretism and pluralism) and to the Chinese social structure which permitted the socio-economic integration of the Jews in Chinese society.

Like the Chinese religions, the general dispositions of Indian Hinduism towards minority religions were syncretistic and culturally pluralistic. The dominant Hindus tolerated other religions which did not threaten the caste system and the supremacy of the Brahmins, but although they were pluralistic in the sense that they did not actively attempt to enforce a Hindu monopoly, the assimilative character of the caste system and the syncretism of the Hindu religion resulted in a virtual monopoly of Hinduism over much of India.[24] Although the Bene Israel had only acquired the status of a low caste, it had presumably been to their advantage to accept voluntarily certain Hindu rituals and the caste system; it was difficult for an alien and therefore impure group, which was not economically self-sufficient, to exist outside the Hindu community. Once the Jews had adopted the caste system and some principal practices of Hinduism, their own distinctive beliefs and rituals were tolerated within the Hindu community itself.

Although the general orientations of Hinduism strongly disposed the Jews to substantial acculturation, the Indian social structure did not strongly dispose them to substantial assimilation. Srinivas has described Indian society as subject to two opposed types of solidarity: the solidarity of village and the solidarity of caste.[25] Indian villages were largely autonomous units; there were no large-scale inter-regional religious institutions in India, and the authority of the secular rulers rarely extended to the internal affairs of the village. For many centuries the Bene Israel resided in the villages of Konkan, and it is clear that their close association with non-Bene Israel occasionally resulted in intermarriage. However, the solidarity of caste reinforced the social boundaries of the Bene Israel and enabled them to increase in number. As in China, the Indian Jews were not singled out for differential treatment as Jews, but unlike in China, the very integration of the Jews into the Hindu religio-social system contributed to their social preservation.

In contrast to the syncretistic religions of the East, Islam developed out of a monotheistic tradition and inherited from it strong dispositions to doctrinism. Islam was flexible in incorporating folk beliefs and practices of the nominal Muslim population, but its syncretism was slight in comparison with the inclusive tendencies of the Eastern religions, and the dominant Islamic groups were consistent in their rejection of distinctive Judaic beliefs and practices. Again, in contrast with Eastern religions, which were generally content to coexist peacefully with other religions, Islam has often been markedly monopolistic; it has sought, often with success, to establish itself as the only religion in a particular area by converting or eliminating non-Islamic religious groups. Islamic monopolism was, however, mainly directed towards pagans or non-monotheists,and the Islamic disposition toward the Jews was, in general, more pluralistic than monopolistic. Mohammed established the general principle that adherents of non-Islamic monotheistic faiths should be allowed

to live under Muslim rule, and although in its early
warrior phase this principle was not consistently
upheld, Arab religious pluralism became firmly
established once the Arabs had conquered vast
territories containing large non-Islamic populations.

The broad pluralist disposition of the dominant
Arabs towards other monotheists was formulated in a
number of treaties which provided for the protection
of the persons, property, and religious observances
of minorities in return for payment to the Islamic
rulers. During the High Middle Ages this pluralism
was interrupted by two outbreaks of monopolism,
limited in time and scope: one in Egypt from 1012
to 1019 under al-Hakim and the other under the
Almohad conquerors of North Africa and Spain in the
1140's. In both cases, Christians, as well as Jews,
were given the choice of conversion to Islam or
death. Such occurrences were, however, very rare
in the Arab world. The general condition of non-
Muslims declined under the rule of foreign "barbarian"
military castes in the fourteenth and fifteenth
centuries, revived under the Ottomon Turks in the
sixteenth and seventeenth centuries, and then
deteriorated again, but over long periods and up to
recent times, the Jews under Islam enjoyed a
comparatively secure existence, free from persecution.

Within the framework of general religious pluralism, the Jews were subject to a certain amount of
differential treatment, although, again, this varied
considerably between periods and provinces. Some,
but by no means all, of this differential treatment
was motivated by a desire to secure the monopoly
of Islam over its nominal adherents and to protect
Islam from "deviant" religions. In order to
demonstrate the superiority of Islam over other
religions, numerous restrictions on non-Muslims were
introduced concerning such matters as modes of dress,
size of buildings, and interfaith contacts. These
restrictions, which applied to Jews, as well as other
religious minorities, were seldom enforced, and in
fact, discrimination was very intermittent.[26] Non-
tolerant and segregationist policies were more likely
to be found where the Muslim population adhered to
a sectarian form of Islam. In the Yemen, under the
rule of the Sh'ites, conditions were particularly
oppressive; Jews were regarded as ritually unclean,
they were subject to many restrictions, and in the

seventeenth century they were forced out of the towns to live in special areas on the outskirts. As the only non-Muslim religious minority in the Yemen, the Jews were without rights, and they were forced to seek Muslim patrons who would provide them with protection in exchange for payment.

Many Jewish communities under Islam were subject to heavy fiscal discrimination, but with a few exceptions, such as the Yemen, other forms of discrimination were slight or non-existent. The Jews had undergone a transformation from an agricultural people to one of merchants and artisans in the seventh and eighth centuries, but since there were few restrictions in the economic sphere, they undertook a great variety of occupations and did not become economically differentiated from urban Muslims. The Middle Eastern Jews shared both in the prosperous mercantile period from the ninth to the thirteenth centuries and in the economic decline in the later Middle Ages and following centuries.[27]

In most cases, the residential separation of the Jews was voluntary: there were no legally segregated quarters, but predominantly homogeneous religious quarters were customary in Muslim towns and there was no degradation associated with living in one. The Jews also had their own semi-autonomous community organisation to which Islamic rulers delegated substantial political authority and which was entrusted with the task of collecting taxes. But despite fairly distinct living quarters and community organisation, close and intimate association with Muslims was not uncommon.[28]

A comparison of the highly acculturated Kurdish Jews of Iraq and the more culturally distinctive Ghardaia Jews of the north-west Sahara shows a considerable difference in the level of social interaction with Muslims. The majority of Kurdish Jews were manual labourers, living in the villages and small towns of Islamic Kurds. In the small towns, they lived by choice in a separate quarter adjacent to the Muslim quarter, but many Muslims lived in the Jewish quarter, and some even lived in Jewish households as lodgers or workers. Jews and Muslims visited each other and ate in each others' houses. In contrast, the Ghardaia Jews were highly segregated both from the neighbouring Arabs, who belonged to the

Malekite sect, and the neighbouring Berbers, who belonged to the puritanical Ibadite sect. The Ghardaia Jews lived in a ghetto-like quarter, performed specialist economic functions for the Muslims, and interacted with Muslims only in impersonal relationships.[29] In general, however, the social boundaries enclosing the Jews under Islam were limited and took mainly voluntary forms.

Like Islam, Christianity was an insular religion with only limited dispositions to syncretism; the Christian church was flexible in incorporating pagan folk beliefs and practices which did not present articulate religious alternatives or challenges, but it was consistent in establishing clear boundaries with alternative religious systems, such as Judaism. The Christian Church differed from Islam, however, in so far as it was far less disposed to take a pluralistic stance towards other monotheistic faiths.

The fact that the Jews were the only deviant religious group whose existence was tolerated by the central organs of the Church is important to an understanding of the situation of the Jews in medieval Europe. Muslims were not tolerated except on a temporary basis in Spanish and Italian areas, and Christian heretics were bloodily suppressed. The Jews were the sole recognised representatives of religious dissent, the only group to fall outside the otherwise complete religious monopoly of the Church. The ecclesiastical doctrine, formulated by the Church fathers and the early popes, stated that the Jews should be tolerated in a submissive state until the end of days, at which time their conversion would herald the second coming of Christ. The Church taught that the exile and submissive state of the Jews was a God-inflicted penalty for the Jewish repudiation of Christ and could thus be regarded as evidence for the truth of Christianity. This doctrine did not mean that the Church should not attempt to convert Jews, but conversion by force was in general officially prohibited.

The policy of limited pluralism with regard to the Jews was held relatively consistently by the Papacy and the higher ranks of the Church throughout the medieval period; with a few exceptions, the central offices of the Church counselled tolerance and restraint during intolerant periods, and they passed decrees whose purpose was to protect Jews and safeguard their property. The Church had little executive power outside the pontifical states and feudal lordships of individual bishops, but the principles of the Church toward the Jews were very influential in determining the policies of secular rulers who generally found that the existence of a Jewish community was congruent with their economic and fiscal interests. The official Church policy of limited tolerance was, however, little appreciated or known by the Christian masses and the lower levels of the Church hierarchy; local and regional clerics, particularly parish priests and wandering monks, were often supporters or leaders of anti-Jewish outbreaks. During periods of unrest, such as the times of the crusades and the Black Death, neither the Church nor most secular authorities were able or willing to prevent massacres of whole Jewish communities. Thus, although European Jews were often protected by sovereign powers, outbreaks of persecution were far more frequent under Christianity than under Islam.

The Church was rarely directly responsible for the persecutions and massacres, but it provided encouragement and legitimation for such activities by its teaching on the Jewish deicide of Christ, as well as its emphasis on Jewish social inferiority and unworthiness. Populist outbreaks against Jews occurred only after the Church had established an effective monopoly in Europe. The first major pogroms in Europe occurred at the end of the eleventh century when the lower stratum of the crusaders extended the principle of revenge on the infidel to native Jews. In the thirteenth century the accusation that the Jews murdered Christian children for their Passover rituals replaced the crusading ideologies as a pretext for massacre, and in the fourteenth century the popular image of the Jew became an integral part of the growing demonology: the Jews were accused of being Satan's associates on earth and widespread large-scale pogroms followed the accusation that the Jews had caused the Black Death by polluting the wells.[30]

It should be emphasised that the massacre of Jews was not an expression of racial or nationalistic antipathy. In the medieval period national self-consciousness was weak, especially in Germany; the Germans thought of themselves as members of a tribe

69

(Saxons, Franks, Bavarians, etc.) or as citizens of
the Holy Roman Empire. The Jews were distinguished,
both in law and in popular beliefs, not in terms of
race or nation, but in terms of religion; they were
seen as "deliberate unbelievers" whose rejection of
Christianity could only be explained by their
association with Satan. The popular beliefs that
conceived of Jews as "monsters" with demonic features
provided clear justification for their destruction
without remorse or guilt.[31]

The tragic side of European Jewish history should
not obscure the fact that there were long periods
when a limited tolerance, sanctioned by the Church,
did prevail. But in order to safeguard its virtual
religious monopoly, the Church found it necessary
to segregate that group over which its religious
authority did not extend. The segregation of the
Jews by the Church began in the early centuries
after Christ when the Church was having little success
in converting the Jews and when Judaism was regarded
as a dangerous proselytising competitor, but the
Church continued its policy of segregation long after
Judaism had ceased to be a threat. The Church
regulations providing for the segregation of the Jews
were extended and elaborated in minutest detail in
the later Middle Ages.

Although the voluntary ghetto was common throughout the medieval period, it did not become an
enforced legal institution until the fifteenth century.
The Jews did not oppose the legal institution of
separate quarters, but many did object to the Jewish
badge,which was first instituted, under the auspices
of the Church, in the thirteenth century and then
took one and a half centuries to become firmly
established. The increased emphasis of the Church on
the segregation of the Jews in the latter part of the
medieval age reflected the fears of churchmen that
the Jews encouraged, directly or indirectly, the
development of Christian heterodoxies and sectarian
deviations.[32]

The majority of European states came to follow
the Church's segregationist and discriminatory
programme, but religious orientations of the dominant
group cannot alone account for the clear legal,
economic, and social separation of the Jews in
medieval society. It is also appropriate to consider

70

the Jews' position and functions in the social and
economic structures of European feudal societies.

In the early Middle Ages, the Jews were welcomed
by many European rulers as a class of merchants who
could provide valuable services in international and
wholesale trade. In the Carolingian period the terms
"Jew" and "merchant" were used almost interchangeably.
The Jewish occupational structure was at first
diversified in trade, crafts, and credit facilities,
and despite the antagonism of the Church, many Jewish
communities achieved social prestige and political
influence by their association with the secular
rulers. From the period of the Crusades, a class of
gentile wholesale merchants grew, and the Jews were
increasingly restricted to money lending, which was
forbidden to gentiles by the canonical prohibition
of the Church. The Jews lost the high status they
held prior to the first Crusade and came to be
despised more and more as a people identified with
usury. Jewish participation in agriculture constantly
declined: many Jewish land-holdings were expropriated,
but in any case, their insecure situation put a
premium on owning property that could be moved. The
prohibition on joining guilds and other discriminatory
legislation and practices prevented Jewish participation in a number of crafts and occupations. In
consequence, the European Jews developed from a people
with a wide variety of occupations to a predominantly
mercantile people with a strong emphasis on the money
trade.[33]

In addition to their economic specialisation, the
Jews were further separated by the corporate structure
of medieval society. Within the feudal system of
estates, the Jews formed a distinct corporation with
their own relatively autonomous jurisdiction. The
legal status of the Jewish "estate" came to be denoted
by the term "serfdom," but the question of who had
jurisdiction over the Jewish "serfs" was much disputed.
The powerful popes of the twelfth and thirteenth
centuries proclaimed the perpetual serfdom of the Jews
to the Church, and they issued decrees concerning the
Jews which they declared were binding on the whole of
the Christian world. This theological doctrine of
Jewish "serfdom" was disputed by the emperor in
Germany and the monarchs of Western Europe. The royal
theory of Jewish serfdom became an actuality in Western
Europe by the end of the thirteenth century, and in

Germany, jurisdiction over the Jews shifted from the
imperial crown to the German princes and cities by the
fifteenth century.

Jewish "serfdom" should not be equated with
villeinage; the Jews were, in many respects, the
"chattels" of the sovereign power, but in a feudal
context they were comparatively free, since they
lived under the sovereign's protection and enjoyed a
considerable measure of corporative autonomy and
independence.

The necessary alliance the Jews had to make with
the monarchs was, in turn, a contributing factor to
their economic differentiation in medieval Europe.
In return for substantial fiscal contributions and
economic services, the monarchs protected the Jews
and their property, facilitated their economic enterprises, and sometimes authorised certain economic
functions, such as money lending, to be performed
exclusively by Jews. Some monarchs exploited other
estates via the mediation of Jewish money lenders;
the monarchs extorted large contributions from the
Jews who in turn charged high interest rates for
their loans. The alliance of the Jews with the
monarchs antagonised both the nobles, who were often
in debt to the Jews, and the burghers, who resented
Jewish economic competition. The combination and
interpenetration of economic antagonism and religious
hatred had tragic consequences for the Jews.

With the decline of feudalism, the growth of the
Christian merchant classes, and the greater emphasis
on national and cultural identities among the Western
European nations, the economic functions of the Jews
were found to be increasingly dispensable. The
massacres and explusions from the Western nations in
the thirteenth, fourteenth, and fifteenth centuries
led to a Jewish migration to Poland and Lithuania
where the continuation of feudal structures, the
absence of a native merchant class, and the greater
ethnic heterogeneity of the general population provided
a more congenial environment.[34] In eastern Europe,
the Jews entered a comparatively wide variety of
occupations, but, in general, they remained a trading
and artisan group, mediating between the nobility and
the peasant masses. Eastern Europe had few cities,
and the majority of Jews lived in small towns and
villages, nearer to non Jews than did the ghetto Jews

of western Europe. Despite this proximity, intimate association between Jews and gentiles was rare.[35]

In the feudal and early modern European states, the Jews had considerable self-government and judicial autonomy; in return for taxes paid to the rulers, the Jews were permitted to elect their own leaders who employed salaried functionaries to administer communal institutions, represented the community in external relations, supervised the collection of taxes, and had certain sanctioning powers to enforce social and religious conformity. The most severe and effective formal sanction within the Jewish community was the cherem (excommunication) which ranged from threatened, and temporary, to permanent excommunication. The excommunicant was excluded from all religious facilities and might also be excluded from economic and social relationships. Since this meant exclusion from all society, the excommunicant was forced into a terribly isolated situation. It was not, of course, possible for a Jew to be unaffiliated with the community and yet remain a Jew; Jewish identity was a corporate identity.

The corporation or kehilla employed a number of salaried functionaries to administer community functions and staff the many organisations which the community maintained. The community employees combined secular and religious roles in varying degrees; the more secular functionaries included the shtadlanim (interceders for the community) and tax collectors, and the more religious functionaries included the rabbis, cantors, beadles, slaughterers, and scribes. Although the kehilla employed professional rabbis, the rabbinate was largely independent and autonomous. The performance of rabbinical roles (scholar, teacher, judge, and ritualistic adviser) was not dependent on an appointment of office, and the professional salaried rabbis often accepted the judgement of the private rabbis who supported themselves by fees. A formal rabbinical hierarchy did not exist; the local autonomy of the rabbinate meant that the only hierarchy was an informal one based on number of followers and recognition of outstanding religious scholarship.[36]

As noted, the Sephardi Jews were less culturally distinctive than the Ashkenazi, and this difference may be related to the more tolerant conditions in

Spain and Portugal up to the end of the fourteenth century.

The Iberian Jews were persecuted by the Christianised Visigoths in the seventh century, but the Arab conquest of Spain in the eighth century brought a long period of pluralistic tolerance which was only interrupted for a short period in the twelfth century by the fundamentalist Almohads. The Church in Christian Spain made many attempts to curtail the rights of Jews, but a combination of circumstances, which included the presence of a large Muslim population, made for a comparatively secure and settled Jewish existence. This came to an end in the late fourteenth and fifteenth centuries when renewed Christian monopolism took the form of massacres, forced conversions, and expulsion.

During the long period of pluralism, the Sephardim were not greatly separated from non-Jews in social or economic spheres, and they played a significant part in the cultural and economic life of Spain. Unlike the Ashkenazim, they were active in most occupations and a few rose to eminence and influence in the Spanish courts.[37]

Where the Sephardi rabbis were more strict than the Ashkenazi in their religious rulings, they were responding to the greater non-Jewish tolerance towards, and social interaction with, the Jews. They made a number of rulings which were intended to counteract the close contact with the Arab population and the concomitant adoption of Arab customs, but it is doubtful whether the Sephardi rabbis, whose authority was not as great as the Ashkenazi rabbis, were very successful in this. Where the Sephardim did observe certain religious practices to a greater extent than the Ashkenazim, these were often observances, such as lustrations, which were also practised by the Arabs.

Where the Ashkenazi rabbis were more lenient in their religious rulings, this reflected the greater persecution and separation of the Jews in central and north-west Europe. The occupational specialisation of the Ashkenazi Jews meant that they had to depend on non-Jews for many goods and services which did not always conform to the religious requirements of Jewish law. For example,Jews often depended on non-Jews for bread and wine, and the Ashkenazi rabbis had to modify the law to legitimise the deviance from certain talmudic injunctions which this involved. The Ashkenazi rabbis also modified religious laws to avoid persecution. For example, they ruled that it was permissible to put out a fire on the Sabbath since it was common in Germany for a Jew to be thrown into the flames if his house caught fire.

Since revenge against the Christian persecutors was not possible and exhortations for a supernatural revenge appeared to have little effect, the Ashkenazi Jews tended to accept persecution as a just retribution by God for past Jewish sins and failure to observe the religious law. They atoned for these unknown sins by abstinence and self-affliction; the number of religious fasts increased and a number of new rituals, such as flagellation on the eve of the Day of Atonement, were introduced. Many laws and customs developed in connection with the martyrs of pogroms, and a new type of religious poetry dealt with persecution and sacrifice.[38]

Early Modern Europe

The important changes in post-medieval Europe - the Renaissance, Reformation, and Counter-Reformation - had comparatively little impact on the cultural distinctiveness and social position of the majority of European Jewish communities. Forced conversions and explusions became less frequent after the fifteenth century, but most rulers maintained or even reinforced Jewish segregation. With one exception, Jewish communities were largely untouched by the development of secularism and individualism among the non-Jewish upper stratum during the Rennaissance period. The exception was Italy where the rich Jewish loan-bankers were socially accepted by the Renaissance Christian elite who were themselves bourgeois and involved in commercial operations. Italian Jewry, and particularly its upper class, made significant contributions to the Renaissance and adopted the Italian language, fashion, and modes of behaviour. In many respects, Italian Jewry was a Renaissance society in miniature; the Jewish patricians who were the nucleus of this society, lived in luxurious houses, commissioned artists, and employed scholars who were versed in both religious and secular knowledge.[39]

In the second half of the sixteenth century, the Counter-Reformation put an end to the tolerance of the Italian Renaissance. Jews were expelled from certain areas, but in most Italian states, there was a return to the segregation of the medieval period: Jews were forced to wear distinctive garb and live in ghettos. The segregation imposed by the religio-political authorities was not reinforced by any vehement anti-Jewish feeling of the Italian people; violent outbreaks were rare and continued friendly association is demonstrated by the number of occasions during the seventeenth and eighteenth centuries when the Church found it necessary to prohibit Christians from joining Jews in social recreations such as dancing. For this reason, and because their segregation was a totally involuntary one, Italian Jews continued to adopt Italian fashion and culture. Those who could not endure the forced segregation and attendant pauperisation either emigrated to northern Europe or converted.[40]

In northern Europe, the immediate effects of the Reformation and the increased independence of the German states from the imperial powers were further anti-Jewish measures and expulsions, especially from the Lutheran states. The expulsion of Jews from German cities in the fifteenth and early sixteenth centuries resulted in a greater dispersal of the Jews over rural districts, but the trend was reversed in the early seventeenth century when the Protestant rulers readmitted the Jews with improved privileges in order to use Jewish commercial and financial skills in the development of their states. The Counter-Reformation introduced measures to segregate Jews, but, as the Church continued to uphold the principle that the Jews should be tolerated until the end of days, there were few expulsions from Catholic lands, and in the Habsburg possessions there was even some improvement in Jewish status.[41]

Comparisons

It is now possible to make a number of statements accounting for the gross differences in levels of Jewish acculturation in the societies discussed. It should be emphasised, however, that with regard to a number of the "isolated" communities, our conclusions will have to be very tentative. The historical data is often sparse and, in some cases, almost non-existent. It is not possible to trace the religio-cultural developments of the Chinese, Indian, and many Middle Eastern communities over the centuries since much of our information derives from Europeans who visited and described the communities after they were "discovered." In many cases, we can only compare a number of static pictures of communities at the end of their periods of isolation and from these attempt to reconstruct their histories. However, what independent historical evidence we do have suggests that, where the distinctiveness of Judaism became highly attenuated, the process occurred over a long period and cannot be explained in terms of the char-acteristics and orientations of the first generation of Jewish settlers. If the original Jewish settlers had been predisposed to cultural and social absorption by the "host" society, the community would not have survived centuries of isolation from other Jewish communities, even in a highly attenuated form.

The size of the Jewish community and the distance from the major centres of Jewish settlement are important variables but should not be overemphasised. Comparatively small numbers, and lack of contact with other Jewish communities, could only make a community particularly malleable to its cultural and social environments. One important cultural dimension was the strength of the boundaries of the dominant religion of the majority. Jewish acculturation was much greater in those societies where the dominant religion was syncretic than in those societies where the dominant religion was insular. Although the differences between Judaism and the environmental religious systems were initially much greater in China and India than in the Middle East and Europe, the syncretism of the Eastern religions contributed to the much greater loss of Jewish religio-cultural dis-tinctiveness in the East.

Another important dimension was the strength of the dominant group's disposition to demand allegiance to its religion within its defined territory. As might be expected, syncretic religions were more disposed to pluralism and insular religions were more disposed to monopolism. The greater the tendency of the dominant group to coerce the Jews into accepting the majority religion, the more the Jews emphasised their religio-cultural distinctiveness. The greater the tendency of the dominant group to accept the existence of Judaism, the more likely the Jews would acculturate to the majority or core culture.

Both religio-cultural and social structural dimensions influenced the extent to which the Jews were separated socially from non-Jews. Where Jews were separated, they were less likely to adopt the non-Jewish religio-culture. Where Jews were not so separated and social contacts with non-Jews were more frequent and intimate, acculturation was far more likely. The extent to which the Jews were separated within a society was often related to the dominant group's disposition to monopolism or pluralism. A total monopolistic policy, if successful, would have resulted in the disappearance of the Jews, but successful monopolism was very rare. Even when Jews were forced to convert to Christianity, they often remained unassimilated, and this drove the dominant group to segregate them still further.

Although attempts at a total monopolism by means of massacres, forced conversions, and expulsions were not uncommon in Christian Europe, periods of pluralism were generally longer. Variations in social separation have, therefore, to be considered within the framework of pluralism, although it is obvious that Jews were more likely to be separated from non-Jews in those societies whose pluralist stance was of a comparatively limited form. In some cases, segregation of the Jews was motivated by the dominant group's desire to impose or retain its religious monopoly over the non-Jewish population. In medieval Europe, however, the Jews were segregated by more encompassing barriers long after Judaism had ceased to be a threat to Christian monopolism.

Some spheres of separation of Jews from non-Jews were little related, at least in any direct way, to the religious motives and orientations of the dominant group. Differences in the social structures of "host" societies were also relevant. The feudal structure of European societies made for the separation of Jews in the economic, social, and political spheres. Jews were less segregated in Middle Eastern societies, but the convergence of religion and state under Islam involved the political separation of religious minorities. In China and India, Jews were not politically separated and corporate Jewish polities did not develop. The Indian caste system did make for some social separation of Jews, but, in contrast to the Middle East and Europe, the Jews were separated within the dominant religious system and not outside it. The social separation of Jews as a caste in India implied a substantial Jewish acculturation, while in the Middle East and Europe, the greater the social separation of Jews from non-Jews, the greater the tendency of Jews to retain or reinforce their religio-cultural distinctiveness.

NOTES

[1]Leslie, 1972: 4-24, 60.

[2]Strizower, 1962: ch 3; Mandelbaum, 1939: 123-60; Strizower, 1971. The Bene Israel claim that they are descendants from the ten lost tribes of Israel and that they reached India about 175 BCE. The Cochin Jews claim that their ancestors came to India after the destruction of the Second Temple in CE 70. There is no independent evidence to support these claims. Although it is possible that there were Jewish communities in India as early as the fifth century CE, the only certainty is that Jews had settled in India before the end of the first millennium CE.

[3]Chouraqui, 1968: 86-97; Goitein, 1955: 109-15, 122-3.

[4]Baron, 1952-1980, Vol 2, 191-209; Vol 5, 3-20; Vol 6, 16-27.

[5]Ibid, Vol 3, 99-114.

[6]Most Middle Eastern Jews spoke Aramaic before they adopted Arabic, but only in the mountains of Kurdistan and Armenia did Jews retain the Aramaic dialect, Goitein, 1955: 131-40.

[7]A number of Middle Eastern Jewish communities developed Judeo-Arabic vernaculars, but they contained far less Hebrew than Yiddish, the language of the Ashkenazi European Jews. Another difference was that Yiddish, a fusion of Medieval German and Hebrew, was transplanted from Germany and preserved in an area, Eastern Europe, entirely foreign to it.

[8] Goitein, 1955: 188-92; Chouraqui, 1968: 67-69.

[9] Slouschz, 1927.

[10] Goitein, 1955: 177-87.

[11] Strizower, 1962: 34-9.

[12] Feitelson, (infra); Briggs and Guele, 1964.

[13] White, 1942; Leslie, 1972: chs 7-9.

[14] Strizower, 1971: 27-30.

[15] Zimmels, 1958: 188-204.

[16] For detailed accounts of the traditional Jewish society see, Jacob Katz, 1961; and Mark Zborowski and Elizabeth Herzog, 1952.

[17] Trachtenberg, 1961.

[18] Zimmels, 1958: 188-204, 251-62.

[19] Weber, 1964: 213-14.

[20] Balazs, 1964: 22.

[21] White, 1942; Leslie, 1971: 108-11.

[22] Balazs, 1964: 41-2, 70-8.

[23] Rhee, 1973.

[24] Weber, 1958.

[25] Srinivas, 1952: 31-2.

[26] Baron, 1952-80, Vol 3, 120-72; Chouraqui, 1968: 42-55.

[27] Goitein, 1955: 73-8, 99-124.

[28] Goitein, Vol 2, 1971: chs 5, 7; Hirschberg, 1958.

[29] Feitelson, (infra); Briggs and Guele, 1964.

[30] Baron, 1952-80; Vol 4, 5-12, 89-149; Vol 9, 3-54; Vol 10, 122-91; Poliakov, 1965: chs 2-7.

[31] Kisch, 1949: 306-16, 323-5.

[32]Baron, 1952-80, Vol 9, 3-96; Vol 11, 77-121.

[33]Ibid, Vol 6, 150-277; Vol 12, 25-197; Kisch, 1949: 318-22, 327-9.

[34]Baron, 1952-80, Vol 9, 135-236; Vol 10, 41-117; Vol 11, 3-76; 192-283.

[35]Zborowski and Herzog, 1952: 66-7, 151-8.

[36]Baron, 1942: ch 11.

[37]Baron, 1952-80: Vol 3, 33-46; Vol 4, 27-43; Vol 10, 118-219; Vol 11, 225-49; Vol 13, 3-158; Baer, 1961.

[38]Zimmels, 1958: 205-32, 237-46, 262-6.

[39]Roth, 1968; Roth, 1959; Baron, 1952-80, Vol 13, 159-205.

[40]Roth, 1946: 289-394; Baron, 1952-80, Vol 14, 114-46.

[41]Ibid, Vol 13, 206-96; Vol 14, 147-294.

BIBLIOGRAPHY

Baer, Yitzak
     1961   A History of the Jews in Christian Spain.
                          Philadelphia: Jewish Publication Society.
Balazs, Etienne
     1964   Chinese Civilization and Bureaucracy.
                          New Haven: Yale University Press.
Baron, S. W.
     1942   The Jewish Community. Philadelphia: Jewish
                          Publication Society.

     1952-1980   Social and Religious History of the Jews.
                          New York: Columbia University Press.
Briggs, L. C. and H. L. Guede
     1964   No More for Ever: A Saharan Jewish Town.
                          Cambridge, Mass.: Harvard University Peabody
                          Museum Publications in Archaeology and
                          Ethnology, Vol LV, No 1.
Chouraqui, Andre N.
     1968   Between East and West. Philadelphia: Jewish
                          Publication Society.

Feitelson, Dina
1959   Aspects of the Social Life of Kurdish Jews.
Jewish Journal of Sociology I: 201-216
(infra).

Goitein, S. D.
1953   Jewish Education in Yemen as an Archetype of
Traditional Jewish Education. In C. Frankenstein (ed.) Between Past and Future,
Jerusalem. (See abridged version, infra).

1971   A Mediterranean Society. Los Angeles:
University of California Press, Vol. II.

Hirschberg, H. Z.
1968   The Jewish Quarter in Muslim Cities and
Berber Areas. Judaism 17: 405-21.

Katz, Jacob
1961   Tradition and Crisis: Jewish Society at the
End of the Middle Ages. New York: The
Free Press.

Kisch, Guido
1949   The Jews in Medieval German: A Study of Their
Legal and Social Status. Chicago: University
of Chicago Press.

Leslie, Donald David
1969   The Kaifeng Jewish Community. Jewish Journal
of Sociology II: 175-85.

1972   The Survival of the Chinese Jews: The Jewish
Community of Kaifeng, Leiden.

Mandelbaum, David G.
1939   The Jewish Way of Life in Cochin. Jewish
Social Studies 1: 423-460.

Poliakov, Leon
1965   The History of Anti Semitism. New York:
Vanguard Press.

Rhee, Jong Nai
1973   Jewish Assimilation: The Case of the Chinese
Jews. Comparative Studies in Society and
History 15: 115-26.

Roth, Cecil
1946   The History of Jews in Italy. Philadelphia:
Jewish Publication Society.

1959   The Jews in the Renaissance. Philadelphia:
Jewish Publication Society.

1968   Jewish Society in the Renaissance's Environment. Cahiers D'Histoire Mondiale 11:
239-50.

Slouschz, Nahum
1927   Travels in North Africa. Philadelphia:
          Jewish Publication Society.

Srinivas, M. N.
1952   Religion and Society Among the Coorgs of
          South India. Oxford: Clarendon Press.

Strizower, Schifra
1962   Exotic Jewish Communities. London.

_____
1971   The Children of Israel: The Bene Israel of
          Bombay. Oxford.

Trachtenberg, Joshua
1961   The Devil and the Jews. Philadelphia: Jewish
          Publication Society.

_____
1961   Jewish Magic and Superstition. Philadelphia:
          Jewish Publication Society.

Weber, Max
1958   The Religions of India. New York.

_____
1964   The Religions of China. New York: The Free
          Press.

White, W. C.
1942   Chinese Jews: A Compilation of Matters
          Relating to the Jews of Kaifeng Fu, 3 Volumes.
          (2nd ed., New York: Paragon Book Reprint
          Corporation, 1966).

Zborowski, Mark and Elizabeth Herzog
1952   Life is with People: The Culture of the
          Shetl. New York: International Universities
          Press.

Zimmels, H. J.
1958   Ashkenazim and Sepharadim. London: Oxford
          University Press.

CHAPTER 4

PATRONAGE AND PROTECTION: THE STATUS OF JEWS IN PRECOLONIAL MOROCCO

ALLAN R.   MEYERS

> Basing himself on Arabic and European his-
> torical sources, Allan Meyers, who teaches
> community medicine in the School of Public
> Health at Boston University, explores one of
> the issues studied by Sharot, namely the posi-
> tion of Jews under Muslim rule. This question
> has attracted attention for contemporary polit-
> ical, as well as scholarly, reasons. In the
> Moroccan context, Meyers argues, different
> relationships obtained in different parts of
> the country. The crucial factors were the
> degree of power which local potentates and
> the central government respectively wielded.
> Communal protection obtained where the govern-
> ment was strong and patrol-client relations
> were forged where the local strongment ruled.

Introduction

·The history of Jewish-Mulsim relations in Morocco
begins with the Islamic conquest of North Africa, in
the 7th and 8th centuries, and continues to the present time. However, until very recently, Moroccan
Jewish studies have fallen into the interstices
between two traditions of scholarly research. On the
one hand, there have been studies of Moroccan history
and ethnography, in which Jews appear as important,
though secondary participants. On the other, there
have been studies of Moroccan Jewish history and social
life with some reference to the broader historical,
social, cultural, and political context within which
this history has taken placed.[1] Each of these scholarly traditions has produced studies of lasting and even
monumental importance, but neither has been able to
adequately set Moroccan Jewish communities in their
Moroccan milieux.

Within the past 10-15 years, the mutual isolation
of these two traditions has begun to break down, as
sociologists and anthropologists who have studied
Moroccan Jews in Israel have tried to reconstruct

SOURCE: Original contribution for this volume.

Jewish life in Morocco, mainly to determine the influence of the Moroccan past upon the immigrants' adaptation to life in Israel (Willner and Kohls 1962; Shokeld 1971) and as North Africanist historians and ethnographers have begun to study Moroccan Jews in the context of Moroccan Islam. In this latter regard, the most interesting development has been an exchange involving Lawrence Rosen, an anthropologist, who has written about Jewish-Muslim relations in Morocco (Rosen 1968; 1972; cf., 1979; Stillman 1973), and Norman Stillman, an Orientalist and historian, who has responded with a short and highly critical note (Stillman 1976).

Both Stillman's and Rosen's papers represent only preliminary efforts, and their respective conclusions may be modified by more intensive research. However, since they are both highly qualified North African-ists, each in his respective discipline, and since they disagree so sharply in their conclusions, it is instructive to examine their controversy in greater depth.

The Controversy

Rosen's papers deal mainly with the town of Sefrou, southeast of Fes, where he did ethnographic fieldwork between 1967 and 1968; he was in Sefrou during the Six-Day War of 1967, when there were rumors and threats of reprisals by Muslims against Jews. Using both direct observation and retrospective data, Rosen studies Muslim-Jewish relations, in normal times and in times of stress. He concluded that under normal circumstances, Jews and Muslims lived together in peace, if not harmony; indeed, he contends that many Jews were able to manipulate their relationships with their Muslim neighbors to considerable economic advantages. In times of danger, on the other hand, each Jewish family had a Muslim guarantor to whom it would turn; this person was supposed to protect them from injury and to avenge them if they were harmed.

To Rosen, dyadic relationships - i.e., relation-ships between two individuals - were of the essence of Sefriwi politics. In reference to Muslim-Jewish relations, a Muslim was the dominant superordinate member of each dyad, the patron; the subordinate member, the client, was a Jew:

...in most of central Morocco...
Jews were able to occupy an inter-
mediate role between (Arabs and
Berbers)[2]... Largely unwilling to
risk any of their independence in
transactions with Arabs and frequently at odds with the urban-
centered and Arab-dominated government of the sultan, Berbers
preferred to have economic relations
with local Jewish merchants and
craftsmen. The relationship was,
characteristically, a very personal
one involving a formal bond of
protection granted a specific Jew
by a specific Berber, a protection
which was jealously guarded lest an
unpunished act by a third party
against a Jewish protege be taken
as a sign of weakness or unreli-
ability on the part of a Berber
protector. The Berber - or for that
matter the Arab - usually developed
a long-term and purely economic
relationship with the Jew and one
which...was generally characterized
by that kind of friendship that so
often attends a clearly symbiotic
relationship (Rosen 1972: 444-5;
cf., Geertz 1979: 166).

Stillman criticizes Rosen for several reasons.
First, he suggests that Rosen has treated Muslim-
Jewish relations in Sefrou as though they were time-
less: i.e., without justification, he has "projected"
the situation prevailing in the 1960's "back in time",
ignoring considerable historical change. Secondly,
he suggests that Rosen has made a serious error by
generalizing the experience of Sefrou to all of
Morocco, because "Sefrou was a notable exception to
the rule even prior to the coming of the French"
(Stillman 1976:13). Thirdly, Stillman states that
Rosen's ideal portrayal of Muslim-Jewish relations
has overlooked some of the most important and least
attractive realities. Finally, by implication, he
denies the importance which Rosen attaches to Muslim-
Jewish dyads. Instead of the pre-eminent role of
partners in dyads, Stillman stresses the Jews' status
as Dhimmîs, members of a subordinate community,

vis-a-vis a superordinate group. Dyadic relationships might have had "a localized, mitigating effect,"
but the essential character of Muslim-Jewish relations
depended upon the Dhimma, a relationship not of
individuals, but of corporate groups (Stillman 1976:
14).

In summary, there are fundamental differences
between Rosen's and Stillman's interpretations of
Jewish-Muslim relations in Morocco, not only in terms
of data, but also in terms of the interpretation of
data and the political uses to which these data are
put. (Cf., p. 89 below). In fact, there is
compelling ethnographic and historical evidence that
both kinds of relationships existed simultaneously
in Morocco, perhaps in the same locales. There was
no single paradigm of Muslim-Jewish relations, but
rather, variations around a common theme. Moreover,
and more importantly, the controversy which surrounds
the interpretation of data, basically a political
controversy, obscures a very important problem in
historical and ethnographic research.

Historical and Ethnographic Background

Jews have lived in Morocco for centuries - perhaps,
millennia (Hirschberg 1974:22) - and they have lived
in as great a range of social, political, and ecological
circumstances as Jews in any other part of the Islamic
world, the Dâr al-Islâm. Like Jews in Medieval Egypt,
Iran, and Yemen, Moroccan Jews lived in imperial
cities, smaller trading and administrative centers,
mountain villages, and oasis towns. There is no
complete continuous roster of the Jewish communities
of Morocco, but there are episodic accounts which
confirm the broad distribution of Moroccan Jews. For
example, at the turn of the 15th-16th centuries,
following the Christian Reconquista of the Iberian
Peninsula, there were at least fifty Millahs (Jewish
communities) in Morocco in all ecological zones
(Epaullard 1956; Mauny 1967:459-462). In the "Modern"
period - i.e., since the establishment of the present
CAlawî Dynasty in ca. 1664 - there is evidence for the
continuous existence of a hundred or more (Zafrani
1972; Foucauld 1888:395-403; Figure 1). These, too,
have been widely distributed throughout the country,
along the major trade axes, ranging in size from a
few isolated individuals to twenty thousand people
and more.

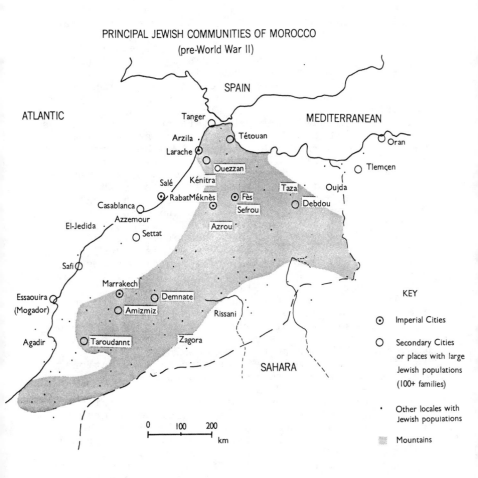

PRINCIPAL JEWISH COMMUNITIES OF MOROCCO
(pre-World War II)

KEY

⊙ Imperial Cities

○ Secondary Cities
or places with large
Jewish populations
(100+ families)

· Other locales with
Jewish populations

▓ Mountains

MAP

Moroccan Jews' subsistence and economic activities varied according to the ecologic zones in which they lived. For much of modern Moroccan history, Jews have controlled much of Morocco's international trade, especially with England, the Low Countries, and France. They have also participated extensively in related fields of government service, as customs agents, interpreters, and European consuls to the sultans' courts. In the cities and administrative and trading centers, Jews were concentrated in lesser forms of commerce, including trading, peddling, money-changing and money-lending, and a certain proportion served their own communities as rabbis, teachers, and scribes. Throughout Morocco, Jews were artisans and craftsmen; they sold and worked precious metals, they were tinkers, embroiderers, shoemakers, and tinsmiths, and in certain parts of the mountains and desert, they were expert gunsmiths, making weapons for both imperial soldiers and dissident tribes. In rural areas, Jews were sometimes farmers and shepherds, and finally, in urban areas, there was a large underclass of carters, day-laborers, bath keepers, butchers, and prostitutes, who lived marginal existences, always on the verge of destitution, vulnerable to any sudden economic change. In summary, occupational inventories of Moroccan Jews (e.g., Flamand 1952: 29-37; cf., 1959-1960) show that they engaged in a broad range of economic activities, excluded only from military service and Muslim religious activities. Correspondingly, their economic states ranged from the broad mass, who were of very humble means, to a small minority, most of whom were engaged in international commerce, who appear to have had untold wealth.

Stillman has properly stressed the historical changes in Jews' status across nine or ten centuries of Moroccan history (Stillman 1976:13-14), but he fails to appreciate that there were also ethnographic and economic differences among Jews in Morocco and that these differences also affected the Jews' status in different parts of Morocco at the same historical epoch.

Dhimma and the Status of Jews in Morocco

At all times and in all places, Jewish-Muslim relations were governed by a single principle, the classical Islamic idea of <u>Dhimma</u> (Goitein 1955:62-87). Put simply, this principle dictated that Jews were

90

subject people who were obliged to pay a tax or tribute to the Muslim sovereign. In return, the sovereign was supposed to guarantee their physical and fiscal security, a measure of religious liberty, and political autonomy in matters of personal status (for example, education, marriage and divorce, and inheritance). However, this principle allowed for wide latitude in its application, depending upon the nature of sovereign authority, Jews' and Muslims' respective subsistence patterns, and the nature of Jewish communal life. In fact, there were several different expressions of Dhimma in pre-colonial Morocco, depending upon the circumstances under which Jews and their Muslim protectors lived.

In the imperial cities, Muslim-Jewish relations most closely approximated the ideal of Dhimma. Jews lived in their own quarter, the Millâh, which was often separated by walls from the Muslim quarters, and they were often obliged to follow certain sumptuary laws; at various times, for example, these laws forbade them to ride horses or to wear visible jewelry or required them to go barefoot outside the Millah or to dress only in black.[3] Jews were enjoined from physically assaulting Muslims, even if they themselves were first assaulted, and they were expected to bear insults without complaint. In a representative passage, William Lempriere, a British surgeon from Gibraltar, described the Millâh of Marrakech in 1789:

> The Jews, who are at this place
> pretty numerous, have a separate
> town to themselves, walled in, and
> under the charge of an Alcaide,
> appointed by the emperor. It has
> two large gates, which are regularly
> shut every evening about nine
> o'clock, after which time no person
> whatever is permitted to enter or go
> out of the Jewry, till they are
> opened again the following morning.
> The Jews have a market of their own,
> and, as at Tarudant, when they enter
> the Moorish town, castle, or place,
> they are always compelled to be bare-
> footed (Lempriere 1804:197).

The Jewish community was also obliged to pay an annual tribute, called Jizîya or Gharâma, to the

sultan or to his local delegate, usually either a
Khalîfa (regent) who was one of the sultan's brothers
or sons, or a Qa'id, a military governor (Michaux-
Bellair 1904). In some cases, the payment was in cash
or precious metal. In other cases, Jews paid their
tribute in kind: in 1648, during a time of great
civil unrest and many domestic military campaigns, the
Jewish communities of Tétouan, Fès, Meknes, Rabat, and
Salé were obliged to pay their tributes in tents,
presumably, their contributions to the war effort
(de Cenival 1931:599). In still other cases, the
sultans exempted a community from paying its annual
tribute in return for an economic service; Lempriere
describes one such case:

> The Jews in general are obliged to
> pay to the emperor a certain annual
> sum, in proportion to their number,
> which is a considerable income, inde-
> pendent of his arbitrary exactions.
> Those of Morocco (Marrakech) were
> exempted by Sidi Mahomet from this
> tax, and in its rooms he compelled
> them to take goods of him, of which
> they were to dispose in the best
> manner they could, and pay him five
> times their value; by which means
> they were far greater sufferers than
> if they paid the annual tax
> (Lempriere 1804:198).

In all cases, the tribute was based upon the community's
size and the financial means of its residents and represented an explicit quid pro quo.

In return for the payment of Jizîya or Gharâma,
the sultans and their officers allowed the Jews a
number of prerogatives: for instance, they were
allowed to collect their own taxes, including taxes
to support Jewish officials and institutions, and they
had watchmen and bailiffs at their disposal to enforce
their decrees. But above all, the sultans guaranteed
the Jews' security and the security of their property
throughout their domains. In fact, when a royal
chronicler wanted to characterize the reign of a
powerful 17th-century sultan, he wrote "(in those days,)
the land was so secure that a woman or a Jew could
walk from Oujda to the Wâd Nûn (in the Moroccan Sahara,
without harm)!" (al-Nâsiri 1906-1907:132).

However, not all sultans were so powerful, nor was the land always so secure. In general, these studies have represented traditional Moroccan politics as a tension between two polar tendencies: Makhzan, central government by the sultan, and Sîba, opposition to centralized authority, embodied in the resistance of towns, tribes, and charismatic holy men (marabouts).[4] In territorial terms, the Bilâd al-Makhzan was the territory which the sultan controlled at any given time, and the Bilâd al-Sîba was the residual category of all regions which were beyond imperial control. The Bilâd al-Sîba included many kinds of government - for example, local dynasties, strongmen, and tribal councils - and there was frequent significant political change. The Bilâd al-Makhzan was territorially discontinuous - for example, two neighboring cities might be under imperial control, while the territory between them was not - and the boundaries were subject to frequent change. Consequently, there were always limitations upon the effective powers of the imperial government. These limitations, in turn, placed corresponding limitations upon the effectiveness of the sultans' guarantees.

The restrictions upon the sultans' powers had a significant impact upon Dhimma protection because many Jews lived in the Bilâd al-Sîba and many others had regularly to travel through dissident regions in pursuit of their livelihoods (Figure 1). The greatest number of Jews almost certainly lived in the major cities, especially the main administrative centers and the commercial ports, which were subject to fairly consistent government authority. But the greatest number of communities was inland, in the mountains and oases, far from imperial control.

People who lived or travelled in these regions had protection needs which were different from those of their urban counterparts. This is not to suggest that the sultans' Dhimma was worthless in the Bilâd al-Sîba. In fact, the sultans often had considerable spiritual authority among dissident peoples, even when their temporal powers were limited, and this respect may have served, in an indirect way, to protect the sultans' protégés. However, people also required more predictable assurances, which only local people with their own bases of independent authority were able to provide.

93

Often, under these circumstances, Jews and Muslims lived together in the dissident regions in much the same kind of arrangement as in the Bilâd al-Makhzan, a kind of microcosmic Dhimma: the Jewish community, through its leaders, paid tribute to the local powers in return for their personal security and partial political autonomy. Although there are only a few data describing such relationships, they seem to have prevailed in many of the smaller Berber "kingdoms" of the Middle Atlas, the Anti-Atlas, and Sûs. Walter Harris, a British journalist and traveller with broad experience in Morocco, describes one such situation, in the Dadès Valley of southeastern Morocco, in 1894:

> Close to the village was a "Mellah," or "Ghetto," of Jews, living by themselves in a separate quarter, which also was undefended, from the fact that they do not in any way participate in the wars. The Jews exist at Dads, as elsewhere among the Berbers, under the system of debeha, or sacrifice, so called from the fact that a sheep or an ox is supposed originally to have been offered to the Berbers in order to obtain protection. The families of Jews here too live in a feudal state, each being dependent upon some Shleh family for immunity from ill-treatment and robbery: in return for this they pay a small yearly tribute to their protector (Harris 1895:173-174).

In other cases, however, Jews derived protection from dyadic relationships similar to the ones which Rosen described in Sefrou. In these cases, individual Jews paid annual tributes in cash or kind to individual Muslim patrons who, in return, guaranteed to protect persons and their property and who foreswore to avenge them if they came to any harm. There are many examples of this kind of agreement from all parts of Morocco; in a recent publication, David Hart has described one such situation among the Aith Waryaghar of the Moroccan Rîf:

> ...in 1953-1955; there were some five Jewish families (all elementary or nuclear in character) located in

94

northern Waryagharland, and two
more at the Monday market of the
Aith Hadhifa.

Every male Jew was either a
silversmith or goldsmith or a
packsaddle maker; the usual pattern
was that there was one of each
resident at or near each market,
and that he and his family were
under the protection of a powerful
amghar or qaid. The keynote of
Jewish behavior was that of safety
in humility; conversely, for a
powerful man to have "his own" Jew
was considered a sign of prestige.
Because the Jews stood entirely
outside of the political system,
and because their occupational
services were much in demand, many
informants said that to kill or
even molest a Jew was an infinitely
worse offense than to kill a fellow
tribesman, for the Jew's protector
would show absolutely no mercy to
the killer (Hart 1976:279-280).

Not all Jewish clients had such powerful patrons,
though, obviously, it behooved them to associate
themselves with as rich or powerful men as they
possibly could: for example, merchants, political
strongmen, or holy men (marabout).

It is not clear how clients chose their patrons -
nor vice versa - but it appears that a number of
factors intervened. First, many protection arrangements were hereditary, in which case, neither party
had much control over the agreement, although,
presumably, even hereditary arrangements might lapse
if dues were not paid (Harris 1895:173; Foucauld
1888:400). Secondly, there was an economic consideration: more powerful protectors probably cost more,
so that only some people could afford the tributary
dues that they might demand. At the same time, not
all people needed the same amount of protection,
and it may have been that those Jews with particularly
high risk occupations - itinerant tinkers and traders,
for instance - needed the greatest amount of protection
and were therefore willing to pay more.

There were also supplementary forms of protection of which these people could avail themselves;
for example, many Moroccan tribes collected a form
of tribute called Zattâta, a kind of highway toll
which ensured a traveller's safety within the tribal
territory but for only a limited period of time,
usually time enough to cross the territory. Zattâta
was assessed upon every foreigner, but it was customarily higher for Jews. Zattâta was especially
relevant to Jews who travelled extensively in dissident territory and was another means by which they
could protect themselves against multiple contin-
gencies (Westermarck 1926, I:518-569; Brunot et
Bousqet 1946:353-370; Geertz 1979:137-138).

What advantages accrued to Jews who participated
in patron-client dyads? The most obvious return was
physical security - security for their lives and
livelihoods - since the Muslim patrons were, in
principal, obliged to protect "their" Jews. In this
respect, they differed but little from their urban
counterparts. The other advantages are less clear;
for example, there is no evidence that Jews who were
in patron-client relationships were assured any
communal political autonomy; indeed, on the basis of
what is known about the political organization of
rural Jewish communities, this was probably not even
a relevant concern. Many individuals were highly
mobile, and most communities were quite small: too
small to maintain synagogues, schools, religious
societies, or even cemeteries of their own (e.g.,
Flamand 1952:1959-1960). This is not to suggest that
rural Jews had no such facilities or that they made
no use of them; only that these arrangements, such as
they were, were not explicitly sanctioned by anything
like a Dhimma. Instead, the pacts of protection were
more limited and specific relationships, not only
because they involved fewer people, but also because
they had more limited ramifications in the Jewish
partners' lives.

Sanctions

Under normal circumstances, Jews in Morocco had
little need for protection. By all accounts, they
lived with their Muslim neighbors in peace, if not
tranquility, and went about their activities unharmed.
However, it was in times of stress that the protection

96

pacts were important, and it was at just such times that the guarantees most often failed. Protectors sometimes punished those who harmed their proteges; for example, Captain John Braithwaite reported that on December 5, 1727:

> Five Moors were crucified for
> robbing and murdering a Jew:
> This was one of the principal Jews
> of Mequinez (Méknès), and great
> Industry and Interest was made by
> the Jews to discover his Murderers
> (Braithwaite 1729:200).

However, there is ample evidence that throughout Moroccan history, imperial troops plundered Jews who had faithfully paid their taxes, tribal marauders robbed Jews who had paid Zattâta, and Muslims injured or killed protected Jews with impunity.

These violations may reflect individual or social pathology; for example, both European and Moroccan sources portray Mûlay al-Yazîd (fl. 1790-1792), the sultan who directed terrible pogroms against the Jews of northern Morocco (cf., Stillman 1978:133-142) as a lunatic and renegade (Lourido 1978:323-33). But what is more important, they also reflect a fundamental contradiction in the entire protection complex: there were only relatively frail and inconsistent sanctions to underwrite the guarantees. Jews, themselves, were powerless to physically sanction recalcitrant protectors or patrons - whence their need for protection - and there is no evidence that higher authorities - tribal chiefs, sultans, or imperial officers - ever did so.

This did not mean that sanctions were non-existent. Such sanctions as existed were social and moral, rather than material, but this is not to say that they were without force. For example, terrific shame befell patrons who mistreated their Jewish clients or who allowed others to do so with impunity. In the former case, they appeared to be bullies; in the latter, weaklings, neither of which was an attractive image before neighbors and kin (Foucauld 1888:400). There might also have been ritual sanctions, particularly if the protectors were holy men or if the protection agreement were sealed by an oath (Âr). In these cases, offenders risked supernatural sanctions, which might be applied to themselves, their families, or their tribespeople without prior warning and at any time (Westermark 1926 (1): 518-564). Finally, the Jews were not totally without practical power; in extreme cases, they could withdraw their services from consistently recalcitrant patrons or protectors and in that way seriously affect their material well-being. Jews were often the only traders, money-lenders, or metalsmiths available. The withdrawal of services would have complicated and perhaps even significantly disrupted local economic life.

There is no evidence of Jewish "boycotts" of towns or tribes or regions of Morocco. This may simply reflect the absence of data or the fact that people were compelled to make a living, even at the risk of their lives. Alternatively, it may also mean that there were relatively few egregious violations of protection agreements, for any number of reasons, and that protection agreements did, in fact, provide the kinds of protection which they were supposed to provide.

Discussion

In principal, the Jews of Morocco were Dhimmis, like their counterparts in other Muslim lands; they were physically and politically vulnerable unless they had Muslim protectors to guarantee their well-being. But in practice, the protection arrangements between Jews and Muslims in Morocco took different forms. In the Bilâd al-Makhzan, the Jews' status conformed closely to that of traditional Dhimmis: Jewish communities, corporate entities, were the sultan's proteges. In the Bilâd al-Sîba, under different social, political, and economic circumstances, the status of Jews was more variable: communal protectorship, but more often, Jews formed patron-client pairs, similar to those which Rosen has described. However, neither Rosen nor Stillman has characterized the situation in all of its complexity, because no single model of behavior can adequately describe the relationship between Muslims and Jews in precolonial Morocco. There were certain general rules of conduct which applied universally in Morocco - for example, Jews always deferred to Muslims - but the essence of Jewish-Muslim relations has been variability: the accommodation of behavior to the prevailing circumstances.

This kind of variability is not unfamiliar to anthropologists, who learned long ago that formal prescriptions for human behavior, whether written or customary, must be treated more as approximate guidelines than as inviolable or inflexible rules. It is essential to understand the formal theoretical statements - in this case, the classical rules of Dhimma, as they may have been modified in Morocco. But these alone are not sufficient; it is also necessary to study the practical applications of these principles, because there are often compromises, violations, and exceptions to the rules.

At the present time, there is no explanation for the distribution of protection regimes, why some Jews formed patron-client dyads and others belonged to protected groups. There are several possible explanations. For example, demography and subsistence patterns played major parts. Where there were small highly mobile Jewish populations, as in the Moroccan Rîf, it would have been difficult to maintain any communal life. Hence, dyadic relationships prevailed. The protectors' relationship with the Makhzan is another factor which may have been significant: i.e., by a process of diffusion, those tribes which were more loyal to the Makhzan or in more sustained contact with Islamic orthodoxy may have been more inclined to practice Dhimma.

Finally, there may have been a social structural explanation for the variation. In fact, a French explorer, Charles de Foucauld, put forward such an explanation about ninety years ago! He suggested that tribes with "despotic" governments inclined toward communal protection, while "egalitarian" tribes were characterized by patron-client dyads:

> Among the tribes which have a democratic style of political organization, for example, the Beràber, each Jew has his own patron. Among those which are governed by a chief with absolute powers, such as the Mezgita or Tazarwalt, the Jews belong to the sheik and have no other sîd (lord or master) than he. In those regions where there are sheiks with limited powers, as at

Tazenakht, among the Zenaga, the
Jew owes him an annual tribute and
cannot move to another place without redeeming himself from him;
nevertheless, he also belongs to a
particular master who has common
rights over him (Foucauld 1888:400).

Unfortunately, no one has tested Foucauld's
hypothesis, but there are several ethnographic settings
in Morocco where controlled comparative studies could
take place: the southern face of the High Atlas
Mountains is one example, the Central High Atlas,
another. In both of these regions Jews lived among
tribal people some of whom were governed by councils
and others by despots. And in both cases, Jewish-
Muslim relations continued, with little outside inter-
ference, until well after World War II. Through a
careful combination of both historical records and
ethnographic fieldwork, in Morocco, France, and Israel,
it should be possible to reconstruct not only the
nature of Jewish life, but also the Muslim context in
which it took place.

Without such a detailed analysis, it is possible
only to speculate about many aspects of Jewish-Muslim
relations in tribal Morocco and also about many aspects
of rural Jewish communal life. What is certain is
that there were several possible kinds of protection
and that they were not necessarily mutually exclusive;
any individual may have been a party to two or more
arrangements or even different kinds of arrangements
at any time.

Finally, since Stillman has accused "American
anthropologists" of presenting an idealized - even
idyllic - view of Jewish life in Morocco (Stillman
1976:13), it is necessary to comment upon the proteges'
perception of the protectors' guarantees. Quite
clearly, it is impossible to know whether Jews were
happy with their status or whether the level of
violations was high or acceptably low. Moreover,
from an academic perspective, it is both irrelevant
and misleading to ask. The data are highly ambiguous.
On the one hand, the combination of personal and
communal protection was remarkably resilient, because
it maintained a viable Jewish community in Morocco
for at least six centuries. On the other hand, it was
clearly defective because Moroccan Jews, since at

least the 17th century, sought the protection of
Western European colonial powers in preference to
that of sultans, marabouts, and tribal despots.

Such data as these are easily amenable to polemical
purposes (Stillman 1977); indeed, they have been used
polemically, to different and contradictory ends. It
is inevitable - perhaps even desirable - that this
be the case. However, they also have an enduring
interest for social scientists and comparative
historians who are interested in functional and
processual analysis. They provide insights into
ethnic relationships in Islamic states, the processes
by which they changed, and the relationship between
the broader political environment and the protection
regimes.

ACKNOWLEDGEMENT

An earlier version of this paper was presented to a panel on
"Anthropological Perspectives on Jewish-Gentile Relations" at
the annual meeting of the Association for Jewish Studies, Boston,
Massachusetts, December 18, 1977. I am grateful to Walter Zenner,
convener of the panel, for his encouragement in the preparation
and revision of this paper and to Shlomo Deshen, Jerry Weiner,
Magali Morsy, and David Hart for criticism and advice.

NOTES

[1]Each of these traditions relies upon very different source
material. The tradition of Moroccan history uses Moroccan
primary sources, mainly imperial chronicles, published accounts
of European diplomats and travellers, and European diplomatic
archives; the best bibliographic guide, restricted to a single
period, is Lourido 1967. Studies of Moroccan Jewish history are
based mainly upon Jewish sources, mainly Rabbinic chronicles
and decisions; the most comprehensive bibliography is Attal
1973:143-227. In more recent years, both traditions have
relied heavily upon ethnographic field work and French and
Spanish administrative accounts.

[2]There is considerable controversy about the distinction
between Arabs and Berbers in North Africa. Simply stated, Berbers

are bilingual, speaking both Arabic and Berber, a distinct
language of which there are three main dialects in Morocco.
They inhabit the mountain regions and some parts of the desert,
they claim to be descended from the autochthonous pre-Islamic
population of Morocco, and, historically, they were often
associated with resistance to the power of the sultanate.
Arabs, on the other hand, speak only Arabic, predominate among
the urban population, and claim to be descended from Arab tribes
who arrived in Morocco beginning in the 17th Century. A more
comprehensive discussion and a more detailed description of
the controversy appears in Gellner 1969:1-34 and Gellner and
Micaud 1972:11-24.

[3]While some of these requirements were clearly humiliating
and disabling, others, such as residential segregation, may
have come about at the request of Jewish authorities or may,
at least, have served their purposes (Corcos 1972; Zafrani 1972:
141-147).

[4]The intensity of the controversy which surrounds the
concepts of Makhzan and Sîba in Morocco resembles that of the
Arab-Berber debate (footnote 1). For a comprehensive and
critical discussion, see Waterbury 1970:15-60.

LIST OF REFERENCES

Attal, Robert
    1973   Les Juifs d'Afrique du Nord: Bibliographie.
         Jerusalem: Yad Izhak Ben Zvi.

Braithwaite, John
    1729   The History of the Revolutions in the Empire
         of Morocco. London: Darby and Browne.

Brunot, Louis, et Bousquet G-H
    1946   Contributions a l'etude des pactes de
         protection et d'alliance chez les Berberes
         au Maroc centrale. Hesperis 33:353-7.

de Cenival, Pierre, ed.
    1936   Sources inedites de l'histoire du Maroc.
         2e Serie - Dynastie Filalienne. France, t.
         IV, Paris: Guethner.

Corcos, David
    1972   Les Juifs au Maroc et leurs mellahs. In
         Zakhor Le-Abraham/Melanges Abraham Elmaleh.
         Jerusalem, 14-78.

Epaulard, A., ed. et trad.
    1956   Description de l'Afrique d'apres Jean-Leon
         l'Africain. Paris: Maisonneuve, 2V.

Flamand, Pierre
1959-1960   Diaspora en terre d'Islam, Casablanca, I.H.E.M., 2V.
Geertz, Clifford
1979   Suq: The Bazaar Economy in Sefrou. In
                 Meaning and Order in Moroccan Society:
                 Three Essays in Cultural Analysis, eds.,
                 Geertz, C., Rosen, L., and Geertz, H.
                 Cambridge: University Press, 123-314.
Gellner, Ernest
1969   Saints of the Atlas. Chicago: University
                 Press.
Gellner, Ernest, and Michaud, Charles, eds.
1972   Arabs and Berbers. London: Duckworth.
Goitein, S. D.
1955   Jews and Arabs: Their Contacts Through
                 the Ages. New York: Schocken.
Harris, Walter B.
1895   Tafilet. London: Blackwood.
Hart, David
1976   The Aith Waryaghar of the Moroccan Rif:
                 An Ethnography and History. Tucson, Arizona:
                 University Press.
Hirschberg, H. Z.
1974   A History of the Jews in North Africa.
                 Leiden: E. J. Brill, v. I.
Lempriere, William
1804   A Tour from Gibraltar to Tangier...and Thence
                 Over Mount Atlas to Morocco. London: Higham.
Lourido Díaz, Ramón
1967   Ensayo historiográfico sobre el sultanato de
                 Sidi Muhammad b. Abd Allah (1757-1790).
                 Granada: Cuadernos de Historia del Islam,
                 Serie Monográfica, I.

1978   Marruecos en la Segunda Mitad del Siglo XVIII.
                 Madrid: Instituto Hispano-Arabe de Cultura.
Mauny, Raymond
1967 (1961)   Tableau géographique de l'Ouest Africain au
                 Moyen Age... Amsterdam: Swets & Zeitlanger,
                 NV, 3 v.
Michaux-Bellaire, Robert
1904   Les impôts marocains. Archives Marocaines,
                 1:56.
al-Nāsirī al-Salawī, Ahmed ibn Khalid
1906-1907   Kitâb al-Istiqsa, trad. par E. Fumey.
                 Archives Marocaines, 9-10.
Rosen, Lawrence
1967   A Moroccan Jewish Community During the
                 Middle Eastern Crisis. American Scholar,
                 37:435-451.

1972   Muslim-Jewish Relations in a Moroccan City. International Journal of Middle Eastern Studies, 3:435-449.

1979   Social Identity and Points of Attachment: Approaches to Social Organization. In Meaning and Order in Moroccan Society: Three Essays in Cultural Analysis, eds., Geertz, C., Rosen, L., and Geertz, H. New York: Cambridge University Press, 19-122.

Shokeid, Moshe
1971   The Dual Heritage: Immigrants from the Atlas Mountains in an Israeli Village. Manchester, U.K.: University Press.

Stillman, Norman
1973   Sefrou Remnant. Jewish Social Studies, 35:255-263.

1976   The Moroccan Jewish Experience - A Revisionist View. Association for Jewish Studies Newsletter, 18:13-14.

1977   In His Cousin's House: The Jew in the Traditional Arab World. Middle East Review, Winter 1976/1977, 37-40.

1978   Two Accounts of the Persecution of the Jews of Tetouan in 1790. Michael, 5:130-142.

Waterbury, John
1970   The Commander of the Faithful. London: Weidenfeld and Nicolson.

Westermarck, Edward
1926   Ritual and Belief in Morocco. London: MacMillan, 2 v.

Willner, Dorothy, and Kohls, Margot
1962   Jews in the High Atlas Mountains of Morocco: A Partial Reconstruction. Jewish Journal of Sociology, 4:207-241.

Zafrani, Haim
1972   Les Juifs du Maroc: vie sociale, économique, et religieuse. Paris: Geuthner, t. I.

CHAPTER 5

JEWISH EXISTENCE IN A BERBER ENVIRONMENT

M. SHOKEID

The hypothesis of the previous chapter
was developed on the basis of literary
sources and ethnographies on Jewish life
in Morocco. This chapter by Moshe Shokeid,
associate professor of anthroplogy at
Tel Aviv University, lends support to that
hpothesis by using oral accounts given by
Atlas Mountain Jews, seven to ten years
after they immigrated to Israel. Shokeid
uses the testimonies of Jews who had
experiences as merchants, peddlers, and
itinerant craftsmen among the Berbers and
who interacted with their patrons and other
neighbors. This data is used in conjunction
with written sources.

INTRODUCTION

During the 1970s historians, sociologists, and
anthropologists have diversely assessed the Jewish
situation in Morocco in recent generations. Polar
answers have been given to the question whether the
Jews were a persecuted minority forced to comply
rigidly with the more humiliating and severe Dhimmi
regulations, or whether their relationships with the
surrounding Muslim society were relatively congenial,
particularly when compared with European Jewry.

The Moroccan debate cannot be isolated from an
assessment of the general scene of Jewish life in
Muslim lands which was permeated with the ambiguity
engendered by the Dhimmi status. That official
charter of rights and obligations, applied to Jews
and Christians alike, has given rise to contrasting
and inconsistent descriptions and interpretations of
tolerance versus oppression is Islamic society.[2]

SOURCE: Actes du Colloque International de l'Institut
d'Histoire des Pays d'Outre Mer, Abbaye de Senanque--
Octobre 1978, pp. 62-91. ©Copyright 1980 by the
Editions du Centre National de la Recherche Scientifique. Reprinted by permission of the Centre National
de la Recherche Scientifique.

Chouraqui was one of the first to emphasize the relatively harmonious elements in Jewish-Muslim relationships in Morocco (1968:54-55). The controversy, however, gained momentum when Rosen (1972) formulated his hypothesis for the sociological raison-d'être of these harmonious relationships. Rosen, who carried out observations in Sefrou, a town in central Morocco, during 1966-1967 identified the role of the Jews as intermediary between Arabs and Berbers. According to his observations the Berbers preferred to trade with Jews, use their services so as not to develop relation-ships with Arabs, which might have jeopardized their independence. Relationships with Jews, it would seem, entailed basically no social commitments or personal dependence. Rosen also developed a theory about the elementary forms of social relationships in Morocco. These, according to his observations are far less group centered than usually assumed; they are mainly dyadic in nature. Also relationships between Muslims and Jews have been geared according to this pattern of dyadic relationships. However, Muslim-Jewish economic-exchange relationships, which were free of the competitive element typical of relationships between Muslims, have enabled, in effect, the development of friendship between a Muslim and his Jewish protégé. These long-term, personal, but non-competitive, bonds demonstrate and explain in Rosen's view, the nature of symbiotic relationships between Jews and Muslims in Morocco. To substantiate his interpretation, Rosen emphasized the security of person of Moroccan Jews. Their property might sometimes have been ransacked - a fate shared by other groups in Morocco - but their lives were usually spared.

This approach to the Jewish situation in Morocco has been challenged by Stillman (1977:forthcoming), who criticizes Chouraqui for idealizing the Jewish position in Morocco and Rosen for distorting the general Moroccan scene through the application of a hypothesis pertinent mainly to the Sefrou case. Stillman reinforces his argument with historical and folkloric sources which depict the humble and vulner-able legal and social position of Moroccan Jews. Pointing to the pariah status of Moroccan Jews, he contends that they were excluded from many trades and consequently forced into occupations forbidden to Muslims, such as gold and silver smithing and the particularly despised occupation of moneylending. Stillman also cites records and brings evidence as to the persecution of Jews.[3]

Against the background of these contradictory
opinions, Meyers (1977) propounds that there has never
been a single paradigm of Muslim-Jewish relations
in Morocco. During different periods, as well as in
different parts of the country, various patterns pre-
dominated, exhibiting different types of co-existence.
According to his view, both Rosen and Stillman represented only a partial perspective of a Jewish
situation which is far more complex. An inquiry into
the ambiguity of patterns and the general ambivalence
in Muslim-Jewish relationships we find in Goldberg's
(1978) analysis of the Mimuna ceremony. This
ambivalence of relationships forms the theme of many
Jewish Moroccan folktales in which contacts with non-
Jews are tense and contentious (Noy 1964:17-18).

Our investigation into the particular situation
of Atlas Mountains Jews revealed that most writers
who have referred to Jewish life under Berber rule
in the Atlas Mountains, and elsewhere, during recent
generations comment on the Jews' relative safety,
emphasizing the cordial relationships with their
neighbors (see for example Flamand 1959:98; Willner
1969:263; Waterbury 1972:27; Hart 1976:280).[4] Some
of these writers refer to symbiotic relationships
between Jews and Berbers. Flamand concentrates on the
economic dimension of this symbiosis, Willner, on the
other hand, is less specific: "The Jews of Ait Ardar[5]
lived in virtual symbiosis with their Berber neighbors,
and enjoyed excellent relations with them and a high
subsistence level" (1969:263). These descriptions
seem surprising considering the unstable political
situation and the more difficult environmental circumstances of Berber tribal areas. The skeptic may query
whether the mere fact that Jews continued to survive
under Berber rule did not give rise to these idealized
descriptions.

Whatever our conclusions on the Jewish situation
in the Atlas Mountains and elsewhere, an important
factor to be considered, both in past and possibly
future debates, is that most of the studies and assessments on Jewish Muslim relationships have been carried
out after the majority of Moroccan Jewry immigrated
to Israel or elsewhere. This factor inevitably cir-
cumscribed investigation, not only in studies of
communities which do not have many written records

107

(particularly communities from southern Morocco), but other communities as well. Moreover, the collective and individual Jewish experience of the twentieth century, particularly the Holocaust, statehood and in its wake mass immigration from Middle Eastern and North African countries to Israel might have colored, in various ways, the views both of Moroccan-born Jews and those who have informed about, or analyze, the situation of Jews in Morocco.

The arguments of the above scientists and our specific reservations evince a problem rarely treated directly by the various disciplines, namely the interpretative dimension in the presentation and analysis of data. The issue was tackled in anthropology by Geertz (1973:3-32) who exemplified his argument with observations he recorded in Morocco. The dramatis personae in his case were a Jewish trader from the highlands of central Morocco, his patron - a Berber sheikh - robbers from a neighboring Berber tribe who had attacked the trader and his guests, and a French officer. The latter, anxious to enforce French law and order, messed up settlement of the dispute according to Berber custom which would have granted the Jewish trader considerable indemnification in sheep by the attackers' tribe.

Discussing the quality of interpretation embedded in the presentation and analysis of observed or recorded behavior, Geertz claimed: "What it means is that descriptions of Berber, Jewish or French culture must be cast in terms of the constructions we imagine Berbers, Jews or Frenchmen to place upon what they live through, the formulae they use to define what happens to them... They must be cast in terms of the interpretations to which persons of a particular denomination subject their experience, because that is what they profess to be descriptions of" (1973:15).

In analyzing my data, I was constantly aware of the limitations in the study of the Jewish Moroccan situation. Through the experiences of a community from the Atlas Mountains transplanted to an Israeli village, which I called Romema,[6] I tentatively suggest some interpretations for the position of Jews in these parts of Morocco. My observations in Romema were carried out over a period of eighteen months - from October 1965 to March 1967, and for three months during the summer of 1976. The people of Romema migrated to

Israel in 1956 from a village, which I named Amran, located in the district of Ait Bou Oulli,[7] about fifty kilometers southeast of Demnate. I refrain from discussing the patterns of social and cultural life of Atlas Mountains Jews and possible cultural symbiotic elements with the surrounding Berber society,[8] but concentrate mainly on basic circumstances of their lives - residence, occupation, and safety. The present anthropological study will, I hope, further contribute to the descriptive and analytical spectrum of Jewish life in Morocco through its assessment of the Jewish situation in some parts of the Atlas Mountains.

The Circumstances of Jewish Life in Amran

When I began to summarize my data on the relationships of the people of Amran with their neighbors (Shokeid 1971:18-23), I realized that these could not be defined in clear-cut terms. The immigrants' spontaneous stories and discussions as well as their answers to my direct questions were sometimes reminiscent of the pathetic descriptions of the position of Atlas Mountains Jews by nineteenth and early twentieth-century travelers and geographers (e.g. Thomson 1889; Slouschz 1927; Montagne 1930). In many of these accounts, the Jew is highly dependent on his Berber patron who protects him for his own interest. At times the patron himself might ransack his Jewish protege's property. Aside from this harsh presentation, there are scores of stories on how the Jews ingeniously contrived to safeguard their wealth and to ensure their personal wellbeing. Often the storyteller, during his narrative, asked God's forgiveness for having duped the Muslims. Others are tales of mutual dependence, based on genuine mutual respect, which stress fairplay and personal friendship between the Jewish trader or craftsman and his Muslim client, partner, or patron.

Amran, an all-Jewish village which prior to immigration had a population of three hundred and fifty inhabitants, was divided into seven family groups. This familial division greatly overlapped the occupational division in the community. At the top of the economic and social ladder were the traders whose ancestor, according to family tradition, had been a merchant from Demnate, who, upon the invitation of a local sheikh, had settled in Amran. His sons and grandchildren, like he, were in trade; they con-

tracted farming partnerships with their neighbors
for whom they put up capital and they owned flocks
of sheep grazed by Muslims with whom they shared the
lambs. However, much of their trade consisted of
nuts and the import of sugar, oil, as well as of
other items. Their senior members in recent generations had headed the community and acted on its
behalf in dealing with the local sheikhs (in Israel
their neighbors have accused them of collaborating
with the Muslims).9

The other families followed various crafts -
cobbling, carpentry, and smithing. The poor and
unskilled worked at odd jobs for the wealthier and
the skilled members of the community. Some of the
craftsmen worked at home - particularly those who
made embroidered shoes - others plied their craft in
near or more distant Berber settlements. All male
members of the community came into direct contact
with the Muslim population on an economic basis.
There were almost no Jewish communal functions which
exclusively provided a livelihood. Also religious
leaders were at times engaged in some kind of economic
transaction or occupation.10

Trade and plying their crafts took the Jews over
wide stretches of territories, crossing tribal
borders, or, as they put it: "We traveled through
different memshalot (governments)", meaning different
systems of tribal organization. A former smith concluded his description of travels in search of work
in Morocco with the sweeping statement, "For us
craftsmen there were no borders".

Their houses and the land the Jews usually rented
from the Berbers. However, some of the merchants
owned property.11 As far as the people of Romema could
remember, they had not paid regular taxes before the
advent of the French administration. The wealthy, however, made costly gifts to their influential neighbors
on the occasion of family celebrations or on holidays.
They also bribed their sheikh to intercede on their
behalf in disputes with their Muslim partners or
debtors. Prior to French rule in the region, the local
Berber sheikh was elected yearly by a council of the
tribal grouping of Ait Mezalt.12

Aside from their local sheikh and landlords, Amran
merchants and craftsmen were not necessarily

permanently bound in business or by patronage to particular Berbers. Though they had sometimes developed special relationships with particular Berber families over a few generations, these ties could be cut off and new ones established without formality. However, their strongest ties were with those Berbers from whom they rented houses and land.[13] Their landlords would intervene in dispute with other Muslim families and in cases of conflict even with other Jewish families. The Jews, on the other hand, held aloof from any strife in which their patrons' patronymic or tribal groupings were engaged. They would stay at home and wait for the tension to cool off. The trader or craftsman might have moved to another close or distant community upon the invitation of an employer or client to live on his estate. This mobility prompted by the search for livelihood may explain the changing size of Jewish communities in the Atlas Mountains from less than ten inhabitants to three hundreds or more (see Flamand's census 1959:329-333).[14]

The landlords and patrons were often intimately acquainted with their Jewish proteges' personal and communal affairs. Thus, for example, the Romemites recall that in settling arguments or disputes between family groups in Amran, particularly between merchants and craftsmen, Berber neighbors were often witnesses or arbitrators.

The itinerant craftsman might have remained with his Berber employer for days, or even weeks. His employer saw to his personal needs. Only on the Sabbath might the journeying craftsman have stayed at a nearby Jewish community or visited the synagogue. The Muslims too might come to visit, stay, and partake of food and drink at their Jewish partners' or acquaintances' homes.[15] Friendship was at times expressed in gestures of physical contact, as in the story of the craftsman whose employer kissed his brow, begging him to stay with him overnight.

During the generation preceding immigration to Israel, two Jews from Amran converted to Islam, both of them had been itinerant craftsmen. The wife and children of one of them immigrated to Israel. Their horrified brethren explained that their Berber employers had practiced "witchcraft" on them while serving them tea. According to the Romemites' stories,

111

however, it would seem that poverty and despair, at a particular hard time (as, for example, drought) drove the two to abandon their religion, family, and community. Individual conversion to Islam was, however, a problem many communities in Morocco had to accommodate with.

The wealthier merchants on their major business trips to Demnate often became the target of robbers; for protection they took on these journeys some robust members of the community. Prior to the establishment of French rule, local sheikhs had ransacked a number of times the property of the family of traders in Amran. According to their account, the last time the family was plundered the women were driven out of the house and the men tied up, but none was hurt. However, since the documents of all financial transactions had been well hidden, the family could renew its business and it continued to thrive. At other times, the merchant could count on his Muslim friends. When the last head of the community was caught by French custom officials with a load of unauthorized fabric, a commodity rationed at that time, he stopped on his way to the police station at one of his Muslim acquaintances' home and managed to leave with him part of his merchandise loading instead sacks of straw. His eldest son, in his frequent references to Amran, has vividly drawn the multi-faceted aspects of Jewish life in Morocco as may be seen in the following succinct comment, phrased in a style often used in Romema in public debates or at ceremonies. This manner of speech interweaves metaphors with a somewhat archaic poetic language.[16] "The Jew even if very rich was stripped of honor in front of the Arab and had to bow down to his will. But the Jew was always better dressed, better fed, and his house better furnished and stocked!"

On the relative safety of Jewish life in the Atlas Mountains, as perceived by the Romemites, we can learn from the following discussion. One evening, in Romema, while leaving the synagogue after the service, a settler spoke of the Negev Beduin who were criss-crossing the borders of Jordan, Egypt and Israel, smuggling into the country dope as well as all kinds of heavily taxable commodities. One of his listeners suggested that those caught should be "slaughtered". Upon which the son of the last head of the community, mentioned above, retorted with astonishment: "But

why? The Arabs didn't slaughter us when we were
living among them!" Yet on other occasions, people
spoke appreciatively of their changed circumstances
in Israel: "It is better to live in Israel because
it is safe. In Morocco, you could be rich, but the
Arab could come any time and rob you of your wealth.
Here you are not afraid of any one; you can shout at,
and even throw out, the Jewish Agency people, if you
want to!" (In rural settlements, Jewish Agency
representatives were responsible in most matters
related to farming, housing, and financial credit).

The ambiguity in the position of Jews in Morocco,
as well as the various modes of relating to their past
existence among the Berbers cropped up also in
references by both former merchants and craftsmen
(though their tone and purpose of mentioning that
point differed) to their manner of dress. Although
the Jewish garb was usually white, the merchants at
times wore fancy and colorful clothes similar to the
attire of Muslims. The craftsmen added, however, not
without a measure of satisfaction, that the proud
merchants were the first to be molested not only by
the highwaymen, but also by their Muslim patrons and
neighbors.

The Intermediary Role of Atlas Mountain Jews

Today, when we try to assess what the Jewish
situation had been in Muslim countries, we often
compare it with the present situation in Israel or in
Western countries. This is done also by the immigrants
themselves, as evidenced by some of the earlier
quotations, or in the following comment by a former
shrewd merchant who was wont to speak of his methods
of fooling his ignorant Muslim clients and who, in
Israel, had become a prosperous farmer: "When we came
to Israel we thought we would be given a small hut to
live in and only bread to eat. I never dreamt we
would have electricity and I would own a refrigerator,
a washing machine, and a tractor! There are Jews who
return to the country of origin, not me. I shall not
go back to Morocco, even if I get thousands in cash.
I shall not return to be cursed again by Arabs". This
former merchant has thus filtered his perspective of
life in Morocco, inter alia, through his comprehension
of personal achievements in Israel which greatly
surpassed his expectations which at immigration had

been highly motivated by Messianic beliefs.[17]

This brings us back to our introductory note on
the interpretative factor embedded in the informants'
apprehension of their past and present situation.
However, as demonstrated earlier, the Romemites'
recollections were not geared into a definitive
formula of positive or negative interpretations of
their social position and their relationships with
their neighbors in Morocco. Consistency in interpretation is, it seems, more typical of outsiders,
including scholars, or to the ideologically motivated
"natives". As mentioned, in the Romemites' view of
life in Morocco the Berbers at times played a prominent
role in relationships of Jews among themselves.[18]

No doubt the Jews of Amran did not leave a
"paradise" behind them, a notion which may be inferred
from those who refer to symbiotic relationships
between Jews and Berbers. They were a low-class
minority; an inferior status, which however, did not
deprive them in all spheres of life. The Berbers
were highly dependent on their many and varied services
which were not confined only to those occupations
prohibited to a Muslim. They were also not the lowest
status group in the Atlas Mountains; lower were, for
example, the blacks, the descendants of former slaves,
who traditionally were servants or followed such crafts
as pottery. Within this framework of economic relationships and interdependence, the prosperous Jew could
own land and prove his economic achievements and the
special social relationships he had established with
influential Berbers through his fancy "non-Jewish"
dress.

To obtain a broader perspective of Jewish life in
the Islamic world we may compare the Atlas Mountains
situation with the position of Jews as observed in
modern Iran.[19] Iran is the only country in the Muslim
world where there is still a large Jewish minority and
where it is still possible to carry out reliable
observations as to the relationships between Jews and
Muslims and on Jewish and Muslim stereotypes and
prejudices. Iranian Jews were confined, well into the
twentieth century, to the most despised occupations
and forced to show humiliating signs of identity and
they were considered a lower moral standing. Bodily
contact with a Jew is still in some places polluting
to his Muslim neighbor. A Jew's property, life, and

honor were never secure. He learned to hide his material possessions, to look destitute and humble. Loeb (1976) argues that the Iranian Jews' occupations as peddler, moneylender, entertainer, vendor of liquor and prostitute, which lead to interaction with diverse social groups might have placed him in a position of communicator or disseminator of ideas. As an outcaste however - humiliated and polluting - he, in fact, served to insulate the various segments of the population from one another and thus performed an important service for the Persian elite.

The potential role of the Jew as mediator between various groups in society has been argued in explaining the position of Jews in the apparently two extremes of Muslim environment: Rosen (1972) who analyzed the intermediary role of the Jew between Arabs and Berbers, and Loeb (1976) who interpreted the Jew's communicatory potentiality as transformed into an insulating function. Though the approach of the intermediary role of the Jew cannot alone explain the complex Jewish situation, as manifest in Morocco or in Iran, it is a key variable in elucidating the Jewish situation in most places throughout the history of the Diaspora. In our case, the Jew cast in an intermediary role clarifies some aspects of Jewish existence in the Atlas Mountains.

In some parts of Morocco the Jew might have played an intermediary role between Arabs and Berbers. In the Atlas Mountains, his role was, inter alia, intermediary between different Berber tribal groupings - a hypothesis which calls for further research. The Atlas Mountains Jews were living in what is known as bled es-siba, or "land of dissidence" and "disorder." The central administration of the Sultan was not effective in these parts of Morocco and even the advent of French rule had little influence. Only at a later stage of French occupation - since the second quarter of this century - were changes imposed. The Berber surrounding society was segmentary, organized agnatically, and in continuous inter- or intratribal conflict (see, for example, Gellner 1972; Hart 1972, 1976; Burke 1976). Basic to the political tribal system were the ingurramen (marabouts), members of holy lineages, who did not belong to the tribal group-ings, mediated in disputes and applied tribal customs (such as the election of chiefs by rotation). They were endowed with baraka (divine grace), pacific and their person was safe (Gellner 1969, 1972). The mosaic of Berber society aside from these indispensable communities of holy outsiders comprised another net- work of communities of pacific and secure outsiders - the Jews - who rendered vital economic services, yet were powerless due to their lower status demonstrated in their humble behavior. Therefore services rendered by Jews or trading with them was not socially committing which would not have been the case had the interaction been with a Berber from another patronymic group which might have been degrading for one party. Lack of commitment was especially significant in partner- ships with Jews who put up the capital in farming and herding enterprises; but also in day-to-day trading with the Jewish merchant who gave credit to his clients. This vital interaction with the Berbers placed the Jewish merchants and traders in Ait Buo Oulli, in an advantageous position evidenced, _inter alia_, by their superior station in the Jewish community.

Hart's study of Jews shortly before immigration to Israel and his recording of comments made by Berbers after the mass departure of Jews, succintly encapsulate some features of Jewish existence observed by the other side: "The keynote of Jewish behavior was that of safety in humility; conversely, for a powerful man to have 'his own' Jew was considered a sign of prestige. Because the Jews stood entirely outside the political system, and because their occupational services were much in demand, many informants said that to kill or even to molest a Jew was an infinitely worse offense than to kill a fellow tribesman" (1976:280).

Although these two sets of records - one from Israel, the other from Morocco - do not originate with the same group of Jews and their Berber neighbors, they reflect complementary interpretations of some elements of Jewish existence in Morocco. As it appears from the Romemites' experience, the Jewish craftsman, peddler and merchant could live in his community or travel with little risk involved and he was welcomed, though he did not enjoy an honored position, in nearby or remote Berber settlements.[20]

The course of peaceful coexistence might have been intermittently interrupted, but the Jew could normally rely on the protection of his patron, employer, or client and draw some sense of security from the local cultural code which specified rules to safeguard the weak and helpless, such as women and Jews. This position of the Jew, comprising both the inferior status and circumstantial advantages, opened the doors of Berber homes and tribal and subtribal territorial borders to the itinerant Jew. "For us, the craftsmen, there were no borders", a remark by one of Amran's former smiths, is most elucidating in this context.

Concluding Note

We started our discussion by presenting a polarity of opinions about the position of Moroccan Jewry. Our case does not fully support either of these viewpoints. It seems as if both Rosen and Stillman have described an objective reality of the Jewish situation. That perception of reality was not modified by the contradictions of daily existence which are apparently "non-data", as, for example, the intervals of economic and social interaction and cooperation between a subordinate ethnic minority and a dominant majority. Accordingly, they have drawn clear-cut conclusions; the harmonious perspective versus the conflict perspective in Jewish-Mulsim relationships. Although I have suggested some situational and structural factors which affected the position of Jews and their relationships with their neighbors, I do not assume to present an objective reality. I emphasized, in particular, the interpretative element embedded in the Romenites' perception of their experience in Morocco. Most striking, however, their perception and interpretations yield a complex image of Jewish-Muslim interaction evidenced by their paradoxical accounts of harmony and conflict. These presentations are genuine expressions of their existential experience which cannot be dismissed because of apparent inconsistency. Thus, while most scholars have tried to formulate consistent paradigms, representative of, at least, some geographical areas, or certain historical periods, such may be non-existent. Disagreement with the various assessments of the Jewish situation in Morocco has emerged also during our conference. Certain rabbinical texts, or other forms of extant records, seem to arouse disagreement when used as sole basis for interpretation. My observations and the verbal communications which I collected about life in Morocco offer a kind of data

117

which is rarely recorded. That type of "non-data",
if it survives at all, is with the passage of time
absorbed into such forms of folklore as folk tales.

I hope that further research both in Morocco and
in Israel - to where the majority of Atlas Mountains
Jews have immigrated - may reinforce the interpretations
of this study and clarify the circumstances of a particular mode of Jewish existence in relative safety
amidst precarious environmental conditions.

NOTES

[1]The study was supported by the Bernstein Israeli Research
Trust, through the Department of Social Anthropology of Manchester University, directed by the late Professor Max Gluckman,
and by a grant from the Faculty of Social Sciences at Tel-Aviv
University. I am grateful to Professor S. Deshen for his
comments and to Mrs A. Sommer who helped with the editing.

[2]See for example Goitein (1955) and Lewis (1973:165) who
commented on that issue.

[3]See for example, Bowie 1976.

[4]In presenting my data, I refer also to a few studies of
various Berber tribal regions, which, though not intending to
study the Jewish population, offer important facts and insights
into the general Jewish situation in these parts of Morocco
(as, for example, Hart 1976).

[5]About ninety kms. east of Demnate.

[6]Pseudonyms are given to the village in Israel and to the
community in Morocco in order to disguise the identity of the
people studied. (This is standard procedure in anthropological
monographs).

[7]To avoid identification of the people studied, I used in
previous publications the name Etgor instead of Ait Bou Oulli.
The district of Ait Bou Oulli comprised a few Jewish communities.
For more details see Flamand 1959, Shokeid 1971.

[8]See my works on kinship, family and religion among Jews in
the Atlas Mountains, Shokeid 1971; Deshen and Shokeid 1974;
Shokeid and Deshen 1977.

[9]Community life in Romema is very much influenced by the conflict and competition between the former traders and the rest of the community (see particularly Shokeid 1971:23-28, 101-164; Deshen and Shokeid 1974:64-94; Shokeid 1976).

[10]For a description of religious leaders in the Atlas Mountains see Shokeid and Deshen 1977:77-92.

[11]Flamand (1959:86) also reports that a few families owned land in Ait Bou Oulli.

[12]See Gellner 1972 and Hart 1972 who describe this system of annual election of tribal chiefs.

[13]See also Hart's evidence on the particular relationships between the Berber landlord and his Jewish tenant (1976:280).

[14]Goldberg's (1971) description of Jewish life in the Gharian Mountains district of Tripolitania reveals considerable similarities in the Jews' economic and social circumstances.

[15]See also Flamand who reports on Berbers drinking in the homes of Jews (1959:99).

[16]See my reference to that manner of speech in Romema (1971:134-135).

[17]See Shokeid 1971:32-33.

[18]See a case presented in Shokeid 1971:26.

[19]This comparison is obviously limited by the particular influence of Iranian Shi'ism on the position of Jews.

[20]The Jews, as other members of pacific groups (of lower or higher status), were exempt from payment of dhazttat, the protection fee a traveller paid to go from his own tribe into the territory of another (see Hart 1976:303-304).

LIST OF REFERENCES

Bowie, C.
1976   "An Aspect of Muslim-Jewish Relations in Late Nineteenth Century Morocco: A European Diplomatic View". International Journal of Middle Eastern Studies, 7:3-19.

Burke, E.
1976   Prelude to Protectorate in Morocco.
                             Chicago: University of Chicago Press.
Chouraqui, A. C.
1968   Between East and West. Philadelphia:
                             Jewish Publication Society of America.
Deshen, S., and Shokeid, M.
1974   The Predicament of Homecoming: Cultural and
                             Social Life of North African Immigrants in
                             Israel. Ithaca, N.Y.: Cornell University
                             Press.
Flamand, P.
1959   Diaspora en Terre d'Islam: Les Communautes
                             Israelites du Sud Marocain. Casablanca:
                             Presses des Imprimeries Reunies.
Geertz, C.
1973   The Interpretation of Culture. New York:
                             Basic Books.
Gellner, E.
1969   Saints of the Atlas. London: Weidenfeld
                             and Nicolson.

_____ 1972   "Political and Religious Organization of the
                             Berbers of the Central High Atlas". In
                             E. Gellner and C. Micaud (eds.), Arabs and
                             Berbers. Lexington: Health and Company,
                             pp. 59-66.
Goitein, S. D.
1955   Jews and Arabs. New York: Schocken Books.
Goldberg, H. E.
1972   Cave Dwellers and Citrus Growers: A Jewish
                             Community in Libya and Israel. Cambridge:
                             Cambridge University Press.

_____ 1978   "The Mimuna and the Minority Status of
                             Moroccan Jews". Ethnology XVII:75-87.
Hart, D. M.
1972   "The Tribe in Modern Morocco". In E. Gellner
                             and C. Micaud (eds.), Arabs and Berbers.
                             Lexington: Health and Company, pp. 25-58.

_____ 1976   The Aith Waryaghan of the Moroccan Rif.
                             Tucson, Arizona: The University of Arizona
                             Press.
Lewis, B.
1973   Islam in History. London: Alcone Press.
Loeb, L. D.
1976   "Dhimmi Status and Jewish Roles in Iranian
                             Society". Ethnic Groups, 1:89-105.

Meyers, A. R.
1977   "Patronage and Protection: Notes on the
                        Status of Jews in Precolonial Morocco".
                        Paper presented to a panel on Anthropological
                        Perspectives on Jewish Gentile Relations at
                        the annual meeting of the Association for
                        Jewish Studies, Boston, Decmeber 1977.
                        (In this volume).

Montagne, R.
1930   Les Berberes et la Makhzen dans le Sud du
                        Maroc: Essai sur la transformation politique
                        des Berberes sedentaires. Paris: Librairie
                        Felix Alcan.

Noy, D.
1962   Jewish Folktales from Morocco. Jerusalem:
                        Bitfuzot Hagolah (in Hebrew, Preface in
                        English).

Rosen, L.
1972   "Muslim-Jewish Relations in a Moroccan City".
                        International Journal of Middle Eastern
                        Studies, 3:435-449.

Shokeid, M.
1971   The Dual Heritage: Immigrants from the Atlas
                        Mountains in an Israeli Village. Manchester:
                        Manchester University Press.

———— 1976   "Conviviality Versus Strife: Peacemaking
                        at Parties Among Atlas Mountain Immigrants
                        in Israel". Political Anthropology, 1:101-121.

Shokeid, M., and Deshen, S.
1977   The Generation of Transition: Continuity
                        and Change Among North African Immigrants
                        in Israel. Ben Zvi Institute (Hebrew).

Slouschz, N.
1927   Travels in North Africa. Philadelphia:
                        Jewish Publication Society of America.

Stillman, N. A.
1977   "Muslims and Jews in Morocco". The Jerusalem
                        Quarterly, 1:76-83.

———— forthcoming   "The Moroccan Jewish Experience - A Revisionist
                        View". In S. Shaked (ed.), Aspects of Jewish
                        Life Under Islam. Cambridge, Mass.:
                        Association for Jewish Studies.

Thomson, J.
1889   Travels in the Atlas and Southern Morocco.
                        London: George Philip & Son.

Waterbury, J.
   1972   North for the Trade: The Life and Times of
                      a Berber Merchant. Berkeley: University
                      of California Press.

Willner, D.
   1969   Nation Building and Community in Israel.
                      Princeton: Princeton University Press.

CHAPTER 6

THE SOCIAL STRUCTURE OF SOUTHERN TUNISIAN JEWRY IN THE EARLY 20th CENTURY

SHLOMO DESHEN

In this chapter, focus shifts to Southern Tunisia. Basing himself on data embedded in rabbinical sources, such as religious law tracts, Shlomo Deshen traces the outlines of the structure and institutions of Jewish society in Southern Tunisia in the early 20th century. The author, professor of Social Anthropology at Bar-Ilan University, describes a situation quite different from that of Moroccan Jewry. Southern Tunisian Jewry has an uninterrupted and relatively peaceful history going back into antiquity. The general Berber population, particularly of the island of Djerba, has since the late 19th century developed a pattern of migrant merchants, who operate throughout Tunisia and retire in their old age to their homes. In this context, the Jews entered local commerce and filled the major local positions. They did not, however, engage in international or in itinerant commerce or trade. Djerban Jewry is therefore extremely sedentary and lacking in geographic mobility. As a consequence, the local community is relatively powerful over its individual members. Social control, particularly in religious matters, is strong because of the high visibility of individuals. Community organs are highly developed in comparison to other Jewish communities in North Africa.

Southern Tunisia is a region of semi-desert. In the past, the general population was mainly engaged in nomadic herding, in fishing and in other occupations

SOURCE: Hebrew version appeared as An Outline of Social Structure of the Jewish Communities in Djerba and Southern Tunisia From the End of the 19th Century Until the 1950's. Zion XL1:1-2:97-105. Copyright © 1976. Reprinted by permission of the Historical Society of Israel.

appropriate to the proximity to the sea. The Jews, by
forming commercial links with groups of semi-nomadic
Berbers, fitted into this set-up. Supplying the Berbers
with articles of trade and craft, Jews wandered in the
footsteps of their customers, and only occasionally
returned to their homes (for a general discussion of
the local economy see Stone 1974). At the end of the
19th century, with the encouragement of commerce by
the French protectorate government, this pattern underwent radical changes. In an attempt to strengthen
their hold over the peripheral areas in the east and
the south, the French established outposts from where
they enforced their administration. Some of these outposts gradually developed into towns which attracted
Jews engaged in the service-trades, crafts and petty
commerce. On the eve of the massive waves of immigration to the State of Israel, the largest Jewish
communities were located on the island of Djerba
(approximately 6,000 people), and on the mainland, in
the nearby city of Gabès (approximately 4,000 people).
Another thousand or so Jews were dispersed throughout
the other communities, and it may be assumed that the
total number of Jews in the entire region of Southern
Tunisia reached about 15,000. On the island of Djerba
the two Jewish communities, Hara Kebira and Hara
Sghira, were separate Jewish towns. These were the
leading communities in the area and our present knowledge is mainly based on information from there.

The little island of Djerba numbered more than
60,000 inhabitants at the beginning of the 1950's, a
population whose needs had not been sufficiently provided for by the island's economy for at least one
hundred years. The Berbers of Djerba, in an attempt
to overcome the natural and economic limitations of
their location, and in order to exploit the commercial
opportunities provided by the French penetration of
the region, developed a unique way of life. The male
members of the population would spend most of their
working lives in other parts of Tunisia where they
would engage in trade. They would return home to
their wives and families after many months of absence,
and then only for short periods of a few weeks. The
fact that these Berbers belonged to a rejected and
ascetic Moslem sect, the Ibadie, combined with their
particular way of life, ensured their success as
merchants, though their neglect of their families
caused them to be regarded as steeped in bad ways.
Towards old age, at the end of twenty or thirty years
of work, the traders retired and returned to Djerba

permanently. There they invested their savings in
their homes and addressed themselves to undemanding
tasks such as the tending of small flocks of sheep,
the income from which supplemented their savings. Although relatively large amounts of money (by North
African standards) flowed into the island, up until the
1950's it was still insufficient to enable the younger
generation to explore new means of earning their living,
and they were compelled, like their fathers, to start
out as migrant traders.

Within this context of migrant traders, it was the
Jews who formed the more settled element. While the
Berbers' trading brought them far beyond the borders
of the island, the Jews restricted themselves to
commerce and handicrafts, such as wool-carding, associated with the raising of sheep, the latter mainly
practiced by the elderly, settled Berbers. The economy
of one Jewish community, Hara Sghira, was based almost
entirely on the skills associated with wool-processing.
Jews also engaged in local trade, in crafts and luxury
items. This economic set-up was stable and continued
to hold within the context of generally peaceful
relations between Jews and non-Jews. The economy of
the other community, Hara Kebira, was more varied. In
addition to the wool-trade, the Jews engaged in the
processing of precious metals, a skill traditionally
associated with Jews in Moslem countries. Furthermore,
the Jews were tailors and shop-owners.

The Djerban Jewish communities were sedentary and
lacked geographic mobility. On the whole, the people
managed to earn their living at the local market or
practiced their trades in their homes. This lack of
mobility, though occasionally characteristic of
traditional Jewish communities, was particularly notable in this case, and was closely linked to the
vitality of the religious and communal institutions
of the Jews of Djerba. Contrary to the situation of
many Jewish communities, whose members were compelled
to remain far from home for long periods of time and
were therefore unable to participate in communal activities on a regular basis, the situation of the Jews of
Djerba was different. As a result of economic and
ecological circumstances which enabled geographic concentration, social control within the Djerban community
was relatively powerful. On the whole, everyone knew
about everyone else's doings. Deviants from the
accepted norms were called before the Dayanim (judges

in the religious court) who might exercise their right
of excommunication in order to impose obedience. This
social control was further strengthened by the large
number of Kohanim (descendants of the ancient priestly
caste). The older of the two communities, Hara Sghira,
was originally entirely composed of Kohanim, a fact
which inspired a sense of holiness and exclusiveness
in its people.

During the last generations, the island of Djerba
developed into one of the most important centres of
Jewish traditional learning in Northern Africa. This
development was comparatively new; from medieval
evidence it appears that the situation then was very
different.[1] From the 16th century onwards, there is
occasional evidence indicating the presence of Torah
scholars in Djerba, and by the end of the 19th century,
traditional learning was flourishing. The large number
of scholarly works by the Sages of Djerba, both printed
and hand-written, indicate intensive study. Participation in the study of the Talmud during the evenings
was popular, on the Sabbath the Sages gave public
sermons of various kinds and levels, and also small
groups met together to study.

There was hardly any male social activity completely beyond the context of the synagogues and traditional
learning. The major other opportunity for socializing
was provided by the gathering of Jews at the Moslem
coffee-houses, and indeed, some complaints pertaining
to the phenomenon appear in the sources. In 1912, a
Hebrew press was established in Djerba which enabled
an increase in the number of works written by local
Sages and the spread of their learning to other communities.

During the first decade of this century, the French
penetrated Southern Tunisia, and in 1905 the Paris-
based philanthropic organization Alliance Israelite
Universelle attempted to establish a modern school for
the Jewish community in Djerba. The local rabbinical
leaders, however, aware of the secularization potential
inherent in modern educational institutions, struggled
to prevent the opening of the school. Eventually, the
first modern school was opened in Southern Tunisia only
fifty years later, when the communities had already
begun to fall apart. Until that time traditional social
institutions remained stable in the south, while in the
north of the country processes of Westernization set

in. Traditional life, even in the city of Tunis which, in the past, had been a famous centre in the Jewish world, began to decline. Thus, the gap between the standard of traditional learning of the Jews of the south and the Jews of other parts of Tunisia gradually increased. Due to the decreasing number of Sages in the north, and the lowering of their standards, the northern communities were compelled to appoint Rabbis and other religious functionaries from Djerba and the south. This further strengthened the sense of exclusiveness among the Jews of Djerba.

The internal structure of the communities of Djerba was notable for its homogeneity. There was, however, a distinction between merchants and craftsmen, and this was reflected in the taxation system that required representatives of both these strata to participate in tax assessments. The distinction does not, however, appear to have given rise to much competitive friction between the two groups, and therefore was probably not clear-cut. In the middle of the 19th century, there were Rabbis who engaged in trade and in the management of workshops alongside their rabbinical activities, for which latter they received no pay. Debates concerning the discharge of Torah scholars and the pious members of the honorary Burial Society from the burden of community taxes recurred during the 19th century. Though the <u>Dayanim</u> concluded that these dignitaries be granted exemption, the community continued to question this ruling. It cannot be concluded, from the sources, whether the Sages to whom these debates referred were scholars whose entire occupation was the study of Torah, or also scholars who worked for their living. At any rate, the picture that emerges during the 19th century is of a community wherein the stratum of Sages was not clearly distinct from the laymen.

The majority of the synagogues were private institutions founded by families or groups of migrants, but the local community committees exercised considerable control over the individual synagogues. In Hara Sghira it is astonishing that no Torah scrolls were kept in any of the nine local synagogues. This practice ensured that during those days in which the Torah was read, the public would be compelled to gather in one single synagogue, the Ghriba synagogue, which was considered especially holy and venerated, and located a little distance from the center of town.

Underlying the practice stood the power of a public capable of overruling the differentiating elements of the various neighborhood synagogues. Similar arrangements existed in Hara Kebira. On order of the Community Committee, ten out of the fifteen synagogues of that community closed down during the High Holy Days. The aim of this ruling was essentially financial: by the creation of large groups of worshippers, the leaders of the community caused competition for synagogue honors to increase. These honors, such as reading from the Torah, or parading the scrolls in synagogue, were most cherished on the High Holy Days. The income from the auctioned honors were on these festivals ordered to be entirely devoted to the general community chest, and not to the benefit of individual synagogues. Even those synagogues permitted to remain open on the High Holy Days were temporarily forced to resign their financial independence.

At the head of the Djerban communities stood the Community Committee and the Beth-Din (Court of Religious Law). The first body was responsible for the collection of internal taxes, and the majority of its income went towards social welfare, the salaries of the night watchmen, and, at a later period, towards the salaries of the Dayanim. The role of the Dayan was, as is common in Jewish tradition, and in Middle Eastern practice generally, not only that of a judge of the law. The Dayan also had great moral and religious authority. Not only did he apply the law, but to a considerable extent also formulated rulings and legislation and moved public opinion. Parallel with this undifferentiated scope of activities in the role of members of the Beth-Din, also the Community Committee was not only concerned with material and political affairs, but also saw itself responsible for general religious matters. Thus the committee employed a man to make rounds of the shops on Friday afternoon in order to ensure that they close their businesses on time. Most of the income of the communities came from indirect taxation, and had its source in the imposition of a 25 percent tax on the price of kosher meat sold locally. At the same time the Committee prohibited the import of meat that might cause evasion of payment of this tax. Direct taxes were imposed on the basis of assessments which were determined by committees composed of merchants and craftsmen. The evaluation for this tax was apparently carried out once a year, and the tax itself collected once a month.

During the twentieth century, the Community
Committee and the Beth-Din underwent formalization.
Contrary to the practice during the previous century,
the Committee began to pay fixed weekly salaries to
the Dayanim. The change was justified by the notion
that a Dayan compelled to seek his living elsewhere
risked public humiliation. This new development was
significant in that it increased social distance
between Dayanim and laymen. Parallel to these new
financial arrangements, it became customary that only
a member of another community and not a local Sage,
could be nominated a Dayan. Thus, the Kohanim of
Hara Sghira appointed their Dayan from among the
community of Hara Kebira; while in Hara Hebira, it
was customary to appoint a Dayan from Hara Sghira.
Also the Community Committee underwent formalization
during this century. In the past, the institution
had had no fixed title and was referred to by various
terms, but during the 20th century, the use of the
hybrid Hebrew French term Vaad Hacomité became permanent. This combination of two equivalent terms
appears frequently in the sources, and is practically
the only term used colloquially by immigrants from
Djerba in Israel when referring to the institution
in the past. Although the Committee acted as an independent body from the Beth-Din, and although it in
fact appointed the Dayanim, the Committee remained
subordinate to the decisions of the Beth-Din. The
latter adjudicated cases in which the Committee was
involved with private persons. In spite of this
the differentiation between the political leadership,
the Community Committee, and the religious-legal
leadership, was not consistent. Thus, the venerated
Dayan of the 1920's to 1940's, Rabbi Moshe Khalfon
HaKohen, was nominated to head the Committee; he,
however, declined the appointment.

Alongside the two principal administrative and
legal institutions, there were many voluntary bodies
within the community which dealt with various spheres
of religion and welfare. The most important of these
was the Vaad Or Torah, the Committee for the Light
of Torah, or more prosaically, the Education Committee.
This body extended financial support to needy Torah
scholars to enable them to devote themselves to study.
The Education Committee also helped children of the
poor in order that they too might study. In addition,
the Vaad Or Torah provided the pupils with books, and
placed students in suitable positions upon the

completion of their studies. By the beginning of this century, Or Torah also had reached a significant degree of formalization, as is apparent in the detailed formulation of its rulings. Due to its widespread activities and the considerable financial sources at its disposal, Or Torah became an important public focal point. Although this caused some friction with the Community Committee, Or Torah retained the enthusiastic support of the Dayanim. Or Torah relied on the activities of its individual members, each of whom was responsible for the collection of contributions from his respective synagogue. Or Torah reached a considerable degree of internal development, a fact reflected in its employment of a "truancy officer" responsible for the attendance of the pupils at the various study groups.

Other institutions in Djerba shared a similar structure to Or Torah. The Vaad Bikur Holim, Committee for Visiting the Sick, extended financial and medical aid to the sick; it too relied on contributions from the various synagogues. There were also many specific activities and roles that underwent processes of formalization at the beginning of this century. The ritual slaughterers and the circumcizers were required to obtain official qualification, which was granted by experts from among the community who had themselves been authorized by the Dayanim. The slaughterers were required to have their knives regularly inspected, and this was done by one slaughterer in the presence of two others. Wine which had been imported to Djerba had, upon arrival at its destination, to be provided with proof of its being kosher. Such proof had to be provided by a person who had accompanied the consignment, but was not accepted from the owner himself, who it was deemed was not trustworthy in such a matter. The person who supplied the proof was also to be a Torah scholar. These issues further illustrate the increasing formalization of communal and religious practices.

By 1920, there is much evidence of the trend toward formalization. The Beth-Din ruled that all those engaged in the meat and wine branches must be declared officially to be men of integrity. During the same year a ruling was passed whereby ritual slaughterers had to be paid the same fee, whether or not the slaughtered animal was found to be kosher on examination. Underlying this ruling was the attempt to ensure that decisions on this matter remained free of considerations other than those imposed by the ritual law. Official qualifications were also demanded of the menakrim, ritual pickers of sinews from butchered meat. In 1922 the arrangements for indirect taxation on meat were changed. Until then, the tax assessment had been carried out by the retailer at each individual sale. It was now ruled that the assessment be carried out at the wholesale stage, by an official assessor appointed by the community. Here too, as with the ruling concerning the proof of the kosherness of the wine, an element of formality penetrated where, in the past, personal integrity had been held to be sufficient. Similar to this was the development in the organization of the honorary Burial Society. It will be recalled that in the past there had been a call to discharge the members of this society from community taxes. Now in addition to this, formal arrangements were introduced into the work of the society, and it was run on the basis of shifts.

There were similar changes in the sphere of rabbinic duties. In the past, the Rabbis appointed by the community were versed in all aspects of the ritual and didn't specialize in any particular sphere. During the later period, however, a Rabbi was appointed who specialized in the law concerning "family purity", and his role was essentially restricted to this sphere, which deals with determining the proper times for sexual relations in connection with the menstrual cycle. In the context of the issue of formalization of roles, it is important to note the above-mentioned refusal of Rabbi Moshe Khalfon HaKohen to accept leadership of the Community Committee, and the opposition to the blurring of the distinction between differing roles that was implied in his rejection of the proposal. Finally, there were attempts on the part of the Dayanim over the last decades to restrict the number of prayer quorums within synagogues, and to ensure that prayer in each synagogue be led by a permanent cantor, at a regular time.

Among the Jewish communities in the region there was a certain degree of competition, nourished by the activities surrounding the Ghriba synagogue in Hara Sghira. A special committee was responsible for the administration of that synagogue, which was the scene of a great annual pilgrimage that brought considerable income. The money was used to support needy elderlies, and also scholars who studied and prayed regularly at

131

the Ghriba synagogue. Though the members of the Ghriba committee were inhabitants of Hara Sghira, they acted independently from their local Community Committee, and commanded relatively large sums of money contributed by pilgrims for the financing of the activities of their synagogue. Relations between the authorities of Hara Sghira, the Beth-Din and the Community Committee, toward the Ghriba Committee, were naturally ambivalent. While the community aspired to control the synagogue's income and to put it to its own use, in particular for aid to the local poor, the Ghriba Committee restricted use of the funds for the development of its own institutions, for the support of scholars affiliated with the synagogue, and for the maintenance of the complex of Ghriba buildings. Despite this conflict, the Jews of Hara Sghira and its Community Committee held the ancient synagogue in great reverence. Besides that, the Ghriba Committee did bring considerable material benefits to the community.

Thus, in spite of the tensions, the people of Hara Sghira and their leaders exerted themselves on behalf of the Ghriba Synagogue. Typically, they were apprehensive that there should be no competition between local synagogues, so that the Ghriba synagogue be paramount among local synagogues. However, the repercussions of internal Hara Sghira strains were felt on the level of the relations between Hara Sghira and Hara Kebira. The latter community, which developed at a short distance from the main market town of Djerba, was not autochtonous. In time, as Hara Kebira became materially established, it attracted more and more Jews from other parts. Among the arrivals was a family of learned Kohanim that claimed descent from Ezra the Scribe (of Biblical renown), whose scholarship was famous throughout Southern Tunisia. On their arrival, the members of this family continued to maintain their own community framework and did not participate in the general taxation system of Hara Kebira. In doing so they followed the pattern of arrangements that existed in Hara Sghira between the Ghriba Committee and the local Community Committee. The friction surrounding this issue apparently continued in Hara Kebira over a number of generations, but eventually it came to an end when the general public of Hara Kebira took control over the independent body that existed in its midst, and forced its disappearance. Strain between the two communities, Hara Kebira and Hara Sghira, arose when members of the Hara Sghira

Cohanim family eventually came to preside over the Beth-Din of Hara Kebira. The new Dayanim expressed criticism of details of the pilgrimage customs held in the neighboring community. Indeed, great Torah scholars over the generations have expressed their disapproval of folk customs practiced at pilgrimages generally. But while the Rabbis of Hara Sghira were inhibited by practical considerations from expressing their views forcefully (because of the economic import- ance of the pilgrimage), the emigrant scholars, res- ident and prominent in the neighboring community, were now vocal in their criticism.

The social structure of the Jewish communities of Djerba remained more or less stable up until the time of the immigration to Israel, and the further unfold- ing of existing trends continued. The communal institutions became increasingly formalized, and organization based on general rules replaced the form- er reliance on particular individuals and groups. Traditional learning and scholarship flourished and the Jews of Djerba inherited some of the prestige that was formerly linked to the center of learning in Tunis. The renown of the community of Tunis was expressed in the concept "ha'iyun ha'tunisi," Tunisian profund- ity, which conceptualized the view that people held of the quality of Jewish scholarship in Tunis. Tunis- ian profundity is a variant of Talmud-study methodology which was customary both in Tunis and in other commun- ities of Tunisia. In time, however, traditional Jew- ish scholarship in Tunis decayed, so that during the 20th century the Jews of Southern Tunisia became the main heirs and practicers of Tunisian profundity (for further consideration of that concept see Deshen 1975). The religious status and sensation of self-respect in religious matters of Southern Tunisian Jews soared as a result of this development. While previously Djerba had been a distant backwater, it now outshone the formerly glorious center of Tunis.

Alongside these developments, the Zionist Move- ment began to make its mark on the Djerban community, at a relatively earlier stage than in many other communities in the Middle East. Already in 1906, a work composed by a sage of Djerba expressed enthusi- astic approval of the Zionist movement, and over the years, there were more Rabbis who lent their vocal and written support to the Zionist cause. In 1919 the Ateret Zion movement was established, which, during the 1940's, organized agricultural training and the learning of modern Hebrew. The membership of the movement grew to two hundred by the end of the 1940's. During those years, there were attempts by Zionist activists to encourage clandestine immigration to then Mandatory Palestine. According to all the evidence, it appears that the Zionist element in its midst did not cause conflict in the community. Indeed, one of its most enthusiastic supporters was the forementioned popular Dayan, Rabbi Moshe Khalfon HaKohen. The status of the Zionist Movement within the general structure of the community was probably similar to that of the other voluntary organizations, such as Or Torah and Bikur Holim, and Zionism was thus readily accepted within the traditional framework.[2]

Let us summarize. The Jews of the region enjoyed relatively calm and peaceful living conditions, and were able to remain sedentary and earn a reasonably comfortable living close to home. These conditions brought forth intensive and dynamic communal life. In terms of traditional Jewish society, communities such as Hara Kebira, Gabès and even Hara Sghira formed relatively large communities, very different from the small communities composed of a few extended families that are the majority in some other Jewish culture areas. Though the family was an important element in social organization in Jewish Southern Tunisia, and especially in the maintenance of links with a particular synagogue over many generations, Southern Tunisian communities displayed conventions that went beyond families' loyalties. Social organization was relatively dependent on the formal written tradition and on abstract rulings, which were given over to the rabbis for interpretation. All this is closely connected to the particular personality characteristic of Jews from Southern Tunisia. The folk morality of the Jews of the region emphasizes the values of modesty, humility, even bashfulness. According to this, it is fitting for a man to humble himself before others, and especially before rabbis. In the traditional writings of local sages, these values recur, and are recommended as motives for action or for desistance. These factors, together with the calm physical conditions, helped mould a quiet and calm personality.

NOTES

[1]Detailed reference to the Hebrew rabbinical sources of the statements made here and throughout the paper can be found in the original Hebrew version published in *Zion* (1976).

[2]See Udovitch and Valenci (1980) for a discussion of the nature of tradition in Djerban Jewry, focusing on conditions of the 1970's.

REFERENCES

Deshen, S.
1975   Ritualization of Literacy: The Works of Tunisian Scholars in Israel. American Ethnologist 2:251-259.

1976   An Outline of the Social Structure of the Jewish Communities in Djerba and Southern Tunisia from the End of the 19th Century Until the 1950's. Zion 41:97-108 (Hebrew).

Stone, R.
1974   Religious Ethic and the Spirit of Capitalism in Tunisia. International Journal of Middle Eastern Studies 5:260-273.

Udovitch, A. L., and L. Valenci
1980   Identité et communication à Djerba. Annales, nr. 3-4, pp. 764-783.

CHAPTER 7

FROM SHAIKH TO MAZKIR: STRUCTURAL CONTINUITY
AND ORGANIZATIONAL CHANGE IN THE LEADERSHIP OF
A TRIPOLITANIAN JEWISH COMMUNITY

HARVEY GOLDBERG

> This chapter by Harvey E. Goldberg, associate
> professor of anthropology at the Hebrew Univer-
> sity of Jerusalem, is the result of both partici-
> pant-observation in a community of Israeli citrus-
> growers who immigrated from a "cave-dwellers'
> village" in Tropolitania and a socio-historic
> reconstruction of the past of these people. The
> situation of this community in Israel is linked
> to the type of leadership which had evolved in
> Libya. Leadership is authoritarian and follows
> in a family tradition. The sheikh in the past
> and the present mazkir refrain, for instance,
> from mutual visiting or participation in domestic
> celebration. This partial detachment has enabled
> the community head to mediate between quarreling
> individuals.

During the past decade and a half there have appeared
analyses of social and cultural "brokers", that is,
"groups of people who mediate between community-
oriented groups...and nation-oriented groups which
operate primarily through national institutions"
(Wolf 1956:1075).[1] Analyses of these broker roles
serve (i) to pinpoint the nature of the relationships
between the local community and "wider" groups and
(ii) to provide a useful focus in the study of change
in these relationships. The present paper proposes
(i) to describe the pattern of leadership in a Tripolitanian Jewish community, delineating continuity
in the structural principles constituting the status
of community leader, and (ii) interpret changes in
the organization of that leadership as a function of
changes in the relationship between the community, on
the one hand, and the political authority and environing society, on the other.[2]

SOURCE: Folklore Research Center Studies I:29-41
(1970). ©Copyright 1970 by Magnes Press, Hebrew
University, Jerusalem. Reprinted by permission of the
Magnes Press.

The group under discussion is the small Jewish
community of the Gharian district of Tripolitania,
Libya during the past century.[3] The Gharian (famous
for its troglodyte dwellings), whose population was
about 55,000 in 1954 (Libya 1959), is composed of
approximately 100 villages. The Jewish population
of the district was concentrated in the villages of
Tigrinna and Beni'abaas.[4] These villages are about
4 kilometers and 14 kilometers respectively from
Garian-town, the centre of the district (Khuja 1960).
Ecologically, they constituted small Jewish hamlets
isolated by several hundred meters from neighbouring
Moslem settlements. The names Tigrinna and Beni'abaas
were commonly used by the Jews while these hamlets
were frequently called Haretelyehud (or Hushelyehud)
and Yehud beni'abaas by the Moslems. In 1944 the
population of Tigrinna was 343 and of Beni'abaas 87
(Guweta 1960:25). Their respective populations were
650-700 and 240 in 1906, according to Slouschz (1927:
127, 134).[5]

Occupationally, the Gharian Jews were mainly
shopkeepers, itinerant hawkers, blacksmiths and coopers
(Goldberg 1967b:211). During the economic development of the region, engendered by Italian colonization,
the number of shopkeepers grew, and several members of
the group became relatively wealthy merchants. Some
Jews owned land and flocks which were usually tended
by Moslems who shared the profits with the Jewish
owner.

Both the natural and social environments of the
Gharian Jewish community were notably unstable.
Periodic droughts and epidemics were supplemented by
successive changes in the political regime. In 1835
Tripoli was retaken from the Karamanli dynasty by the
Ottoman Empire (Féraud 1927:366-371). From 1839
through 1858 the Gharian was intermittently involved
in revolts against Ottoman rule by tribal leaders of
the Tripolitanian Jebel (Slouschz 1908:433-453;
Féraud 1927:380-382, 388, 411). The Ottoman regime
gave way to the Young Turks in 1908 (Féraud 1927:443-
444), who lost Tripolitania to the Italians several
years later. Italian "pacification" of the Gharian
took place in 1922 and in the 1930's colonial agricultural settlements were established near Tigrinna
(Italian Library of Information 1940:62-78; Epton
1953:96). During World War II German troops were
stationed in the region which was lost to the British

at the end of 1942. During the British Military
Occupation, which lasted till Libyan independence in
1952, Tripolitanian Jewry faced violent riots in
1945 and 1948. These riots were a significant factor
in stimulating mass migration to Israel in 1949-1951,
resulting in the complete dissolution of the small
Jewish communities of the Tripolitanian hinterland.
At the present, about 90 percent of the Gharian
Jews live in the moshav[6] of Even Yosef (the name is
fictitious) in the central part of Israel.

One of the important socio-cultural mechanisms
which facilitated the adaptation of this small
minority community to its environment was the
concentration of the political interchanges with the
environing society into one status (and role), that of
the community leader. The incumbent of that role,
known as the shaikh in Tripolitanian and the mazkir
(secretary) in the Israeli moshav, is the political
"broker" of the community par excellence (Goldberg
1967b:214-215; 1969a).

The discussion of leadership in the Gharian
Jewish community will begin by considering the case
of the mazkir of Even Yosef and then discussing the
Jewish shaikh under Turkish, Italian and British rule.
In each instance the discussion will focus on three
aspects of the leadership pattern which, though clearly
interrelated, are analytically distinct. These are
(i) the relationship of the community to its socio-
political environment, (ii) the role of community
leader, and (iii) the leader as an individual. The
discussion will conclude by outlining the structural
characteristics of the status of community leader
that have persisted despite major changes in the
community's socio-cultural and even geographical
environment.

The Mazkir of Even Yosef

Even Yosef, like other moshavim, is dependent
on many governmental and other centralized bureaus
that provide resources essential to the development
and functioning of the community (Weingrod 1962:
75-76). Virtually all of the channels to these
bureaus are linked to the status of mazkir. The
incumbent of this role, Hai Halifah Hajaaj (the names
of all living people are fictitious), thus has great

control over the flow of resources and information to and from the village. This is one of the major sources of the power he exercises in running the village in an autocratic fashion as he has for the past 19 years (Goldberg 1969). This power is not completely "naked", however, but is legitimized to the villagers in a number of different ways.

Most of the villagers state that Hai, the mazkir, has the ability and knowledge to fulfill his role, a set of skills not possessed by the majority of the community. He is one of the two people who completed the Italian elementary school in the Gharian. His house boasts a wall covered with books, both religious and secular, which contrasts to the small collection of prayer books to be found in other homes.

The possession of the required intellectual skills is a necessary but not sufficient condition for fulfilling the role of mazkir. The mazkir must be trustworthy, an attribute that is stressed when the villagers discuss how Hai Halifah has managed the village during the past 19 years. The more the villagers rely on the mazkir to manage their communal and individual affairs, the more the attribute of trustworthiness becomes crucial to an incumbent of that role. Hai communicates his trustworthiness to the villagers in several different ways.

Hai exemplifies the religious values of the community. Not only does he observe traditional law and ritual, as do other members of the community, but these observances hold a central place in his life. He is frequently accorded the privilege of leading communal readings in the Synagogue on festivals. He is a ba'al teqi'a, or one who sounds the ritual ram's horn on the High Holidays. His reputation for knowledge extends to the religious realm as he is respected for his religious learning by other members of the community.

Hai is a "quiet" person. He is distant from the other villagers with regard to recreation, visiting and so forth. He rarely appears at the village kiosk in the evening where men gather to drink, chatter and play cards. Also, he rarely attends the celebration of a wedding, bar mizva or circumcision. Because it is not apparent who are his close friends it is difficult to charge him with favoritism. "If there is

140

favoritism", some people say, "at least he does not show it." Showing favoritism publicly would be an affront to the social values of the community (Goldberg 1969).

A similar stand is taken by the villagers with regard to any personal benefit accruing to Hai from his handling large sums of money going in and out of the moshav. For example, many people feel that Hai takes "commissions" for himself from the money paid for materials that he brings into the village. Once, when this was discussed by the villagers, Hai posted a notice in the village store that he was deeply hurt by the current rumors and that, so far as he was concerned, the villagers could be responsible for acquiring their own materials in the future. The rumors quickly subsided as people preferred to leave this task in Hai's hands rather than assume the responsibility themselves. The villagers claimed that it is "natural" for someone to take a small commission, so long as the amount is reasonable, and asserted that others in Hai's position would take a great deal more.

Hai is financially secure. For this reason he is not as tempted as would be a poorer man to tamper with public funds. Also, his own financial security frees him of potential pressures from other wealthy individuals and groups.

Lastly, the mazkir of Even Yosef occupies an interesting position on a kinship chart of the village. His father was a Hajaaj,[7] his mother a Hasaan and his wife is from Beni'abaas. He has no brothers nor did his father have any brothers. He thus occupies a "balanced" position with regard to the patronymic and village-of-origin groups. This fact also helps structure the villagers' perception of the mazkir as being fair to all.

The Turkish Period

During the period of Turkish rule the most salient political problem was that of physical security. The members of the Jewish community considered themselves surrounded by "thousands of Moslems" who, under certain circumstances, might be incited to acts of anti-Jewish violence. Law and order were the responsibility of

141

the Ottoman Empire whose seat of power, however, was in Tripoli, a distance of two and one half days across the desert. (The old men of Even Yosef, in explaining the term osmanli, liken it to "the police".) The shaikh, therefore, had to be a skilled diplomat, sensitive to threatening changes in relationships among the groups. He had to be well-informed about the "outside world", and to be able to present, convincingly and eloquently, the case of his people to the wielders of power. Financial resources were important so that the shaikh could devote time to communal affairs (he received no salary), and could put forth bribes in the form of cash, or lavish hospitality, if necessary.

The government expected of the shaikh that he would collect the "head tax" from the members of the community which supposedly was in lieu of army service (Hacohen ms:77b, 229b). He himself was not obligated to pay the tax (Hacohen ms:213a). (The tax was known locally as the miri.)

Because the community was dependent on the political skill of the shaikh, he had to be a person who could be entrusted with the community's interests. This trust was grounded in the fact that the shaikh upheld the social and religious values of the community and, in the case of the last shaikh under the Turks, the shaikh was also the Ḥakham Bashi (Head Rabbi) of the district.

Shaikh (Rabbi)[8] Halifah Zubit Hajaaj served as leader of the community from approximately 1885 to 1913 (Hacohen ms:229a-b). He is described in some detail by both Hacohen (ms:228b-230a) and Slouschz (1926:37-40; 1927:132-153), the former stressing his skill as a physician and the latter his talent as a poet. He was granted a license to practise medicine by modern Turkish authorities (Hacohen ms:229a). In 1885 he was instrumental in securing permission from Istanbul to build a new Synagogue in Tigrinna (Hacohen ms:230a). He was "wealthy" owing to his medical practice. Halifah died about 1913, leaving one male son named Huatu.

Huatu, the son of shaikh Halifah, died in his early twenties. After the death of Huatu, Halifah brought an orphan from Tripoli named Berchani Zigadon (Berchani had French citizenship) to work in his household. Berchani married one of Halifah's daughters. Another daughter was married to a local Gharianite, an older individual named Ya'aqov Humani Hajaaj. A few years after this marriage, Halifah passed away and the shaikhship devolved upon Ya'aqov Humani who served as shaikh for about seven years.⁹

During the period of 1912 to 1922 the Gharian was controlled by local Arab leaders as Italian power was confined to the coastal towns. Ya'aqov's shaikhship more or less coincides with this period. Few memories of him survive among the people of Even Yosef except that he was a physician, as was Halifah. Ya'aqov Humani died without male offspring and afterwards the shaikhship passed on to Berchani.¹⁰

One characteristic that was shared by Halifah Zubit, Ya'aqov Humani and Berchani Zigadon was that they all entered into polygamous marriages. In order for them to do so they had to obtain the permission of the rabbinical court in Tripoli (Hacohen ms:9a). In the cases of Halifah and Ya'aqov permission was granted because their first wives did not bear male offspring. In the case of Berchani permission was granted to take a second wife because his first wife was crippled and was unable to carry on her normal domestic-conjugal activities. The only other case of polygamy of which I am aware also involved one of the community élite.

The Italian Period

During Italian rule the political situation of the Gharian Jews grew more secure. The government went to great lengths to secure civil order and was quick to execute political insurgents (Khadduri 1963:25). Tripolitanian Jews are quick to describe the improvement of their security under the Italians who "ruled with a strong hand". Older people of Even Yosef describe how they could no longer bribe local officials as they did under the Turks. The stability during Italian rule is frequently contrasted to the insecurity during the successor British administration.

The shaikh, therefore, during this period, did not have to be as skilled a diplomat as his predecessors. However, he still was the main link between the government and the community. He advised the government in

143

assessing the taxes of individual families and, in general, was consulted in all instances when members of the community were involved with the administration.

Berchani assumed the status of shaikh at the beginning of the period of Italian rule and retained the position till the British occupation. In accordance with the changed role of the shaikh, Berchani filled the position differently from Halifah. He hardly learned to speak Italian and did not excel intellectually in either the religious or secular realms.

In the early years of Italian rule the local officials imposed a corvée on the Jewish community, forcing them to work on the construction of public buildings. Berchani did nothing to oppose this corvée even though it had no legal basis. The corvée was eventually abolished through the efforts of another member of the community. No attempt was made to replace Berchani, however, despite his yielding nature toward the administration, because, for the most part, the rights of the Jews were insured and there was no need for a "strong" shaikh.

In other ways the status of community leader remained the same. For example, Berchani upheld the religious values of the community even though he was not a religious specialist. In his role as shaikh he played an important part in communal religious affairs. He would encourage individuals to study at religious academies in Tripoli in order to acquire the skills of shohet (ritual slaughterer) or mohel (ritual circumcisor) if these specialities were lacking in the Gharian. He maintained contact with the Jewish communal institutions in Tripoli to make sure that the Gharian was provided with teachers for the Synagogue school. He thus worked for the religious welfare of the community despite his lack of special religious training.

Berchani had no relatives in the Gharian other than his children. None of the families nor the patronymic groups could claim that he showed favoritism.

Berchani also was fairly well off. He had a shop in which he sold spices and dried goods. Financial resources were necessary to entertain "official"

visitors to the community (e.g. government officials,
local leaders, Rabbis from Tripoli or Palestine).
Funds were also important in fulfilling another
function of the shaikhship, namely the resolution of
disputes between members of the community.

The organization of the shaikhship during the
Italian period throws into relief another important
task of the shaikh, that of a mediator of conflicts.
It is in this aspect of the role of shaikh that
Berchani primarily is remembered by the Gharian Jews
today. There are a number of stories relating that
Berchani would give his own money to disputants in
order to settle minor conflicts. The community
exerted pressure on its members not to resort to the
government courts but to submit disputes to the
arbitration of the shaikh and other community notables.
Once a person had sought Berchani's arbitration it
would be an insult to the honor of the shaikh to
dispute his decision (Willner and Kohls 1962:228).
The people of Even Yosef point out that his yielding
nature made Berchani a successful mediator. This is
the same quality which made him a "weak" representative to the Italian government.

At the end of 1942 the British army entered the
Gharian. British officers approached Berchani who
was then old and infirm and asked him to name a
successor. He first named Hai Halifah, the present
mazkir of Even Yosef. Hai, under pressure, accepted
the office for a number of months but afterwards
transferred the responsibility to Hlafu Hoga Hassan
who remained shaikh until the members of the community
migrated to Israel.

The British Military Administration

During the British occupation the political
position of the Jewish community reverted to the pre-
Italian situation. The relationships between British,
Moslems and Jews were aggravated by contemporary
political events involving corresponding groups in
Palestine. Many Tripolitanian Jews claim that the
British were ambivalent in their attempts to stem the
anti-Jewish riots of 1945 (Zuaretz et al. 1960:207-
213). Because of this situation the Gharian Jewish
shaikh, though maintaining the same formal status as
during the Italian period, was called upon to make

145

his primary contribution in the role of diplomat.

Hlafu Hoga Hassan was one of the more educated members of the community. He was a gifted speaker and spoke Italian fairly well. In his home he set up a small restaurant where he would entertain British officials and sell them handicraft items produced by members of the community. These activities gained him influence among the British and were financially lucrative. He became a locally important political figure. Jews and Moslems would seek his intervention with the authorities and he served as a go-between for bribes extended to administration officials. As his ties with the British grew stronger, his power within the community also increased. For example, he took the liberty of using the Synagogue's funds in carrying out his political role.

Hlafu's power, however, was not without legitimation in the eyes of the community. He was the son of one of the local religious specialists. His father, Rabbi Yitzhak Hoga, read from the Torah and delivered sermons in the Synagogue. He led prayers on the Day of Atonement and was called upon to write marriage contracts. As Rabbi Hoga grew older some of these activities devolved upon Hlafu who thus served as a religious leader simultaneously with his fulfilling the duties of shaikh.

Hlafu had but one sister and his father had no siblings so there were few close relatives who could press him for favors not extended to other members of the community.

Hlafu's political activities were more or less known to the members of the community. His use of communal funds was justified by the good ties he maintained with the British and local Moslem leaders. During the 1945 riots he was instrumental in preserving Jewish life in the Gharian and property losses were also minimal. This political skill was sensed by a visitor to the Gharian in 1948 who reported:

> Shaikh Hlafu's (the name is fictitious)
> authority remained undisputed even in
> the widespread anti-Jewish rioting of
> 1945. Probably this had something to
> do with the diplomatic qualities of
> the shaikh. When I asked what he
> thought of the events in Palestine he

did not appear to hear the question
and showed me some of the attractive
carpets woven by his wife and selling
for about Ŀ3 (Kimche 1948:4).

Conclusions

The changes in the social environment of the
Gharian Jewish community, attendant upon its migration
to Israel, were greater than any of the earlier
changes discussed. Shopkeepers and artisans who
serviced a local peasant market became farmers linked
to a national economy and international market.
Members of a confessional minority, insecure as to
life and property, became citizens of a national
state in which they formed part of the majority.
An Arabic speaking shaikh, whose prime function was
that of diplomat, became a Hebrew speaking mazkir
whose main task is to maintain and develop the
economic links between the community and its environment. Nevertheless, there are a number of characteristics of the status of community leader which
remained constant along with the changes in role
described above.

1. The majority of the members of the community
are content to leave communal matters dealing with the
"outside world" in the hands of a single community
leader.

2. There are few attempts to transfer leadership to another individual once a person has formally
attained the status of leader, that is, the shaikh
(or mazkir) maintains his position throughout his
lifetime.

3. The leader is much more knowledgeable about
the world outside the community than are the other
members of the group.

4. The leader upholds and exemplifies the
religious values of the community.

5. The leader does not have close personal or
kin links with other individuals or groups in the
community.

147

6. The leader of the community is relatively wealthy so that:
(a) he can acquire and maintain those symbols of social rank appropriate to the shaikh (mazkir) as representative of the community to the outside world,
(b) he can be free from financial dependence on other individuals or groups within the community,
(c) he will not be tempted to excessively misuse his power in the interest of personal gain, and
(d) he can muster financial resources, in times of need, to bolster the community and aid individuals.

With regard to the last point (6d), the mazkir of Even Yosef has _moshav_ funds at his disposal and does not use his personal resources for these purposes. Likewise, the mazkir uses _moshav_ money to entertain official visitors. Still, Hai Halifah, the mazkir, is the individual who decides on the disposition of funds for these various purposes (Goldberg 1969a). Again, the Tripolitanian shaikh had to be wealthy so as to have time to devote to community matters while the mazkir is paid for his work. Despite these organizational changes in the role of the leader, the mazkir of Even Yosef is clearly the structural "descendant" of the Gharian Jewish shaikh, a status that has "survived" in a new social environment.

NOTES

[1] Other examples of these analyses are found in Fallers (1955), Geertz (1960), Baer (1961), and Silverman (1965).

[2] This analysis utilizes Firth's (1951:35-36) distinction between "social structure" and "social organization" which seems to parallel Linton's (1936:113-114) less systematically developed distinction between "status" and "role". Very briefly, "structure" (and "status") is concerned with "principles" and "models", while "organization" (and "role") refers to "dynamics" and "concrete activity".

[3] The present paper is based mainly on research conducted between October 1963 and April 1965 and supported by a U.S. Public Health Fellowship (MH-07876) from the National Institute of Mental Health. Some additional data were collected in 1968 during the tenure of a post-doctoral fellowship (MH-15,902-01) from the same source.

[4]The Gharian and its Jews are depicted by following
nineteenth century explorers: Lyon (1821:28-32), Barth (1858:
59-65) and Rohlfs (1874:32-38). More recent systematic description can be found in Brandenburg (1911), Norris (1953),
Khuja (1960) and Suter (1964:223, 264-265), while special
attention is paid to the Jewish community by Hacohen (ms:226a-
230a), Slouschz (1927:115-153) and Goldberg (1967a; 1967b;
1968; 1969).

[5]Much of Slouschz' work is drawn directly from the manuscript of Mordechai Hacohen (ms.). See, for example, their
descriptions of events in the Gharian during the revolt of
Ghoma (Hacohen ms.:86a-87b and Slouschz 1927:151-152). This
makes it quite often impossible to consider Slouschz an independent source. Hacohen, who was familiar with the community
over the course of many years, also states that there were
about 800 people in the two villages so I tend to accept this
estimate over the lower ones of the Alliance (1902:41) and
Agostini (1917:388-389). There may well have been demographic
changes between the time of Slouschz' visit and Agostini's
survey (see n. 10). For more demographic data see Attal (1967:
234-236). The Jewish population of the district was reported
at 550 in 1886 (Ish S.D.H. 1886:735), and Benjamin (1859:243)
tells of 120 families in the "Ghurian" (probably referring
only to Tigrinna). The Jews of Garian-town mentioned by Guweta
(1960:25) originated from Tripoli and set up stores and shops
in the Gharian after the establishment of Italian rule.

[6]Descriptions and analyses of Israeli moshavim, or small-
holders' cooperatives may be found in Ben-David (1964) and
Weingrod (1966).

[7]Most of the villagers are included in one of three
patronymic groups (Goldberg 1967b). The Hajaaj and Hasaan who
come mainly from Tigrinna constitute 35 percent and 28 percent
of the village, respectively, while the Guweta, who come from
Beni'abaas, constitute 15 percent.

[8]Tripolitanian Jews commonly accord the title "rebbi" to
anyone who assumes a special religious function such as ritual
slaughterer, Synagogue school teacher and so forth.

[9]The shaikh was generally appointed by a local official
after consultation with the community notables. The status
was not inherited though it is quite possible that leadership
of the community remained in the hands of a small group of
families over the generations (Goldberg 1968). Thus it is
likely that Ya'aqov Humani was related to the shaikh Humani
Hajaaj of the 1850's (Benjamin 1859:243; Slouschz 1927:151-152).

[10]The Turkish-Italian "interregnum" in the Gharian is a
period about which memories are unclear and often contradictory
among the people of Even Yosef. It is possible that there were
other "temporary" shaikhs during this time. Insofar as there
was no stable government there could be no stable position of
shaikh. The period saw an epidemic, sea blockade, drought and
famine. Many(?) peopld died. The whole community of Beni'abaas
abandoned their village about 1915 and moved to Tripoli. After
two years part of the community returned.

LIST OF REFERENCES

Agostino, Enrico De
    1917   Le populazioni della Tripolitanaia: notizie
                    etniche e storiche. Tripoli.
Alliance Israelite Universelle
    1902   Les Israelites de la Tripolitaine. Revue
                    des Ecoles de l'Alliance Israelite Universelle
                    7:41.
Attal, Robert
    1967   The Jewish Population in Libya. In Jewish
                    Folktales from Libya (D. Noy, ed.).
                    Jerusalem.
Baer, Gabriel
    1961   The Village Skaykh in Modern Egypt (1800-
                    1950). Scripta Hiersolymitana 9:121-153.
Barth, Henry
    1858   Travels and Discoveries in North and Central
                    Africa. New York: Harper and Brothers.
                    Vol. I.
Ben-David, Joseph (ed.)
    1964   Agricultural Planning and Village Community
                    in Israel. Arid Zone Research 23. Paris:
                    UNESCO.
Benjamin, Israel Joseph
    1859   Eight Years in Asia and Africa from 1846 to
                    1855. Hanover, 238-245.
Brandenburg, E.
    1911   Die Troglodyten des Djebel Garian. Oriental-
                    ische Literaturzeitung 14:1-14.
Epton, Nina
    1953   Oasis Kingdom: The Libyan Story. New York:
                    Roy Publishers.
Fallers, L.
    1955   The Predicament of the Modern African Chief.
                    American Anthropologist 57:290-305.

Feraud, L. Charles
1927   Annales Tripolitaines. Paris: Libraire
                     Vuibert.

Firth, Raymond
1951   Elements of Social Organization. London:
                     Routledge, Kegan Paul.

Geertz, Clifford
1960   The Changing Role of a Cultural Broker: The
                     Javanese Kijaji. Comparative Studies in
                     Society and History 2:228-249.

Goldberg, Harvey
1967a   FBD Marriage and Demography among Tripolitanian
                     Jews in Israel. Southwestern Journal of
                     Anthropology 23:176-191.

1967b   Patronymic Groups in a Tripolitanian Jewish
                     Village: Reconstruction and Interpretation.
                     Jewish Journal of Sociology 9:209-226.

1968   Elite Groups in Peasant Villages: A Compari-
                     son of Three Middle Eastern Communities.
                     American Anthropologist 70:718-731.

1969   Egalitarianism in an Autocratic Village in
                     Israel. Ethnology 54-75.

Guweta, Amishadai
1960   The Institutions of the Jewish Community of
                     Tripoli. In Yahadut Luv (Frija Zuaretz
                     et al., eds.). Tel Aviv: Va'ad Kehilot Luv
                     BeYisrael, 20-25 (Hebrew).

Hacohen, Mordechai
ms.   Higid Mordechai (Mordechai Told). Manuscript
                     in the National and University Library.
                     Jerusalem, No. 8º 1292 (English version
                     appeared as Mordecai's Story, Philadelphia:
                     Institute for the Study of Human Issues, 1980).

Ish, S. D. H.
1886   Tripolitania in Africa. Knesset Yisrael
                     (S. P. Rabinovitz, ed.) Warsaw I:730-735
                     (Hebrew).

Italian Library of Information
1940   The Italian Empire of Libya. New York.

Khadduri, M.
1963   Modern Libya: A Study of Political Develop-
                     ment. Baltimore: Johns Hopkins University
                     Press.

Khuja, Mahmud
1960   Garian Town. In Field Studies in Libya (S. G.
                     Willmett and J. I. Clarke, eds.) University
                     of Durham Research Paper Series, No. 4.

Kimche, Jon
1948   Oldest Jewish Underground.   Palestine Post
                       No. 6724, 30 May, p. 4.
Libya, Government of the Kingdom of
1954   General Population Census of Libya, 1954:
                       Report and Tables.   Tripoli.
Linton, Ralph
1936   The Study of Man.   New York: Appleton-
                       Century.
Lyon, G. F.
1821   A Narrative of Travels in North Africa in
                       the Years 1818, 1819, and 1820.   London:
                       John Murray (Reprinted in 1966).
Norris, H. T.
1953   Cave Habitations and Granaries in Tripolitania
                       and Tunisia.   Man 53 (Old Series):82-85.
Rohlfs, Gerhard
1874   Quer durch Afrika: Reise vom Mitelmeer
                       nach dem Tschad-See zum Gulf von Guinea.
                       Leipzig: F. A. Brockhaus.
Silverman, Sydel
1965   Patronage and Community-Nation Relationships
                       in Central Italy.   Ethnology 4:172-189.
Slouschz, Nahum
1908   La Tripolitaine sous la domination des
                       Karamanli.   Revue du monde musulman 6:
                       58-84, 211-232, 433-453.

_____
1926   In the Libyan Mountains.   Reshumot 4:1-76
                       (Hebrew).

_____
1927   Travels in North Africa.   Philadelphia:
                       Jewish Publication Society.
Suter, Karl   "
1964   Die Wohnholen und Speicherburgen des
                       tripolitanisch-tunesischen Berglandes.
                       Zeitschrift für Ethnologie 89:216-275.
Weingrod, Alex
1962   Administered Communities: Some Character-
                       istics of New Immigrant Villages in Israel.
                       Economic Development and Cultural Change
                       9:69-84.

_____
1966   Reluctant Pioneers: Village Development
                       in Israel.   Ithaca: Cornell University.
Willner, Dorothy and M. Kohls
1962   Jews in the High Atlas Mountains of Morocco:
                       A Partial Reconstruction.   Jewish Journal
                       of Sociology 4:207-241.

Wolf, Eric
    1956   Aspects of Group Relations in a Complex
                        Society: Mexico. American Anthropologist
                        58:1065-1078.
Zuaretz, Frija et al. (eds.)
    1960   Yahadut Luv. Tel Aviv: Va'ad Kehillet Luv
                        BeYisrael.

CHAPTER 8

JEWS IN LATE OTTOMAN SYRIA[1]: EXTERNAL RELATIONS

WALTER P. ZENNER

Using a variety of historical sources
supplemented by the accounts of Syrian Jews
in both Israel and the United States, the
author reconstructs the social life of Syrian
Jews in late Ottoman Syria. The complex
nature of the political and economic forces
which affected the lives of Jews in Aleppo
and Damascus are underlined. These included
the Ottoman state, European states, the
world market, and the Christian and Muslim
neighbors of the Jews. The presence of
large numbers of Christians gave intergroup relations in places like Syria a
different character from that of Muslim-
Jewish relations in Morocco.

Historical Background

While Syria has played a role in Jewish history
from the beginning of the Hebrew tribes, the modern
Syrian Jewish communities may be said to begin in
the 16th Century. First, the Ottoman Turks conquered
Egypt and Syria from the Mamluke Sultans. Syria
remained under Ottoman control until the First World
War. Second, with the circumnavigation of the Capes,
the Atlantic European powers came to control world
commerce and begin the establishment of the "modern
world system" (Wallerstein 1974). Third, after the
explusion of Jews from Spain and Sicily, large numbers
immigrated to the Eastern Mediterranean, including
the cities of Aleppo and Damascus.

The Ottoman regime resembled the Muslim empires
which had preceded it in a number of ways. The
rulers adhered to the Sunni branch of Islam. Persons
with the legal status of slave held high positions
in the civil and military bureaucracies. Even in the
Arab provinces, many officials, including the governors, were Turks, Circassians, Albanians and Slavs

---

SOURCE: Article written expressly for this volume.

who did not speak Arabic. The entire population of Syria, Muslim, Christian, and Jew, was thus subject to an administration of strangers. At times, the local governor was practically independent of the central government. But whether rule was by such a local Pasha or directed from the central government, it tended to be exploitative and arbitrary, since the rulers were not generally responsible to the local populace.

The decline in Ottoman power became visible in the 18th Century. The late 18th Century was highlighted by the Russian advance southward and the French invasion of Egypt under Napoleon, which led the way to Westernization of the Empire. Various attempts at internal reform culminated in the Young Turk revolt of 1909, the transformation of Turkey by Ataturk in the 1920's, and the Arab nationalist movements.

The Ottoman period was marked by the increasing involvement in a European-dominated economic system. During the 16th, 17th and 18th Centuries, Aleppo was one of the principal centers of the European Levant trade. In this period, the French, the Dutch, the English, and the Venetians maintained consulates and factories (agencies) in the North Syrian city. The caravan trade continued, even though East Indian goods reached the Middle East via Europe in the 18th Century. Aleppo exported such Middle Eastern goods as local cotton and Persian silk to Europe (Lutzky 1940; Wood 1935:145-6; Sauvaget 1941:192-204). Initially this was a trade in luxury goods, but it was increasingly a trade dominated by the Europeans. In the past two hundred years, the commerce of Syria suffered several severe blows. By the end of the 18th Century, the commerce of Aleppo had diminished greatly with exports to Europe less than imports. With the Industrial Revolution, the Middle East was considered as a market for cheap European manufactures rather than as a source of luxury goods, as it had once been (Bowring 1840:83-5). After 1869, the great caravans to the East, which had once been a major vehicle of trade, could not compete with the Suez Canal with its cheap East-West transit (Braver 1945/6). These caravans had been important for both Aleppo and Damascus. The instability of the Ottoman Empire contributed to this deterioration. Under the Mandate, there was no essential change in the state of commerce and industry in Syria, although there was a beginning of modern industry (Himadieh 1936: passim). Westernization, however, affected the internal demand for goods. For instance, the adoption of European dress caused a demand in woolens (ibid. 143-4). The competition of cheap Japanese imports, the closing of the border between Syria and the Turkish Republic, which included a part of Aleppo's hinterland, and the Great Depression made the interwar period difficult.

The fact that the Jewish communities in the 16th Century had been augmented by refugees with connection in Italy and the Balkans helped them supply interpreters to the European merchants in Syria. The division between the immigrants and the indigenous, Arabic-speaking, Mustarib Jews took time to resolve. Differences between the groups such as different prayerbook texts, marriage contracts, and customs for the various festivals persisted even after the immigrants had become arabized. By 1900, however, the groups had merged.

The Jews and the Christians of Aleppo served the European merchants as brokers and dragomans. While most of the men from these minorities worked as retailers and craftsmen, a number of well-to-do individuals were involved in international commerce or worked for the Ottoman authorities. The Jews benefited from commercial relations with the Jews of Livorno. Jews from Livorno and elsewhere in Italy came to settle in Aleppo. During the 18th Century, the number of European Jewish merchants, known as Signores Francos, increased, while the Christian merchants declined. Most of these Jewish merchants came from Italy. They reached the height of their prosperity around 1740. After 1775, there was a sharp decline in Aleppine trade in general (Lutzky 1940; Sauvaget 1941:204-207).

The European Jews took advantage of the Capitulations, the treaties made between the Ottoman Government and the European states, granting subjects of the latter certain extra-territorial privileges. Chief among these was a measure of freedom from the extortions, fines, and taxes which Ottoman subjects were forced to pay. It also entitled the bearer of a foreign passport to a trial before his own Consul, rather than before the local courts. The Europeans

paid lower duties on exports and imports. Indigenous
Christians and Jews often acquired these privileges
through purchasing a certificate granting them these
immunities and privileges. They were frequently
extended to consular dragomans, but the right was
often abused. In 1793, the pasha of Aleppo reported
that there were 1500 persons claiming to be consular
dragomans. All but six were deprived of their
certificates of immunity (berat) after an investigation (Gibb and Bowen 1950:I:122, 310-311). The
European Jews in Aleppo had passports from several
European states, including Britain, the Netherlands,
Venice, Austria, and especially France. Relations
with the local French merchants and priests were,
however, far from cordial (Lutzky 1940). In the
late 18th Century, Austria appointed as Consul the
scion of an Italian Jewish family residing in
Aleppo (H. J. Cohen 1971).

The European Jewish merchants were a distinct
group with the Jewish community. They maintained
handsome residences in the vicinity of the Baḥsita,
a section near the Market and the Jewish quarter.
They did not form a separate synagogue, although they
may have conducted separate prayer services. Since
Consular protection was granted to them, they did not
recognize the authority of the local Jewish community
to tax them. A controversy on this broke out in the
mid 18th Century. The Sephardic Chief Rabbi Solomon
Laniado tried to force the Francos to adhere formally
to the local Jewish community and its sanctions,
including payment of taxes to the Ottoman government.
Rabbi Judah Kassin maintained that the Francos
were correct in maintaining their customary privileges
and aloofness. They did, however, contribute money
to the various community institutions, including the
Great Synagogue. A special agreement regarding the
payment of a special tax levied by the local community
on non-residents, Ottoman and Frankish Jews, had
been signed with the French consulate.

These Frankish Jews maintained a European way of
life in this Levantine city and may have influenced
the indigenous Jews. While the Frank merchants
continued wearing beards, which were unfashionable in
the 18th Century Europe, their women-folk would stroll
in public unlike the Oriental ladies. The Signores
Francos hired many indigenous Jews as agents, clerks,
and workmen. Their own children studied together

with those of the Must'aribim. It should be pointed
out that this Must'arib group of the 18th Century,
now included the descendants of the Spanish and
Sicilian Jews who had immigrated in the 16th Century,
who were Ottoman subjects. These still retained the
Sephardic rite.

During the early 19th Century, there were some
minor migrations. After the Aleppo earthquake of
1822, many Halebi Jews moved to Damascus[2] (Paton
1844:39). As a result of a blood-libel, the Jews
of Hamah were expelled and many went to Aleppo
(Burton 1898:129). From the second half of the 19th
Century onwards, many sought their fortunes in
Beirut, Cairo and Alexandria. By the early 20th
Century, Syrian Jews and Christians were emigrating,
often to such far-off places as New York, Argentina
and Hong Kong. These migrations continued into the
Mandatory period.

There were Jews from other parts of the Middle
East moving to Syria and vice versa. After World
War I, many Jews from Urfa, Gaziantep, and Diyar
Bekir migrated to Aleppo, often as a way-station to
the Americas or to Palestine. There were also small
numbers of Ashkenazic and Persian Jews who became
assimilated into the larger Sephardic-Must'arib
population. Estimates of the Jewish population in
Ottoman Syria vary. According to the Ottoman Census
of 1893, there were 9,356 Jews in the Province of
Aleppo (including the City of Aleppo) and 6,265 Jews
in Damascus and its vicinity (Karpat 1978:263; 265).
Some travelers estimate that the population of each
city was somewhat larger.[3]

The Syrian Jews and the Ottoman State

An outstanding characteristic of Ottoman government was its "lack of a complex, all-embracing
political organization." As Gibb and Bowen suggest
(1950:I:209), Muslim society in the Arab provinces
may be visualized as composing "two co-existing
groups, the relations between which were for the most
part formal and superficial." One group was the
governing class of officials and soldiers, which
lived on a certain percentage of revenues, while the
other "class" consisted of merchants, artisans,
and cultivators who accommodated themselves to those

159

who ruled. It is not surprising that the main impression of Ottoman administration conveyed by European travelers is that of a rapacious and corrupt tax-collecting bureaucracy. What is forgotten in this description is the large number of residual and customary rights allowed both to the Muslim Arabs and Kurds and to the members of non-Muslim communions. The reforms of the central Ottoman government during the 19th Century may be seen as attempts to achieve an all-embracing political organization of the society along European lines. These reforms had the consequence of invading the customary privileges which various corporate groups had enjoyed. This found fuller expression in the attempts of the Young Turk regime (1909-1918) to build a national state out of the authoritarian but pluralistic Ottoman empire.

Just as relations between the Turks and their fellow Muslim Arab and Kurdish subjects were formal and superficial, so were they with the Jews and Christians. The Jews and Christians in the empire, of course, were dhimmi or protected communities, provided that they submitted to the Islamic state. For protection, however, they had to abide by regulations which indicated that they were inferior to the Muslims (eg. not building new houses of worship and maintaining a low profile). These communities were given autonomy for regulating their internal affairs, too. They were also obliged to pay special taxes. The burden of taxation weighed heavily upon the people even in relatively prosperous communities. In the late 18th Century, leaders of the Jewish community considered selling the quasi-sacred synagogue ornaments in order to pay taxes (S. Laniado 1774/5: OH 13:23a; I. Antebi in A. Antebi 1842/3:YD3:21b).

During the Mohammed Ali occupation of the 1830's taxes also were oppressive. The reforms of that regime and the Ottoman administration which followed changed the rules of taxation. Certain customary exemptions, such as those for religious scholars, were removed. The manner of assessment was altered as well. Taxes were assessed by the number of men in the community, but if an individual moved from Ainteb (Gaziantep) to Aleppo, the community of Ainteb would still be liable for his taxes. For a time in Ainteb, Christians, Jews and Muslims were listed in the same tax roll, until Christians protested that the Muslims were making them pay more than their just

160

share. As a result of such exactions many fled from the Egyptian occupied areas in the 1830's, but some of these taxes remained after the Egyptian forces of Mohammed Ali withdrew in 1840. In the responsa, the rabbis were asked if these new taxes were dina d'malkhuta, the law of the land, i.e. legitimate taxes, or gazlanuta d'malkhuta, state robbery (Antebi 1842/3:93b-100b; Dwek 1909/10:11b; Laniado 1951/2: 164; Taoutel 1960:56-9).

The Jews themselves were involved in the collection of revenues and other governmental activities. In the late 18th and early 19th Centuries, Jews and Christians were employed as bankers for the provincial governors, which, in effect, meant acting as tax-farmers. They provided the surety for the Turkish tax-farmers and governors who had to pay for their posts. The banker guaranteed payment to the Treasury of the tax-farmer's obligation. These bankers (Sarraaf, sing., Sayaarif, pl.) profited from the high interest rates, while the need to repay the Sarraaf was one reason for the heavy tax burden. Still, the influence, wealth and high position of the minorities in this period has been highly exaggerated. The majority may have perceived the minority banker as representative of his group, but the members of the minority itself benefited little from his activities, since he himself had to identify with the official's interests in order to protect his investment (Bodman 1963:ix, 32; Fischel 1944; Gibb and Bowen 1957:II:23-24; 26).

The collection of taxes was particularly hard on the peasantry. Those living on government (miiri) land paid their rent according to the lunar calendar, which rarely coincided with the agricultural cycle. Thus, they were frequently obligated to borrow money to pay their taxes. The taxes also affected the prices within the city and many blamed the bankers for inflation and other economic hardships (al-Maghribi 1929).

The other position which was commonly occupied by Jews and Christians was customs collector (or kashaaf). Here, the exactions were made of foreign merchants rather than indigenous peasants and others. They, too, could become so oppressive as to cause a decline of commerce (Gibb and Bowen 1957:62-4). For both positions, there was competition between Jews and

Christians and among the Jews themselves. This can be
illustrated through cases found in the responsa. An
example is a case which came before the rabbinic
court of Aleppo in the 1760's. There the collection
of customs had been in Jewish hands for many years.

> The brothers, Aaron Bekhor Sason
> and Moses Sason had been serving to-
> gether with their uncle's sons, Hayim,
> Abraham, and Moses Sason and another
> partner, Abraham HaKohen. According
> to the contract, they received one-third
> of each ghruush[4] (piastre) taken in by
> the agha. The total revenue was divided
> in four parts: HaKohen received one
> part, one for the senior Sason brothers,
> one for the sons of their uncle, and
> one for the Harari family which had
> formerly served in this capacity. The
> principle of hereditary familial rights
> was in operation here.[5]

> After a time, the senior Sasons and
> HaKohen retired, although the junior
> Sasons continued to serve. The agha
> then gave the shares of those no longer
> employed to the current kashaaf. A
> former Dragoman of the Venetian Consul,
> Hanna Diba, a Christian, worked his way
> into the service. The junior Sasons
> and the heir of HaKohen were accused of
> embezzlement. The Sasons succeeded in
> regaining their position through bribery.
> After the Sasons had been restored, the
> Kohen and Harari families claimed their
> original share of the revenue. The
> Sasons held that the original contract
> had been cancelled when they were removed;
> therefore the others deserved no share.
> The responsum supported this contention
> (Shama' 1820/21:37:70a et. seq.).

This case shows how the Jewish community handled
such matters. Families were treated as units. Among
the sanctions employed was the threat of excommunication if the parties did not take an oath. Excommunication, or ostracism, was one of the ultimate
punishments used by Rabbinic courts in dealing with
recalcitrant members of the Jewish community. The

oath was sworn by the Sason brothers in 1767 and the case was settled after fifteen years of litigation.

The rivalry with Christians for these positions was often intense. In Egypt, Syrians belonging to the Greek Catholic church succeeded in displacing the Jews in 1763, under Ali Bey al-Kabir (R. M. Haddad 1970:51n.; Livingston 1971). The above case shows that in Aleppo there was alternation between the Christians and Jews. This was also the case with regard to the office of saraaf. Even the Farhi[6] family which had dominated that office in Damascus during the early 19th Century could be displaced. In 1825, Raphael Farhi was forced to flee and was succeeded by a Christian from Homs. In 1830, when Mohammed Ali, the Pasha of Egypt, conquered Syria, Christians were given preference (al-Maghribi 1929; Bodman 1963:32; Russell 1794). After the return of full Ottoman rule in 1840, the situation changed (see below).

Jews and Christians were rivals for favors from the European Powers as well as from the Ottoman state. Increasingly the Europeans were able to exercise real power within the bounds of the empire. At first, Christians and Jews served as interpreters and agents for the European trading companies, some even acquiring the extra-territorial rights of foreign subjects. This rivalry was many-sided, since the European powers, the Ottoman authorities, and the protected minorities each sought favors from the other parties. For instance, after the Syrian Greek Catholics wrested the Egyptian customs administration out of Jewish hands in the late 18th Century, they were given "first rank in Egyptian commerce as well as a virtual monopoly over European consular positions in Egypt" (Haddad 1970:51n.).

In Aleppo, a Jewish family from Livorno achieved such a near monopoly on consular positions for much of the 19th Century, although its power was not as great as that attributed to the Syrians in Egypt. Rafael Picciotto became Consul in Aleppo for the Holy Roman Emperor and Duke of Tuscany in 1788; in 1806, he was knighted. His son succeeded him as consul and the de Picciotto family provided consuls for most European powers (save Britain) for much of the 19th Century. During the Napoleonic wars, one duty of the Austrian consul was to protect Greek

Catholic rights in Aleppo, even though the Greek
Catholics were often rivals of the Jews (Segall 1910;
H. J. Cohen 1971; Bowring 1840:192).[7]

The de Picciottos, however, also protected
Jewish interests. The consuls (called **Signores
Francos**) obtained the governor's assistance in re-
building the synagogue at the shrine of Ezra the
Scribe at Tedif al-Yahud near Aleppo (Laniado 1951/2:
15-16). In Damascus, the Mohammed Ali regime, which
ruled there from 1831 to 1840, tended to favor Greek
Catholics--then favored by Mohammed Ali's French
allies, over the Jews. In 1840, both the rivalry
of the Greek Catholics and the Jews and between the
French, backing the Egyptian pasha, and the other
European powers came to a head. The latter made
moves to force Mohammed Ali to return full control
to the government in Istanbul.

In Damascus in that year, the local authorities
and the French Consul accused the leaders of the
Jewish community of having murdered a Corsican
Catholic priest. A number of Jewish notables were
arrested. One, Isaac de Picciotto, son of the late
Austrian consul in Aleppo, found refuge in the
Austrian consulate. The case aroused Jews throughout
Europe to assist their co-religionists. The British
and Austrian governments also aided the imprisoned
Jews. These two governments were among those interested in restoring Syria to the Sultan in Istanbul
and in blocking the growth of Egyptian and French
power. This presence helped obtain the release of
the surviving Jewish prisoners (Braver 1936). That
same year Mohammed Ali withdrew his forces from
Syria and Palestine.

Wealthy Jews, although only a small percentage
of the population, recognized the value of consular
protection. In Damascus, after 1840, Jews sought
British protection. In 1860, for instance, some Jews
were imprisoned, charged with complicity in the anti-
Christian pogroms of that year, but they were re-
leased with British help. The British consuls
themselves were often lukewarm or hostile towards the
Jews. Several reasons may account for this. One is
that consular protegees often took advantage of
their extra-territoriality in commerce, moneylending
and other activities, something which the consuls
resented. Another is the anti-Jewish prejudices of

the consuls themselves.

The explorer, Richard F. Burton, sought to with-
hold consular protection from certain Jewish bankers.[8]
Burton's treatment of Jews holding British passports
may have been related to the efforts which the central
Ottoman government was making to restrict foreign
protection of those holding foreign passports. For
instance, in 1867, foreign subjects were allowed to
own real estate in the empire, but had to submit to
the control of the Turkish courts and pay the usual
taxes. Similarly a nationality law was passed in
1869 which made it more difficult for Ottoman subjects
to claim foreign nationality and which imposed more
stringent passport control on both Ottoman and foreign
nationals.

While the number of foreign subjects claiming
extraterritorial rights was small, they did obtain
rights which gave them many advantages over the
Ottoman nationals. Of those born locally, the vast
majority were Christians and Jews, claiming a variety
of nationalities including Austrian, British, French
and Italian (Braver 1945/46; Baron 1933, 1940;
I. Burton 1879:264-5; Davison 1963:260-3).

In the mid-19th Century, the Ottoman government
began to westernize its administrative apparatus.
Attempts were made to abolish tax farming. For
instance, in 1840 all the leading sarrafs were called
together in Istanbul and informed that their contracts
were cancelled. Yet abuses in tax collection continued and tax farming was reintroduced two years
later. Despite repeated promises to abolish this
system, it persisted into the late 19th Century.
After the return of central government administration
in Syria in 1841, Raphael Farhi, a member of the
famous family of Jewish ṣayaarif, was appointed
Banker to the provincial treasury. He was, however,
superseded two years later, but Jews and Christians
in Syria continued to serve the new Ottoman financial
administration. Other minority members worked as
civil servants dealing with such new bureaus as those
dealing with sanitation, education, the police, and
the registration of real estate. In Damascus around
1900, a Jew was the inspector general of real estate
(Paton 1844:40; Davison 1963:55, 105, 111, 116, 137,
141, 307; Krikorian 1977; Franco and Gottheil 1903;
Maoz 1968:206).

The westernizing reform of the Ottoman regime also resulted in the introduction of incipient representative councils and the establishment of a state-sponsored chief rabbinate. The former institution was set up on a French model in the early 1840's. Previously Muslim officials and dignitaries who formed the governor's _divan_ had been consulted by the governor, but this body had no formal authority. The new councils were, however, invested with considerable powers, including the assessment and farming out of taxes, and customs, supervision of tax collection, supervision of agricultural production and marketing, management of public works, and helping to maintain public order, as well as the administration of justice. While the vast majority of members were members of the Muslim upper class, including religious officials and large landowners, the religious leaders of non-Muslim communities were appointed to these councils, as well as some Jewish and Christian notables. While underrepresented, some of these minority leaders could gain real power (Maoz 1968: 87-107; Davison 1963:48-9, 140-2).

Most of these officials were appointed or self-appointed. A law promulgated in 1864 did provide for the election of district (kaza) councillors, at the lower level, but it was a complex indirect system of representation. There were several levels of voting, beginning with male citizens over 18 and ending with the selection of councillors by elders from a list prepared by administrative officials of the district. Such a mixture of autocratic, oligarchic, and democratic principles prevailed during the 19th Century (Davison 1963:148-151, 374-5).

The _ḥakham bashi_ or chief rabbi was one member of the provincial council. Unlike the Armenian, Greek Orthodox and Catholic churches, Jews do not have a hierarchical system by which Jewish communities are united into a single ecclesiastical organization. Utilizing certain Jewish legends about the close relationships of early rabbis in Constantinople with Sultan Mehmed the Conqueror, the Ottoman reformers sought to make the Jewish subjects of the empire comparable in organization to that of the Christian churches. Therefore they set up the chief rabbi (_ḥakham bashi_) of Istanbul as head of the Jews of the empire as a whole and appointed comparable chief rabbis or _ḥakham bashis_ in the various provincial capitals.[9]

The appointment of ḥakham bashis gave power to
the governors and their Jewish clients and secularized the Syrian rabbinate. In some communities,
such as Saida (Lebanon) and Mosul (Iraq), there are
reports that unqualified individuals who were
favorites for the governors were appointed ḥakham
bashi, over the protests of the local Jewish
communities. In Aleppo, the hakham bashi was generally a respected rabbi, but even here he could
become a controversial figure. Such was the case,
when Abraham Dwek Halusi became ḥakham bashi, during
the reign of Abdel Hamid II. He wore a medallion
from Istanbul on his hat and was known for knowledge
of Turkish. This rabbi was feared by Jews because
of his influence with the government and he tried to
force the wealthy to pay taxes on behalf of the poor.
According to one informant, the notables sought his
removal for that reason. Like other leaders of
minority communities, such as the Christian bishops,
the ḥakham bashi participated in the local provincial
council (field notes; Adler 1905; I. Abulafia 1886-7:
Pt. III:YD:no. 16:40b-45a).[10] Thus the chief rabbi
became a mediator.

In addition to the new offices, the westernization
of the Ottoman empire impinged on the lives of its
subjects in other novel ways. As part of the reform
of the government, it now required the registration
of land and the payment of fees upon receiving an
inheritance. Such registration is not mentioned in
responsa from the 18th or early 19th centuries, but
does appear after 1860, in the late responsa of
I. Abulafia (1896/7:V:37:127b, 141a, 156a).[11]

Like other non-Western states which were drawn
into the European state system in the 19th Century,
the Ottoman government began to finance its operations through the sale of bonds in both Europe and
its own realms. When it deferred payment on several
bond issues in 1895 and 1876, its bankruptcy had
wide ramifications for both European and Ottoman
bondholders. A European financial administration
was set up, while many of its bondholders were ruined.
This included wealthy Jews in Damascus and Aleppo
and the bankruptcy of the government contributed to
the rapid decline of these communities (Braver 1945/6;
Abulafia 1886/7:III:HM:8:30a; I. Dayan 1902/3:HM29:
45a seq.; Blaisdell 1929).

Until the Young Turk revolt in 1909, Jews and Christians were not conscripted into the Turkish army. During the 1850's and 1860's, the principle that non-Muslims could serve in the army as equal Ottoman subjects alongside Muslims was proclaimed, but, in practice, Jews and Christians paid a special exemption tax while Muslims were conscripted (Davison 1963: 94-95). Reference is made to three Jews who served in the army during the Russo-Turkish war of 1876-78 in one responsum, concerning one of these Jewish soldiers who had converted to Islam (Abulafia 1885/6: II:83b-92b). After the Young Turk junta was installed, conscription for members of minority groups was introduced. Escaping the draft was one of the motivations for the emigration of many young Jewish and Christian males from Syria (Hitti 1924: 51). During the Balkan wars and the First World War, many Syrian Jews served in the Turkish army, many of whom died. By the end of the war, the empire had collapsed and many conscripts had deserted the army. One man, born in Killiz, told of how he remained hidden in his family's home in Aleppo; a Damascus Jew related the story of how his brother deserted and fled to Jebel-el-Druze and how he went from Damascus to see his brother there. Later the brother fled to Argentina. One informant went to Germany with the Ottoman Navy.[12]

Several aspects of the Jewish situation in the Ottoman state become clear. First, Jews, like other non-Muslims, were subject to differential treatment. They were excluded from certain positions, favored for others, and subject to special taxes. Second, the gradual involvement of the Ottoman empire into the European state system had its effects on the Jewish subjects. Some Jews were able to obtain special extra-territorial privileges. New laws changed the kinds of governmental posts open to Jews and Christians and transformed the nature of the game for government favors. The consequences of bankruptcy and the disastrous military campaigns of the "sick man of Europe" affected Syrian Jews adversely. Thus the Jews were involved in the conflicts which upset the old balance between Muslims and non-Muslims in the empire.

Jewish-Gentile Relations

In traditional Middle Eastern society, Jews, Christians and Muslims lived distinct lives. Each had its individual style of dress, its own courts of law and its own norms, and loyalties. Each had a set of stereotypes about the other groups. The Muslim concept of the world outside the Islamic state as daar al-harb, the enemy camp, epitomizes some of the feelings which each group had towards the other. Nevertheless, they were economically interdependent. In Syria, they shared Arabic as their everyday language, as well as many values and customs. All lived under one monarch, although the Ottoman sultan was not recognized as fully legitimate by large segments of the population, both Muslim and non-Muslim. The readiness with which non-Muslims sought the protection of foreign consuls was a sign of this.

Religion is a deep boundary separating ethnic groups in the Middle East, particularly between Jew, Christian and Muslim. Each group had its own laws governing inheritance, cousin marriage and divorce. No group permitted unrestricted intermarriage. The Muslim law which states that Muslim men may marry Christian and Jewish women is only apparently permissive and, in fact, is an assertion of Muslim and male dominance. The Islamic form of prayer, the various Christian liturgies, and Jewish individual and synagogue prayer are quite different, one from the other. Muslims are forbidden to drink alcoholic beverages, permitted to Jews and Christians. Jews and Muslims have similar, but not identical, dietary laws. While similarities might exist in having periods of abstinence, the times and manner in which they were observed were not the same. No one would mistake Ramadan, Lent and the Jewish Days of Awe for one another.

Each religious tradition had its own indicators of identity and idiom and was expanded and transmitted by its own network of communication.[13] The Greek Orthodox and Greek Catholic Churches used Greek, the Armenians, Armenian, the Muslim Ulema used Classical Arabic, and the Jews used Hebrew. An Armenian Catholic (Uniate) priest would be connected with the Mekhtiarist monastery in Venice, while the Armenian Apostolic priest might correspond with a bishop in Echmiadzin. The Sunni qaadi (judge) had contacts

169

with Cairo, Istanbul, and Mecca. The rabbi had his books printed in Livorno and received Jewish pilgrims from Poland as guests, as they travelled to the Holy Cities of Jerusalem and Safed. Modernizing styles moved along similar "religio-ethnic" lines. A Maronite might receive a modern western education in the French clericalist atmosphere of St. Joseph University, while an Armenian would go to an Armenian nationalist school and a Jew would receive the European tradition in a French laicist form in the school of the Alliance Israelite Universelle.

The separate sets of norms, embodied in separate legal codes and enforced by different judges, whether bishops, 'ulema, or rabbis, each with their social networks, form the basis of the "communal system", which has sometimes been labeled the "millet" system. The term, milla (Arabic) or millet (Turkish) is a term meaning either religious or ethnic community. Since the 19th Century, it has been applied to the formally recognized religious communities, who were granted the right to deal with the personal law of their own adherents. It was seen by historians to have originated in the arrangements which the Ottoman authorities made with the various Christian and Jewish communities at the time of the conquest of Constantinople. It implied parallel administrative hierarchies. Braude (1977) has convincingly argued that, while an "organic" system of communal pluralism did exist prior to the 19th Century, no single formal administrative structure governed the various non-Muslim communities nor were the hierarchies of the different groups parallel. In the 19th Century, of course, the Ottomans did demand confirmation of communal heads, like the ḥakham bashi. In practice, the Ottoman bureaucracy allowed local authorities, including the rabbis, much freedom in dealing with the everyday affairs of their own communities.

The Jews of Aleppo could ask the government's participation in the ritual area of their life. It was customary for the Jews in that North Syrian city to "rent the city" from the governor for a specified time. This was done so that they could symbolically enclose the city in such a way so as to enable them to "carry" within its wall on the Sabbath. According to Jewish law, one may not carry anything, even a hankerchief, on the Seventh Day except within an enclosed area, such as a home. The question came up after the deposition and death of Abdul Aziz in 1875 and a change in governors (I. Dayan 1902/3).

Despite the separatism, it should be stressed that there was a shared ideology. All groups professed belief in one God and adhered in some fashion to the tradition of Abraham. On the popular level, there was a shared idiom. All told jokes and stories about their own and each other's religious dignitaries and all knew something about the different traditions associated with Moses, Jesus, Mohammed, Ali, and Omar (Zenner 1970; 1972).

Two anecdotes will show the sometimes concealed hostility with which this mutual knowledge was manipulated.

Once a Jew was eating in the market on the first day of Ramadan and a Muslim reproved him for doing this. So he refrained from eating publicly that day and for two days thereafter. On the fourth day, however, he started eating again and again the Muslim came to him. The Jew replied, Muhammed wrote, don't eat for three days, but a fly came along and made a dot next to the three (the Arabic zero is indicated by a little dot; obviously this is anachronistic, since Arabic numerals were not used in Muslim Scripture). So why should I fast on account of a fly.

A Damascus Jew related that once a Shiite, of whom there were few in Damascus, came to a rabbi and asked, how can it be that we will be the donkeys of the Jews when the Messiah comes, since Jews are many and Shiites are few. The rabbi, replied chanting in the Quranic mode, that Shiites would be such big asses that they could carry all the Jews.

Part of the shared interfaith ideology is a fatalism, marked by such phrases interspersing Arabic speech as "if God wills" (in sha'allah), "Thank God" (al-hamdah l'llah) which Jews and Muslims in the Middle East share. This fatalism is balanced by a belief in the efficacy of religious and magical practices. For instance, all groups were concerned over envy of an individual's good fortune, which could be prevented by certain measures against the "evil eye." Muslims, Jews, and Druzes used the color of light blue and the number five (often in the form of a hand) against the evil eye. A Jew might call in a sheikh in order to

171

obtain a cure, while a Christian might resort to a
rabbi. At times, the relationship between the religio-
magical specialist and the member of another communion
was more of a commercial than a moral transaction.
In a period of crisis, the religious leaders of all
groups did come together to pray. The recurrent
droughts of the Middle East were such occasions
(Russell 1794:II). A Lebanese Jew recalled such an
incident during his youth:

> Another rabbi prayed for rain to come
> down. All the Mohammedan and Christian
> religious leaders and "schools" were
> praying and it didn't come down. They
> came to the rabbi, and said he should
> pray and blow the shofar (ram's horn).
> He declared a fast and took the children
> from the Talmud Torah (Jewish school) to
> the cemetery and before they finished
> (their prayers), the rain came down.
> They honored him and came to him. Then
> (after his death) they went to the
> rabbi's grave. He is powerful like.
> He was the teacher of my oldest brother.

The graves of saintly men were honored by all.
Many stories are told of Muslims' attempts to steal
the bodies of saintly rabbis. There is a legend that
Muslims tried to bury Moses Kohen, the first ḥakham
bashi of Aleppo in their cemetery, but were prevented
from doing this by the Consuls Picciotto who had him
interred in their family tomb. The common reverence
for saints comes out in the history of the synagogue
in Tedif al-Yahud which was restored in the 1830's
with aid from Ibrahim Pasha's regime (Laniado 1951/
2:15) and was saved from destruction in 1947 by an
Arab.

Visiting in the homes of members of different
groups was limited. It was probably more common in
Aleppo quarters where Jews and Muslims shared court-
yards than in Damascus. When Jewish peddlers traveled
in rural areas, they often had to spend the night in
Gentile houses. The relative degree of intimacy, no
doubt, depended on the current degree of hostility or
amity between the groups. There were Gentile guests
at Jewish weddings. Russell reports that Turkish
ladies came to view the booths built by Jews for the
Festival of Sukkot; those who were guests of the

family would be entertained and served coffee, sweet-
meats and sherbet. Such guests were probably more
common among the well-to-do (Russell 1794:II:58-88).
At the end of Passover, according to one informant,
Muslims would bring their Jewish acquaintances bread
and cheese. In the Mandatory period, men would meet
Muslim and Christian acquaintances in cafes, but
they rarely invited them home.

In those occupations where there was ethnic
specialization, economic interdependence was obvious.
However, rivalry would also be established along
group lines, as in cases where both Jews and
Christians served as bankers to the Turkish pashas.
Some Jews were employees of non-Jews: One Jew
worked as an accountant for a Muslim mercantile
family, and some Jews worked as printers for a Christian firm in the 20th Century. Jews generally
preferred not to enter full partnership with Gentiles.
Certain tasks for Jews were performed by Gentiles.
According to Russell, Christian and Bedouin servants
did work prohibited to Jews on the Sabbath, and the
attendants in the bath-house were Muslims. All the
groups had rules (with loopholes) against lending
at interest to members but each group lent to outsiders
usuriously.

Intergroup rivalry in the 19th Century and later
resulted in interethnic conflict. Christians sought
to displace Jewish sarrafs and tax farmers and
accused Jews of ritual murder. Muslims resented the
intervention of European powers on behalf of the
minorities, especially the Christians, and resented
the grant of equal rights to them. The Damascus
pogrom and the Druze massacres of 1860 were an
expression of this sentiment. In the effort of 19th
Century Christians to gain more rights on the Ottoman
empire and to utilize European intervention, the Jews
took an equivocal position. They tended to side more
with the Muslims than with their Christian competitors,
but they also utilized the European consuls on their
own behalf when they could. During the anti-Christian
pogroms of the mid-19th Century, Jews were at times
accused of helping Muslims loot the Christians (Braver
1936; 1945/6; Baron 1933, 1940; Gidney 1897:128-9;
Maoz 1968:205-210; Jessup 1909:II:424-5; Taoutel
1960:69).

The Jews in Aleppo and in hinterland were

witnesses to the Armenian Holocaust during the First World War. As with regard to other Christians, the Armenians were rivals, and little love was lost between them and the Jews. This comes out in testimonies by old people from that area in Jerusalem. A man from Chermik (Cermik) in Turkey told of a Jew who had a vision that the Armenians were planning to kill the Turks and the Jews and who warned the Turks. A woman related a story of a Jew who was mistaken for an Armenian. He saved himself by showing the Turks his şişit which showed that he was a Jew.[14] A man from Urfa said that the Turks had ambushed the French, when they occupied the southeast Turkish town after the First World War; after finishing with the French, they massacred the Christian population. One informant did claim that his mother had told him that the Jews in Anteb did help the Armenians. After the war, there were fights between the many Armenian refugees and the Jews in Aleppo.

While the Jews were not directly involved, the south Turkish Jews in what had been Aleppo's hinterland before the fall of the empire felt less secure than before and were now among the few non-Muslims in the area. Many left Turkey for Syria, Palestine, and the Americas. They had finally shared the unease of their Christian neighbors.

Ottoman religious and ethnic pluralism was a complicated web of individual, group, and international relationships. Economic competition between individuals from different religious groups could, as we have seen, have its effects on the Ottoman government, the European states intervening in the Middle East, and on their own groups. What is crucial here is that the Ottoman communal system was dynamic and that relationships between individuals, groups and governments were constantly shifting. While individuals could be treated as members of the corporate religious bodies to which they belonged, they could also manipulate these relationships to their own benefit. An examination of the economic sphere will show how this could occur.

Ways of Livelihood and Trade

The pervasiveness of ethnic identification in the Middle East, as Coon (1951:1-9) had emphasized, is shown by occupational specialization along ethnic lines. There are several classic examples of this from Damascus in the early 20th Century. Among the shoemakers, Muslims made certain kinds of shoes, while Christians only made another variety, and Jews made a third variety, while there were some kinds which were made by shoemakers of all three groups (Gibb and Bowen 1950:294, n. 2). There was also a factory there where Jews specialized in metal work, and local Christians processed mother-of-pearl, while Armenians did the woodwork (Goitein 1955:117).

The picture of a static mosaic of ethnic specialties is the product of observing Syrian society as a series of snapshots, such as the ones above. Even the portrait of the shoemakers, however, suggests that there was competition between individuals of different origins. Such competition is alluded to in a legend:

A number of gravediggers had uncovered the grave of a man who had died thirty years previously, but it was like the corpse of one who had been dead for only a few days and it had a sweet perfumed aroma. Since the gravediggers did not understand, they consulted Rabbi Raphael Solomon Laniado (a well-known 18th Century sage). He too did not understand. That night the dead man appeared to him in a dream and told him his story. The dead man, a button-seller, had gone to work at an early age and had saved his money. One day a new qaimmaqam (official) came to Aleppo to collect taxes. Before his arrival, 200 Jewish women and orphans had worked at making buttons, but now the local Christians asked him to give them the monopoly. When the widows and orphans learned this, they asked the button-seller for help. After the Sabbath, he put on his finest clothing and went to the qaimmaqam. He persuaded him to let the Jewish widows and orphans retain their trade by giving the Turkish official his savings as a bribe. Now the rabbi understood (Rabi 1966).

Whatever the historicity of this story, it shows that competition between individuals and groups was not limited to the ṣayaarif, but that economic conflict extended to craftsmen and petty traders as well. The division of labor among the shoemakers shows one way around such rivalry, which incidentally served as a way of maintaining the group borders. In 1893,

when a group of young Jews showed interest in
Protestant teachings, they were excommunicated and
thrown out of work. Because of the ethnic-speciali-
zation, Christians would or could not employ them
and the ban succeeded in returning them to the Jewish
fold (Gidney 1897:131-3).

The Jews of Damascus included many craftsmen
such as dyers, sandlers, weavers, smiths, upholsterers,
barbers, and later army tailors (Franco and Gottheil
1903). During the inter-war period in Damascus,
an informant said that 40 percent were peddlers,
20 percent workers with a large proportion working as
engravers on metal (especially copper) and marble,
15 percent merchants, 10 percent artisans, 15 percent
living on charity. The copper-engraving industry
attracted many. It is said that this craft was
brought to Damascus in the early 19th Century by a
Jew from Baghdad. During the depression of the 1930's
this industry suffered great losses, especially
because of competition from Japan.

The Jews of Aleppo worked mainly in commercial
occupations. Russell (1794:II:58-88) reports that
the wealthier members of the community were bankers
or merchants, while the others included brokers,
grocers or peddlers. This is the general impression
one received of the Halebi community in the 20th
Century as well as the 18th. There were some
exceptions, however, such as the goldsmiths.

During the early 19th Century, one Halebi rabbi
deplored the concentration of Jews in commercial
occupations as opposed to the crafts (A. Antebi 1960,
61:33, 111). There were some Jewish craftsmen in
Aleppo and its vicinity. One occupation which was
Jewish was that of goldsmith. It seems to have been
mainly in the hands of one family, which handed down
its traditions and "secrets" from generation to
generation. One member of this family claimed that
there were 48 shops of goldsmiths belonging to the
family: grandfather, father, uncles, cousins, were
all in one craft. One man would apprentice his son
with his brother or in his own shop. Jews from other
families would also learn the trade with them. One
informant who learned the trade after World War I
said:

There were about 20 Jewish goldsmiths in Aleppo. They had a "market"

176

to themselves, sharing it only with
Christian silversmiths. Jews worked
in gold, Christians in Silver. Anyone was free to open a shop if he
wanted to; there was no organization
stopping him. Muslims used to come
in, especially on Friday, to buy.
Christians working in silver, accepted
commissions to make ornaments for the
Torah scroll. Jews were also buyers
of gold. In the winter, men did not
work much, but would stay home, eat,
and drink cognac.

He said that the apprentice learned without a
contract. It was informal. There were those who
learned for two to three years and then opened their
own shops. Perhaps one would work for half a year
before getting a contract. He himself worked for
seven years, much of the time only running errands
and then he began to grasp what was needed. After
10 years he opened his own shop, but he still gave a
commission to a contractor.

This informant spoke of a Jewish-owned courtyard
used by silver-and goldsmiths, a sheikh supervised
the market and took a commission from the smiths.
This sheikh was Muslim. After the First World War,
Christians, especially Armenian, replaced the Jews
as smiths. The craft of the goldsmiths among the
Jews was organized in an informal manner. It is
difficult to find traces of a formal and ritualistic
guild organization for the Jewish goldsmiths or for
any other occupation from the reports of informants,
although Gibb and Bowen (1950:I:281-299) claim that
such guilds existed in Syria.

One can be sure that twenty to fifty Jewish goldsmiths in a city of one hundred thousand would be
aware of each other's existence, especially if there
was a familial tie. In a small market area reserved
to a single craft, such informal relationships would
be reinforced. If, in addition, there is a sheikh
for this bazaar, though he be more inspector or tax-
collector than guild official, a common identification
with the occupation would be increased, although a
more formal guild might not exist. Himadieh (et. al.,
1936:170) confirms the suspicion of the atrophy or
lack of guild organization by Mandatory times. There

177

was still an honorary sheikh for some crafts, but this was little more than an honorary title that was passed down from father to son. In general, Middle Eastern crafts were suffering from unemployment, in this period and facing foreign competition.

There were Jews involved in the trade of agricultural products such as livestock, dairy products, grain, fruits and vegetables. This involvement of Jews in the trade of agricultural goods made them into the partners of the peasant and the herder. They provided the peasants with the capital for buying animals, paying taxes and buying manufacturered and imported goods. This process was connected with money lending. The peddler, or rural retailer, was stocked with goods by an urban merchant on credit. He, in turn, sold the goods to the farmer on credit or received payment in kind. Some dealers took risks by buying the agricultural products themselves (Himadieh 1936:208-212). This is the type of arrangement which Jewish merchants sometimes referred to as partnership with the peasant. Interest was usually implicit in these transactions. Individuals from Aleppo, Tedif, Urfa, and Diyar-bekir have spoken of this type of arrangement, as well as references to such loans in Southern Syria (al-Maghribi 1929; I. Burton 1879).

The Jewish merchants often owned sheep and goats, although it was the Muslims who were the shepherds. On one occasion the question arose as to whether the butter and cheese which the Bedouin made was permitted to be eaten by Jews, since the Bedouin might have mixed it with that of the camel, an animal forbidden to Jews (A. Dayan 1849/50:6-8:39b seq.; I. Dayan 1902/3:9a). A. Dayan permitted the butter from these Bedouin.

As this indicates, the rabbinate intervened in commercial affairs. On another occasion, the Jewish cheesemakers were accused of having worked on the Sabbath and were threatened with excommunication. A court order was issued and the Jewish cheesemakers all signed a statement of adherence to the ruling dated in 1876 (Laniado 1951/2:165).

Jewish slaughterers were ritual functionaries who were ordained by the local rabbinate since they had to be acquainted with the technicalities of the

Jewish dietary laws. Proceeds from ritual-slaughter were contributed to the income of the Jewish community as payment to the slaughterers and as charity for the poor (Russell 1794; Franco and Gottheil 1903). The manner of slaughtering was under rabbinic supervision and might be brought to the rabbis' attention (e.g., Abulafia 1870/71:I:YD5, YD6). In one case, other slaughterers accused one man of having pressed his knife against the animal in a forbidden way (according to the Jewish law). The accused slaughterer claimed that the testimony of the plaintiffs was invalid, since they were relatives. This precipitated a long controversy in which opinions were rendered first in favor of the defendant, and later for the plaintiffs (I. Dayan 1902/3:12b-13a).

In Aleppo, according to Gibb and Bowen (1950:I: 294), Jewish slaughterers were considered part of the Slaughterers' Guild. According to rabbinic informants, kosher meat in Aleppo was stamped and then was sold by Gentile butchers in the market. The torso of the animal, with limbs, had to be sold at one time because the limbs were not so stamped.

In addition to the occupations mentioned above, there is some information on other vocations in which Jews of Aleppo and the North Syrian-South Turkish region were engaged. In Antioch there were tinsmiths and musicians (Segall 1910). A Jewish group of musicians and singers also existed in Aleppo. There were also Jewish bakers who made the flat Arab bread. By the early 20th Century some Christian bakers made European bread as well, but Jewish bakers did not make this type of bread.

Another Jewish enterprise was a soap factory in Killiz, south-central Turkey. This town is in an area which produces an excellent type of olive oil. According to an informant born in that town before World War I, the soap factory employed both Jews and Muslims (also see I. Dayan 1903/4:HMI:1a).

In the towns of south-central and south-eastern Turkey, the Jews were traders either of manufactured textiles, which they brought from Aleppo, or of agricultural goods, which were shipped to the city. This was the case with regard to the Jews of Urfa and of Killiz. The Armenians are said to have been the craftsmen. In Killiz there were one or two Jewish tailors and barbers and one Jew made burlap bags. The others were traders.

Up to 1860, there had been Jewish communities in such Lebanese towns as Deir al-Qamer and Hasbaya. Some of the Jews in these once predominantly Druze areas were cultivators, but they were also involved in the contacts between this area and the outside. In the early 19th Century, when Lebanon exported silk to Europe, Jews were involved in the silk trade. A Jew in Deir al-Qamer was involved in the manufacture of soap from local olives (Ben Zvi 1930/1; 1965:450). With the polarization of Lebanon between the Christians and the Druzes, the Jews left this area for Beirut and other cities.

In Aleppo, women generally did not work outside the home, although some girls and women were domestics in Jewish homes or seamstresses. In Damascus, where the Jewish community was poorer, there were some Jewish dancing girls, as well as women who worked as copper engravers.

As noted above, the late 19th Century marked the culmination in the general decline of commerce flowing from the Middle East to the West and it was marked by a reversal of flow of goods from Europe into Western Asia, as well as the rest of the world. Jews no longer participated in long-range caravans to Baghdad and Basra as they had previously (Antebi 1842/3: HM 9, HM 11:42b-43b). Now they joined those Syrians who were emigrating to Egypt and the Americas. A high percentage of Jews in Aleppo and Damascus were either beggars or otherwise lived off charity.

The Jews were often intermediaries both for native and foreign products. This applied both to the head of an export-import firm with representatives in Manchester and to the peddler in the anti-Lebanon or in the Kurdish villages near Diyar-bekir. The peddlers were members of the Jewish poorer classes and they worked both in the city and its suburbs and in the outlying areas, including agricultural villages and nomadic camps. Peddlers sold from house to house in the city and to passers-by. Many made circuits in the villages and stayed out of the city, where they maintained their domicile all week, coming home for the Sabbath. If the peddlers had longer routes, they might stay away for several months during the

summer. In winter, they stayed at home. The winter
in North Syria and Anatolia can be severe; thus it
is a season of leisure. The peddlers were members
of the low-status group, known in Aleppo, as being
rough and bold.

There were techniques for buying, selling and
providing credit for long periods of time and over
long distances. These methods could be applied even
though there were restrictions and prohibitions on
usury, which Judaism, Christianity and Islam all had
imposed on their adherents. In Damascus merchants
had a council, or <u>shuuraa</u>, a Tribunal of Commerce
which regulated the trade of the city. This tribunal
at the time of Ibrahim Pasha's occupation used the
French Code of Commerce when concerned with questions
of European trade. This tribunal had representatives
from merchants of the three religious groups. In
the 1850's, the Ottoman authorities established such
councils in the major cities, including Beirut and
Aleppo. Purchases and sales between merchants were
made through their brokers (factors or <u>fators</u>).
Transactions were made for ready cash or credit,
which was usually extended for two, three, or four
months (Bowring 1840:44f, 77-80; Maoz 1968:91-2).

The Jewish legal responsa reflect these
commercial practices, since cases involving such
transactions reached rabbinic courts. Cases are
quite similar whether found in Salonika in the 16th
Century (Goodblatt 1952:47-54), or Damascus and
Aleppo in the 18th Century (e.g., Galante 1808/09:32:
114b-115a; Shama' 1820/21:44b). Certain differences
of usage do appear from time to time. For instance,
18th Century responsa refer to the promissary note as
<u>temosuk</u> (<u>tamusuk</u> in Arabic, Wehr-Cowan 1961:909).
While this instrument was used in the 19th Century
(Abulafia 1895/97:V:159a), 19th Century responsa
refer more and more to the <u>cambiale</u> or to the <u>polizza</u>
(the Hebrew spelling of these Italian words varies)
which operated more as negotiables than the <u>temosuk</u>
appears to have been (Abulafia 1908/09:VI:HM4:18a-
19b; I. Dayan 1902/03 11b-12b).

Isabel Burton (1879:135) writes that while there
were no banks in Damascus up to 1879, one could cash
checks of the Imperial Ottoman Bank with Jewish
money-lenders in Damascus. By the end of the Ottoman
period, banks of the modern type existed alongside

the more traditional currency-exchanges. The widespread use of the cambiale and the polizza concerned
the moralists; one rabbi deplored resorting to Gentile
courts in order to collect debts and warned people
against becoming involved in usurious dealings (J. S.
Dwek 1913/14:93b-111a).

Businesses were usually located in the bazaars
of the older parts of Aleppo. After World War I,
there were shops, especially groceries, in the new
extra-mural section known as the Jamaliye, too. More
prosperous Jews were beginning to reside in this
quarter at that time. In Aleppo, unlike smaller
communities such as Urfa or Killiz, shops were
specialized for dry-goods or other forms of merchandise.
Partnerships and similar arrangements were often made
with kinsmen: fathers and sons, uncles and nephews,
cousins and brothers. One son might be the father's
partner, while another would open his own shop with
another partner. Men were accustomed to economic
ups and downs; failure was not uncommon. In this
century, a man could also emigrate and seek his fortune
elsewhere. If he failed abroad, he could return.
Partnerships and agencies between kinsmen were not
always stable. The litigation of the brothers who
were threatened by a third brother over the income
from the customhouse is a case in point (supra).

Modernization

     Since the contacts between the Levant and Western
Europe have been many through the centuries, it is
impossible to set a particular date and say that the
"Westernization" and "modernization" of Syria begins
at that time. The view which Wallerstein (1974) has
of a European-centered world economy,[15] based on a
regional division of labor and unequal exchange between
the various states and regions which compose it makes
a great deal of sense in understanding Ottoman Syria.
At some point, between the fifteenth and nineteenth
centuries, the luxury trade between merchants of equal
power in Europe and the Levant was transformed into an
exploitative relationship between the regions.
Perhaps the export of cotton and silk from Palestine
and Lebanon in the 18th and 19th Centuries and the
later importation of finished textiles from Europe
mark this alteration.

As noted above, Syria was very much affected
by the Industrial Revolution. It became an importer
of textiles, but also railways, telegraph services
and modern arms were introduced into this country.
The introduction of bonds sold at European exchanges
and negotiable instruments drawn on European banks
show how commerce was affected. The building of the
Suez Canal, an achievement of Western technology,
marked the demise of the caravan trade, while ports
like Beirut, Haifa and Jaffa served the new steam-
ships. They also became the destination for internal
migrants and the embarkation points for those who
sought their fortunes in neighboring Egypt[16] and
faroff America.

The various attempts at reform undertaken by the
Ottoman government were desparate efforts to trans-
form the empire into a state which could withstand
European control. The building of a new civil service
and establishing representative councils on European
models were part of this process. It culminated
in the Young Turk regime which ruled the Ottoman
empire from 1909 till its collapse during the First
World War. Conscription of minority members into
the army and genocide directed at the Armenians and,
to some extent, other Christians helped encourage
further emigration on the part of Syrian Jews and
Christians. The large colonies of Syrians and
Lebanese of all religions throughout the Americas
and West Africa were initially formed in this final
period of Ottoman rule.

NOTES

[1]This and the following chapter are a thoroughly revised
version of Chapter II: Jews in Ottoman and Mandatory Syria from
Zenner 1965. It is based both on written sources, which are
specified, and testimonies of former residents of Syria, inter-
viewed in Israel and the United States. I would like to
acknowledge Shlomo Deshen's critical reading of an earlier version.

[2]On this earthquake, see Ben Zvi Institute file on Syria;
also Dayan 1849/50 and D. Laniado 1951/52:17-18.

[3] The other estimates of Jewish population seem to be based on unreliable and often contradictory reports. In the late 18th Century Russell (1794:II:58) reports 5,000 Jews in Aleppo. In the 1830's, British Consul Barker reported 60,000 Muslims, 14,000 Christians, 8,000 Jews (total 80,000) in 1838; Bowring estimated 60,000 Muslims, 16,000 Christians, 3,500 Jews and 500 Franks (Bowring 1840:112). The difference is attributed to the effects of Mohammed Ali's demands on the Muslims in particular, this being during the Egyptian Pasha's rule over Syria. Around 1900, Adler (1905:166) and Gidney (1897:111-112) give estimates of approximately 10,000 Jews out of 127,000 persons in Aleppo. Gidney estimates that there are 10,000 Jews in Aleppo, 100 in Antioch, 1,500 in Beirut. Rosanes (1930) quotes an estimate of 8,000 Jews in post-World War I Aleppo. Schechtman (1961:132) cites a Jewish newspaper claiming that there had been more than 50,000 Jews in Syria, the majority residing in Aleppo and Damascus. According to Neeman (1927), Aleppo had 8,000 Jews (officially 6,900), Damascus had 7,000 after the Druze rebellion, and Beirut had 4,500; before World War I, Damascus had had 20,000. Himadieh (1936:405) gives the following figures: 505,419 Christians, 1,514,725 Muslims, 16,526 Jews for both Syria and Lebanon (3,372 Jews in Lebanon)... The entire first half of the 20th Century was a period of emigration and immigration, much of which was illegal. Jews from Turkey entered Syria illegally and Syrian Jews left Syria in order to go to Lebanon, Palestine, Israel, and overseas illegally. With the spread of modern medicine, the birth-rate was generally rising and the death-rate falling, save for the epidemics at the end of the First World War. These statistics do give us a rough idea of the number of Jews living in Syria (also see H. J. Cohen 1973:78-80).

[4] The _ghruush_ or piastre was a silver coin. On Turkish currency and its approximate values, see Gibb and Bowen (1957:II:49-50).

[5] Other cases in which members of families holding either the kashaaf or sarraaf positions charging usurpation are found in Shama' 1820/21:33:58b-70a and Galante 1808/9:27-28:104a-107b; cf. Zenner 1965:43.

[6] On Farhis, see I. Burton (1879); al-Maghribi (1929), Fischel (1944); Gibb and Bowen (1957:II:69); Ben Zvi (1955:342-3); Shiloah 1971.

[7] In the 18th Century, part of the Greek Orthodox Church in Syria broke with the Patriarchate in Istanbul and joined the Church of Rome. Of this process, see Haddad 1970.

[8]Richard Burton, after his ouster, actually authored an anti-Semitic work in which he accused Jews of committing ritual murders (1898). Ritual murder accusations and beliefs persisted into the 20th Century, especially among Christians (H. J. Cohen 1971; 1973:12; Gidney 1897:120-135).

[9]Here I am following Benjamin Braude (1977). Previous to his work, Gibb and Bowen (1957:217) argued that this institution had existed in the 15th Century and Baron saw the 19th Century institution as a revival of an older office, not an innovation (1942:195-9). From a close reading of the responsa, I had already concluded that no such office existed at the provincial level and Braude has made clear that the evidence for this office and the associated picture of a millet system has been weak.

[10]According to one rabbinic informant, the rabbis who participated in the local council of Aleppo (al-majlis al-adliyah) were as follows: Abraham Antebi, Mordecai Levaton, Moses Kohen, succeeded by Rahamin Nehmad, a layman. Then Abraham Dwek Halusi, succeeded by Solomon Safadieh, Jacob Dwek, Yehezkel Shabbtai, and Shabbtai Bahbut. Moses Kohen was the first to bear the title, hakham bashi.

[11]For further information on land registration, see Gibb and Bowen 1950:I:239; Davison 1963:99-100; 256-262. Unlike most of these treatments which deal with rural areas, the responsa show the effects of registration on urban real estate.

[12]Conscription continued in the Turkish Republic (Zenner 1965a:55).

[13]Personal and family names often labelled one as a Jew, a Christian or a Muslim. H. J. Cohen (1973:13) notes that Damascus Jews, unlike other Middle Eastern Jews, did use Arabic names like Bakrii, Majiid, Arif and Abdu for men and Badriya and Bahiya for women.

[14]A comparable story is told of Jews being saved from death during the Druze and Muslim rampage against Christians in Lebanon in 1860 (Malachi 1934-5).

[15]This is not the place to argue about the date when the "world economy" began, although a case could be made for starting it before 1450, although its nature may have been quite different. Also, an acceptance of Wallerstein's analysis of the past does not mean that I accept his prediction of the "future demise" of this system. Coincidentally, our period (1750-1914) marks the transition in the Western European core of the world system

from "agricultural capitalism" to "industrial capitalism" to use Wallerstein's terminology. This period also marks the Ottoman loss of control over trade within their empire. The fact that the Jewish and Christian protegees of the European consuls also often were the collectors of customs is a symptom of this process.

[16] Some reflections of the emigration to Beirut and Egypt in the 19th Century appear in Abulafia's responsa. One man left Damascus to find work in Beirut (Abulafia 1885/6:II:54a). There were questions from Egypt, regarding the permissibility of using a cable car on the Sabbath, the kashrut of Egyptian cheeses, and the use of cisterns and waterpipes for ritual purification (1896/7:V:1a-8b; 9a-12b; 32a-34b). These inquiries obviously reflect the new technology and I infer that they are also related to the attractiveness of Egypt in that era as a destination for Syrian Jews. On Syrian Jews in New York City see Sutton 1979.

Bibliography and List of Citations for chapters on Jews in Late Ottoman Syria will be at the end of the following chapter.

CHAPTER 9

JEWS IN LATE OTTOMAN SYRIA:
COMMUNITY, FAMILY & RELIGION

WALTER P. ZENNER

In this chapter, Zenner provides us with a
reconstruction of internally oriented institutions. It should be noted that some of the
sources which he used show the way in which
Western influences impinged on Syrian Jews in
major cities in the 19th Century. For example,
British doctors and missionaires are among
his sources.

In this chapter, I will describe the internal
aspects of the Jewish communal life in Syria.

Jewish Communal Organization

The Jewish groups in the larger Syrian cities
were not directly dependent upon other Jewish
communities. Despite the imperially confirmed
hakham bashi, each Jewish community was not bound to
a hierarchy, unlike the Roman Catholics who are
organized in relation to their Church's hierarchy.
Jews in small towns, such as Killiz, Marash or Urfa,
were forced to bring cases before rabbinical courts
in the larger cities. They could, however, choose,
as those in Diyarbekir did, whether to send the case
to Aleppo, to Baghdad, or to Istanbul. It is true
that Halebi Jews considered southeastern Turkey as
part of their hinterland, but this was not enforceable
by law.

The factor integrating all Jews was the common
acceptance of one body of tradition as authoritative.
Like traditional Jews everywhere (outside of sects
such as the Karaites), Syrian and Turkish Jews considered the Hebrew Scriptures (Old Testament) and the

SOURCE: "The Inner Life of the Jews in Late Ottoman
Syria" (Hebrew) Peamim No. 3:45-58 (1979). © Copyright
Ben Zvi Institute 1979. Reprinted by permission.

Talmud as sacred. The common body of law or lore, to which rabbis in Aleppo, Izmir, and Warsaw referred, made it possible for them to communicate. All wrote in Hebrew and were concerned with similar problems. Many of the responsa and other works of Syrian rabbis were published in Livorno, Italy, while other works were published in Izmir, Istanbul, Aleppo, and Jerusalem. The shared identification and the common tradition made it possible for Spanish, Italian and even East European Jews to be assimilated into the Syrian Jewish communities.

In Aleppo, rabbinic authority was strong until the First World War. Russell writes of the great authority of the ḥakham (Kakhan):

> In general the Jews were more sober
> than (native) Christians. Many were
> secured from intemperance by poverty,
> besides which their attendance twice
> a day at the synagogue, on all festivals,
> and their living so much under the eye
> of their Kakhans render it more diffi-
> cult to conceal debauchery, than it
> would be under a more numerous people.
> (Russell 1794:61).

The ḥakham was distinguished by the size and color of his turban and by the long-wide sleeves of his outer garments. He was, according to Russell, more respected by his community than the Christian bishop was by his flock. His civil jurisdiction was restricted and parties could appear before the maḥkama, the governmental Muslim court. This privilege of appeal was exercised warily, since it might result in having to pay many bribes (Russell 1794:64; Shama' 5581:39; I. Dayan 1902/3:HM29; 45a seq).

The cases which came before the rabbinic court were of many types--Jewish rituals, marriages, divorces, inheritance, business contracts, loans, torts, build-ing regulations (especially with regard to placement of windows opposite a neighbor's house). This can be best seen by examining collections of responsa such as I Dayan (1902/3) or S. Laniado (1774/75) or Saul Dwek (1909/10).

The penalties available to the rabbinic court in enforcing its decisions were excommunication, fines, and corporal punishment. These, especially corporal punishment, were used by individual teachers and rabbis. The story is told of a father who was drunk from arak. He protested to his son's schoolteacher because the ḥakham had had the boy bastinadoed. The teacher had the father given the same punishment. There is a story that a ḥakham once had some young men given for violating the Sabbath (see below). These practices continued into recent times. A woman teacher at the Alliance School in Aleppo in the 1920's reported the following: A father brought his adolescent son, whose hands were bound, to be whipped for disobeying the father. This modern teacher refused (also see Neeman 1927:24 et al).

The quasi-magical powers of the rabbis added to the respect which they received. Legends of the miracles rabbis worked were told (cf. Na'aneh 1960/61: V:260 et. seq.; Zenner 1965b). It was told of one rabbi that the Court ordered him to curse a certain sinner; the man died because of his curse and the rabbi refused to use his holy powers in such a manner thereafter. Rabbis said prayers at the bedside of the sick and wrote amulets against the evil eye. During a period of drought, the Muslim authorities called on the rabbi and the Christian bishop, as well as on the sheikh to pray for rain (Russell 1794:86). After his death, people would pray at the grave of a saintly rabbi. This reinforced the powers of the rabbinate and made a rabbinic ban of excommunication particularly forceful.

The rabbis were divided into those who were members of the rabbinic court, headed by the Head of the Court (Av Bet Din), the teachers at various levels, and private scholars. Teachers at the primary school level (kuttab) had a relatively low status. What is called here 'private scholar' is an individual who is known for his erudition, but does not hold office as teacher or judge. He may work as a shohet (slaughterer), or as a businessman. It was not uncommon for a wealthy businessman to go into a partnership with a scholar, who was thus insured an income. Such a scholar might be the son-in-law of the merchant or a brother. A merchant might hire a scholar to tutor his children or he might endow a small yeshivah, where scholars would assemble and study.

189

Selection of the Court, the various heads of the Community, including the Chief Rabbi (who was confirmed imperially) and assessment of taxes were the functions of what was later known as the Committee. This body was made up of both 'notables' and the Rabbis of the Court. In Aleppo, the notables were a self-perpetuating body, since there were no elections to the Committee, or Council. Wealth and family position played an important role in appointment to these posts. Over the years similar names recur. The dispute in 18th Century Aleppo about whether the Signores Francos should pay communal taxes was example of this (Lutzky 1940). In the small community in the Lebanese city of Saida (Sidon), discord arose over the appointment of two judges to the rabbinic court. There were only two potential candidates in the city who were "fit to present (a legal opinion)". One was opposed by a faction in the city who suggested choosing the judges by lot, out of a panel of seven scholars, even though several of these were unqualified. The majority were prepared to appoint an unqualified judge, but the minority appealed to a rabbi in Damascus who supported their position (Abulafia 1886/7:HM9:35a-40b). If the controversy revolved around an individual with powerful connections, such as a Pasha'a banker, a consul, or a ḫakham bashi, the power of the state might be invoked against the leaders of the community (Fischel 1944; M. Nehmad 1941).

The income of communal organizations was raised from several sources: the sale of kosher meat, taxes assessed by the Committee, voluntary contributions pledged in the synagogue at the Torah readings and on other occasions, and fines. From the World War I period to the present, a large part of the community's finances came from foreign remittances sent by Syrian Jews who had emigrated. On minor festivals, such as the 15th of Ab (July-August) or Lag B'omer, there were celebrations in the evening at which songs were sung and contributions made. These were on behalf of charitable societies such as the Burial Society, Food for the Poor, Clothing, Dowries (for needy girls), Study, Visiting the Sick, and the synagogue. Another source of income for communal institutions was the endowment known in Arabic as waqf, and, in Hebrew as heqdesh. By use of the endowment, an individual could dedicate property for a sacred purpose or a religious institution. For instance, a man could

190

provide that the rental from a building he owned would
be used hereafter on behalf of a school. In Damascus,
on one occasion, a son challenged his father's will,
in which money was dedicated for such a goal (Abulafia
1886/7:III:HM13; Franco and Gottheil 1903; Lutzky
1940).

Before World War I, the rabbis had issued an order
of excommunication against a violator of the Sabbath
and had made a proclamation of warning to the community
(J. S. Dwek 1913/4:117a-124a). At that time, only a
few had violated the Sabbath. After the First World
War, communal discipline weakened.[1]

Traditionally boys were sent to school at the age
of three or four. Many, however, did not complete
the full curriculum of studies. Those whose parents
were poor often left school before the age of thirteen
and could barely read. In small communities, such as
Urfa, schooling was irregular, since teachers did
not stay in the town for extended periods of time.
During the First World War some schools in Aleppo were
closed for a period of time.

The curriculum of the kuttab, as the elementary
school was called, started with the Hebrew alphabet,
followed by vocalization of the Hebrew letters (Hebrew
letters represent consonants, not vowels), then the
benedictions and prayers, the weekly portion of the
Torah which is read in the synagogue, then the
Pentateuch, followed by the Prophet and Hagiographical
sections of the Hebrew Scriptures. In Saida, this
was followed by reading a book called Hoq LeYisrael,
which gives a daily selection to be read from the
Pentateuch, the Prophets, the Hagiographic, the Talmud,
and the Zohar.

In Aleppo as elsewhere in the world, Leviticus
was the first book of the Pentateuch that was taught.
This was followed by the book of Genesis and the
remainder of the Pentateuch and Scriptures. Scripture
was accompanied by sharh, a traditional translation
of Scripture into Literary Arabic. At the beginning
all was taught by rote, since even the translation
was in a dialect different from their spoken Arabic.
Scripture was followed by 'Ein Ya'aqov a collection
of the non-legal sections of the Talmud. At about age
ten or eleven, the student began the study of Gemara
or Talmud, first using Rashi's commentary and then

proceeding with the more advanced commentaries of the Tosefot.

After this point, most boys quit school, while others continued into the midrash or yeshivah, the advanced rabbinic school. The students, in their adolescence, were expected to learn independently without the help of a teacher or rabbi. Two differences between the Halebim and the Ashkenazim are that the latter studied only the Pentateuch in school and not the rest of the Scripture, while the Halebim emphasize dialectical casuistry less than the Ashkenazim do. According to one informant, a characteristic of Halebi learning was 'iyun Halebi (Halebi deliberation or concentration), which meant that thorough learning of the text received more weight in study than making casuistic distinctions. One Halebi rabbi believed that the Sephardic superiority in learning lay in their more thorough knowledge of texts, while an Ashkenazi criticized Syrians for "reading the Talmud like a story," rather than studying it through argumentation.[2] There were several such schools in Aleppo, but only one in Damascus (H. J. Cohen 1973:137-8).

The teacher or his assistant would collect the boys in the morning by going to their home. They would be in school all day. There were study sessions on the Sabbath. They were not allowed play outside of school; the pupil was accountable to the teacher on that as well. Severe means of corporal punishment, including the bastinado could be applied. In former times, the students sat on the ground before the teacher. Arithmetic was the main secular subject taught. In more recent generations, the traditional school added Arabic, French, and similar subjects to the curriculum. This was partly due to competition from the other schools which had been opened.

In important areas of life, Jews, during the Ottoman and Mandatory periods, were isolated from their fellow inhabitants of Syria. Certain taxes were levied through and by Jewish organs; in religion, they had their own institutions, including separate schools for their children. This separate organization contributed to their feeling of identification as Jews.

The Family and Household

As elsewhere, the family and household was the
basic unit of social organization of Syrian Jewry,
as well as the initial base of socialization.

At least until the 20th Century, the home in
Aleppo or Damascus was generally in a courtyard. This
was the case for people of all religions. Often
several families shared a courtyard. Lodgings were
often overcrowded. Travelers often complained about
the impoverished condition of the Jewish quarter in
Damascus.

One reason for the poor appearance of the Jewish
quarter was the Middle Eastern pattern of an impoverished public facade, which contrasted sharply with a
private display of luxury. Isabel Burton (1879:
102ff, 129) described such a traditional Jewish home
with its "mean" doorway, its narrow winding staircase
which led into a luxurious home.

Even when the motivation is not to conceal one's
wealth from the tax-collector or the beggar, the
traditional Middle Easterner desires the privacy of
his home and the veiling of his women. A number of
legal responsa deal with the problem of who should
bear the cost when one property-owner or tenant
intrudes on the privacy of a neighbor by installing
a new window or opening a shop opposite a courtyard
entrance. Such privacy is protected by Talmudic
Law (I. Dayan 1902/3:HM21-24:33a-37b; Babylonian
Talmud: Baba Batra).

Bowring in the 1930's reported that the lot of the
ordinary Syrian compared favorably to that of the
working class in England (then at the height of the
Industrial Revolution (1840:49-50). Mutton was
eaten several times a week, sometimes with rice or
bulgar pilaff. Bread would be eaten daily. Clothing
was mainly of cotton in the warm season. Lodging
consisted usually of a separate set of rooms per
family. The cost was relatively low. Wages were
low, and epidemics frequent. By the turn of the
century, however, many Syrians of all religions faced
extreme poverty and sought better conditions abroad.

193

The attitude of children towards their parents in the traditional household was one of respect. Children were expected to obey their elders. It was customary for a son to kiss his father's hand when greeting him. On the Sabbath, the father blessed his children and grandchildren by placing his hand on their heads. A father in Syria could punish even an adult son bodily. He could turn a son over to a teacher for punishment. Older brothers had authority over their younger siblings as well. One female informant said that in Syria children did not drink coffee or crack pistachios until they were mature.

The birth of a son was a time for rejoicing, while feelings at the birth of a daughter were mixed. Before the opening of the Mission School in Damascus and the schools of the Alliance, girls did not go to school. Girls from poorer families worked as domestics in wealthy Jewish homes, sometimes beginning at the age of eleven or twelve (Russell 1794:84). Inferring from the Halebim in Israel and elsewhere, the movement of young girls was carefully controlled.

Many boys began to work in their adolescent years. Some continued their studies, but most became apprentices either in commerce or with craftsmen. Unless they emigrated, they were expected to live in their parents' home. Their income belonged to the family.

The role of the family in determining an individual's occupation was significant. Certain positions in the community, such as the moreh ṣedeq (leader of the Must'arib group), had a quasi-hereditary nature. Business concerns were often partnerships organized along familial lines. Posts such as financier to the Pasha and those of the customhouse were often passed on in the family. A trade, such as that of goldsmith, was generally learned from one's father or uncle. Obviously the positive role of the family in this realm could only apply when a skill could be learned or a position could be passed on. The many unskilled workers in Aleppo and Damascus could not always rely on their kin. As the court cases concerning inheritance show, Syrian Jewish families could be arenas for competition as well as refuges from a hostile world.

Marriages were generally arranged by the parents, although a young man might indicate to his mother his interest in marrying a particular girl. According to Russell (1794:II:79), Jews married at a younger age than the Turks. Some bethrothed their very young children, while others waited until a few months before the marriage. Most were married before they reached the age of 18 or 20. By the Mandatory period according to informants, men frequently married in their late 20's when they were established in business.

Cousin marriage of all four varieties was practiced. In Aleppo, there does not seem to have been a particular preference for the father's brother's daughter. In Urfa, as is customary in other rural areas of the Middle East, a man had a right to demand his father's brother's daughter as late as the period of the First World War.[3]

In Aleppo, there was an exchange of gifts between the family of the groom and the family of the bride, as well as between the bride and the groom. The emphasis of the exchange was on a dowry which the father of the bride gave his son-in-law. In southeastern Turkey, on the other hand, the property exchange at marriage emphasized a 'bride-price' from the husband's family. In Urfa at the time of World War I, an informant said, the dowry was beginning to receive more emphasis than the bride-price. In Aleppo, there was a society to provide dowries to poor and orphaned girls, but these women were often wed without substantial dowries.

Marriage contracts contained clauses for the protection of the women. The Must'arib contract gave the man the right to divorce his wife without her consent, as well as giving him the right to take a second wife without his first wife's consent and without having to divorce her first. The Sephardic contract on both these points favored the woman. The rabbinical informant stated that a woman who accepted a Must'arib, rather than a Sephardic, contract had to be a strong, confident woman. The use of a particular contract did not depend on the Sephardic or the Must'arib origins of the parties involved. There also was a contract known as the "Frankish" contract which had provisions slightly different from the Sephardic, and a mixed contract containing provisions of the others. Polygyny was rare; it occurred mainly in cases of childless couples. The clause forbidding a man to take a second wife was applied even to the situation of levirate marriage:

> According to Jewish law, if a man
> dies childless, his wife is obligated
> either to marry his brother or to obtain
> a release (ḥaliṣah) from the husband's
> brother, before she can remarry an out-
> sider. A complication occurred in one
> case in which a man married his
> brother's widow, thus violating the
> clause of his first wife's marriage
> contract; he had also impregnated the
> widow (Galante 1808/9:No. 13-20:54
> et. seq.)

Other clauses in the marriage contract protected a woman and her heirs. In Damascus and elsewhere, a husband could not force his wife to move from her home city except when the husband wanted to immigrate to the Holy Land (Galante 1808/9:51a; A. Dayan 1849/50:1:9b; Abulafia 1885/86:11:54a-64a). In marriage contracts in Aleppo and Damascus, provision was made for returning property exchanged at the time of marriage to a woman's heirs. Under some conditions, a woman's father would return to the husband gifts which the husband had given him, while the husband would return to the father what the latter had given the husband (known as Hishavon). Under a provision called Minhag Damaseq (the term the Damascus custom, was used in 16th Century Salonika, Goodblatt 1952), there was a division of the property in question. There were ordinances making it necessary for a couple to be married before a quorum of ten men in order to prevent elopements, such as the levir taking his brother's widow to be a second wife, or otherwise deceiving the woman into a marriage (Zenner 1980).

Once married, the couple would generally live with the husband's parents. They might share a kitchen and have a separate room in the courtyard. There were cases where the couple was so young that the husband's parents had to help them. One woman related that her parents were thirteen when they were married. The husband's parents had to entertain his bride because the boy could not yet consummate the marriage. This type of arrangement of "two women in one kitchen" often resulted in conflict. On holidays, generally a man's sons and daughters-in-law would eat at his table.

There were situations in which couples lived with the wife's parents or in a separate apartment or house. In any case, the couple usually lived in the same city with one set of parents or both; mutual visting was frequent. In Aleppo after the First World War, many Jews moved to the Jamaliyeh, a new quarter outside the walls of the city. Proximity facilitated close relationships between the parents and their married children. A woman could frequently obtain support from her own family if she had trouble with her husband's, assuming she had not shamed her own kin.

According to Russell (1794:II:63), Jewish women were veiled in the presence of strangers and did not eat at the same table with the men, except on holidays and the Sabbath. "From the common circle of several families living in the same house and inter-marriage among near kindred, it happens that Jews live more familiarly with women than Turks or Christians and women are more negligent in veiling before persons of their own nation."

During the 18th Century, the European Jewish ladies in Aleppo would stroll in public unveiled, thus scandalizing the rabbis of that period. In the 19th Century, one ḥakham wrote harshly about the laxity of Jewish women in their dress and their negligence in covering their faces. He also complained about the new trend toward men and women's eating together at the wedding feast (A. Antebi 1960/1:118-121). By the First World War, European styles for both men and women were becoming popular in Aleppo but had not completely replaced traditional dress (Segall 1910).

According to Russell, a physician who recorded his impressions of Aleppo life, women domestics remained in service until they were with child. Jews, more than Christians, used wet nurses. They seldom continued to suckle after the next pregnancy, he writes. Otherwise the child was kept at breast from eighteen to twenty months. Jews were more prolific than Christians or Turks. He claimed that intrigues among Jewish domestic servants were more common than among Christians, but that Jews were no less chaste, only more often exposed to temptation. Matters were handled discretely so as to prevent a scandal or the exaction of a fine. An unmarried girl with child might be sent to another town, or was provided with a husband. Poverty made it difficult for the poor to marry. Venereal disease, however, was rare, according to the physician, Russell (1794:II:84). Abraham Antebi warned the wealthy about the dangers of having male domestics in the house and saw dangers of leaving a maid and a bachelor servant alone in the house, exposing them to temptation (A. Antebi 1960/61:32-33).

Information on extra-marital affairs is most difficult to obtain. One person reported that a married couple had a widow as a neighbor. The husband became ill and it was determined that the widow was performing love-magic so he would have to come to her. The wife permitted this affair. Divorce could only be initiated by the husband and was in any case considered shameful. In the discussion of married life in Aleppo and Damascus, features such as divorce and inheritance are emphasized, while normal interaction of course is neglected. Our reconstruction is based primarily on court cases and memories rather than on observation, although some inferences are made on the basis of oral testimonies (also see Zenner 1980).

A wife could precipitate divorce. Such is the case of the moredet, a woman who rebels against her husband. She may flee her husband's home and return to that of her father. If she does this, she is liable to lose the rights guaranteed her in the marriage contract. She may also provoke her husband's anger, in which case, he may threaten to leave her an agunah[4] "till her hair whiten", that is, without the possibility of remarriage. Even if the moredet is granted a divorce after forfeiting her rights, she may still try to claim the return of gifts to the couple from her side of the family (A. Dayan 1849/50: 29b).

In other cases of divorce, too, the provisions of the marriage contract are what is of issue in the court cases, not the rights or wrongs of actually granting a divorce (see above). Cases include ones in which husbands wished to force wives to move to other cities, as well as instances of childlessness and sterility (Abulafia 1885/6:II:46b-54a; 1885/6: II:83b; 1909:VI:4; 1896/7:V:19:EH5:65a-69a; I. Dayan 1902/3:EH24:34a-37a; Antebi 1842/43:12:51a, 56b;

198

I. Dayan 1902/3:EH15:19b, 22b).

The internal stresses and strains which families were subject come out in inheritance cases too. According to Jewish law, sons are the first in line to inherit, followed by daughters if there are no sons, then brothers of the deceased (Num. 27; Shulhan Arukh-Hoshen Mispat 276:1). Men could insure that members of their family not in line to inherit would receive gifts such as providing for a daughter's dowry (I. Dayan 1902/3:EH19-20:27a-32b). These legal provisions for widows and orphans often became the issues on which litigations were based. A man's half-brothers and his full sister might battle for property which he inherited from his and his sister's maternal grandmother (I. Dayan 1902/3:HM26:42b). A man may claim a full third of the profits from a business which his brothers started, while he was still a minor, with their father's estate (I. Dayan 1902/3:HM21:32a). On the occasion of contracting a second marriage, Reuben makes a bequest to his sons from the first marriage, so that they receive a full share of his property (Abulafia 1886/7:III:11:45a-54a; I. Dayan 1902/3:HM30:47a).

These cases were produced by a combination of circumstances stemming from death and other conditions and human acquisitiveness. They serve to illustrate the imagery of "peril and refuge" which Gulick (1976:39) sees as a theme running through Middle Eastern institutions, including the family. Kinsmen are both an individual's "first line of defense" and his "last resort". While they must be relied upon, this high expectation often cannot be met and "over-dependence breeds disappointment, which in the absence of alternatives perpetuates overdependence." The bitter quarrels of kinsmen, as well as the factiousness of communities, can thus be explained.

Religious and Leisure Activities

Syrian Jewry in the 19th Century lacked the compartmentalization of the sacred from the profane and the magical from the religious which character-ized Western Europe in that period. As I have noted elsewhere, noted rabbis were considered charismatic figures who helped bring rain and otherwise provide direct supernatural aid to their people (Zenner 1965; above paragraph).

The interweaving of the religious with the
secular occured in many aspects of life. All areas
of existence could be adjudicated by a religious court
or would be subjected to comment and censure by a
preacher. Aleppo, however, was not a sacred society
in the sense that some nostalgic religious families
in Jerusalem today remember it as "a community of
saints and scholars".[5]

The use of leisure-time can be used to illustrate
the connection of what to us are separate realms.
As Antebi wrote, the most extreme attitude was that
every moment not needed for subsistence was to be
spent in some form of sacred activity, whether prayer,
learning, or song. Hymns to God, even if written
to the music of Arabic or Turkish love songs,[6] were
praiseworthy, but the songs on which they were based
were deplored by the moralists (Antebi 1960/1:10).

While the young men sought physical prowess,
there was little time for this and doing it on the
Sabbath was a violation. Again, Antebi wrote:

"It is necessary to erase that which Jewish
bachelors, lads empty of Torah and misvot (obligations),
for these also go out on the Sabbath without license
to walk in the gardens, to swim in the water, and to
hurl stones to each other and to violate the Sabbath
in public" (1960/1:96).

Legend has it that Rabbi Saul Dwek eliminated
this custom several decades later by forcefully
punishing these young men and then forming them into
two teams for the purpose of singing vigorously in
the synagogue for a pittance. Thus the competitive
urge and song were harnessed to the worship of the
Almighty.

The conversion of dancing was more difficult.
Dancing in mixed company was considered immoral by
the rabbis. One rabbi denounced what he considered
to be an innovation, when women danced before the
bride at a wedding with male musicians playing
(Antebi 1960/1:119). In the early 20th Century,
Jacob Saul Dwek severely upbraided those who took
their families to cabarets to watch dancing girls
(Dwek 1913/14:17b; Adler 1905).

Gambling, particularly backgammon, dice and playing cards, was a common form of recreation. As elsewhere, it led to abuse, including theft and was a cause for divorce (Antebi 1960/1:10). In the early 20th Century, women of means spent much time at card parties.

The sacred and what we moderns would call leisure also came together during Sabbaths and holidays. As indicated above, a clash could occur here, too. Antebi (1960/61:10; 96) condemned the Sabbath walks which many men, women and children took to the gardens, vineyards and orchards around Aleppo. He feared both violation of the Sabbath and that this will lead to something illicit. Instead, he counseled the men to study sacred lore and sit at home.

Travel and performing a sacred duty were combined in pilgrimages. Jerusalem, Safed and Tiberias were in reach of many Syrian Jews during the Ottoman period. Aleppo Jews also went to Tedif al-Yahud, the reputed resting place of Ezra the Scribe on his way to Jerusalem. The favored time for visiting that shrine was the period between the Fast of the 9th of Av (July-August) and the High Holydays (September-October).

While a separate realm of leisure was not recognized in the modern sense, there were professional entertainers, as noted above, including musicians, dancing girls, clowns, singers and storytellers. People also would come together to listen to a good teller of tales, especially on Saturday night.

Creeping Westernization

With the incorporation of most of the world into a single political and economic system and with the improvement of communications, the 19th and 20th Centuries have been marked by a tendency to cultural homogenization. The introduction of Western education institutions was part of this development. The Protestant London Society for Promoting Christianity amongst the Jews maintained a mission in Damascus during most of the 19th Century and into the Mandatory period. At first, the rabbis fiercely opposed the activities of this mission, but by the First World War a modus vivendi had been reached.

201

Jewish children thus obtained a modern English education with Christian overtones, while a rabbi came to the school to provide Jewish religious instruction (Gidney 1897:107-135; 1908:101-108; H. J. Cohen 1973:137; informants).

The Alliance Israelite Universelle founded a boys' school in Aleppo in 1869, followed by the establishment of schools for both boys and girls in Damascus and Beirut and a girls' school in Aleppo in 1889 (J. Bigart 1903:421 f). In 1900, more than half of the students did not pay tuition and were supported by foreign philanthropy (Adler 1905; Cohen 1973:137-140). Both Christian and Jewish schools often helped prepare Syrian Jews for foreign trade and emigration, since they taught French and English, as well as Hebrew and Arabic. The rabbis initially opposed the Alliance schools as well as the missions. Stories are still told about the religious practices of the first Alliance principal who came to Aleppo, pretending to be an observant Jew. A rumor was circulated that he put on phylacteries, but when the phylacteries examined, the scroll in each phylactery was missing. The rabbis similarly opposed the founding of Masonic and B'nai Brith lodges in Aleppo.

In the areas of fashion, taste, and morals, Westernization was gradual and still very incomplete by the end of the Ottoman period. Syrian Jews had European models, such as the Signores Francos in the 18th Century. The laxity of which moralists complained with regard to veiling and sexual segregation may have been influenced by these wealthy sojourners. It is only in the period just preceding the First World War, however, that a missionary notes that Western fashion and dress had become common (Segall 1910:99-104). There is also a shift in the remonstrances of the preachers. Whereas Antebi in the early 19th Century complained of women dancing at weddings in the presence of men, Dwek in the early 20th Century condemns the cabarets where men, women and children watch dancing girls. It was only in the 1920's and 1930's, however, that mass media, such as films and radio, were introduced into the Levant. The mass media have undoubtedly speeded the process of homogenization, although it should be noted that they also help sustain a modern form of Arabic music.

Berger (1976:186) has defined "modernization" as "a shift from giveness to choice on the level of meaning." What had previously been unquestioned as a "fact of life" now becomes an individual option. By the end of the Ottoman period, this process was well underway in the cities of Syria. The Jews continued to adhere to their traditional Jewish and Middle Eastern patterns, but they had been profoundly affected by European culture. They knew that while they continued many of the old ways, they were to do so under the shadow of a powerful modern civilization.

NOTES

[1] Many of the rabbis had emigrated, as had many of the wealthy. In the Mandatory Period (1920-1940), synagogue attendance on the Sabbath was still generally observed. On other issues, however, that of women going to cafes outside the home, the rabbis had more difficulty (Ne'eman 1927). During the 1920's there was serious quarrelling between the rabbis and the younger men on this kind of issue. An informant who was from Jerusalem and visited Aleppo said that she was shocked when she saw girls belly-dancing at a party in Aleppo and when she saw that card playing was a major leisure-time activity.

[2] How 'iyun halebi actually differs from Ashkenazic forms of studying Talmud requires further examination. Deshen informs me that there is also an 'iyun tunisi.

[3] In the Islamic Middle East, there is a preference for marriage between the children of two brothers (Father's brother's daughter marriage). Indeed, in the customary law of some groups, a man has the right to marry his Father's Brother's Daughter; if she or her parents refuse him, he can veto her marriage to another. If my source's statements are correct, this was the case among the Jews of Urfa. Unfortunately, no statistics back up a hypothesis that Urfali Jews had a higher ratio of such marriages. For further discussion of patrilateral parallel cousin marriage, see Patai 1955 and Marx 1967:110-113.

[4] An agunah is a woman whose husband is missing without proof of death, or who has deserted her without a divorce, thus not releasing her from the status of being a married woman.

203

⁵This view already existed in the early 19th Century, when Rabbi A. Antebi wrote about a former generation which rose early at night to study and to pray and which used each spare moment for sacred learning (1960/1:3-5).

⁶On such songs using Arabic melody-types but in Hebrew, known as baqashot, see Zenner 1980; and Katz 1970.

LIST OF REFERENCES

Abbady, Mordecai
   1957/8 (5718)   Sefer Ma'yan Ganim. Part I. Jerusalem.

   1960/1 (5721)   Sefer Ma'yan Ganim. Part II. Jerusalem.
Abulafia, Isaac
   1980/71 (5631)   Pene Yiṣhaq, Aleppo. I.

   1885/86 (5646)   Pene Yiṣhaq, Livorno, II.

   1886/87 (5667)   Pene Yiṣhaq, Izmir III and IV.

   1896/97 (5657)   Pene Yiṣhaq, Izmir V.

   1908/09 (5669)   Pene Yiṣhaq. Jerusalem, VI.
Adler, E. N.
   1903   Aleppo Jewish Encyclopedia. I, 338.

   1905   Jews in Many Lands. Philadelphia.
Al-Maghribi, Sheikh
   1929   The Jews of Damascus (Sham) 100 Years Ago. Revue de l'Academe Arabe. 9:641-653 (Arabic).

Antebi, A.
   1842/43 (5603)   Mor Ve'oholot. Livorno.

   1960/61 (5721)   Ḥokhmah uMusar. Jerusalem.
Baron, S. W.
   1933   The Jews and the Syrian Massacres of 1860; Proceedings. American Academy for Jewish Research, New York. IV. 3-31.

   1940   Great Britain and Damascus Jewry in 1860-61. Jewish Social Studies, New York, II, 179-208.

   1942   The Jewish Community. Philadelphia. Jewish Publication Society.

1957   Social and Religious History of the Jews. (Rev. Ed.) III. New York: Columbia University Press.

Ben Zvi, Yitzhak
1931/2   The Jews Among the Druzes in Lebanon. Tarbiz III:436-51 (Hebrew).

1960   Eretz Yisrael under Ottoman Rule, 1517-1917. In (L. Finkelstein ed.) The Jews: Their History, Culture and Religion. Philadelphia, Jewish Publication Society I:602-689.

1965   Shaar Yashuv: Remnants of Ancient Jewish Communities in the Land of Israel. Jerusalem: Yad Ben Zvi (Hebrew).

Ben Ya'akov, A.
1961   Qehillot Yehudei Kurdistan. Jerusalem: Ben Zvi Institute.

Berger, Peter L.
1976   Pyramids of Sacrifice. New York: Doubleday.

Bigart, J.
1903   Alliance Israelite Universelle. Jewish Encyclopedia, V. I. 418-422.

Blaisdell, D. C.
1929   European Financial Control in the Ottoman Empire. New York.

Bodman, Herbert L., Jr.
1963   Political Factions in Aleppo 1760-1826. Chapel Hill: University of North Carolina Press. James Sprunt Studies in History and Political Science, No. 45.

Bowring, John
1840   Report on the Commercial State of Syria. Parliamentary Papers, Vol. 21, Reports of Commissioners, London.

Braude, Benjamin
1977   Myths and Realities of the Ottoman Control System Before the Tanzimat. Paper presented at the Middle East Studies Association Annual Meeting. New York City: November 10, 1977.

Burton, Isabel (Arundell)
1879   The Inner Life of Syria, Palestine and the Holy Land. London.

Burton, R. F.
1898   The Jew, the Gypsy, and El-Islam. London: Hutchinson.

Braver, A. J.
1936   New Material on the Damascus Blood Libel,
                     Sefer HaYovel Le Prof. S. Krauss. Jerusalem,
                     261-302. (Hebrew).

————
1945/46   The Jews of Damascus After the Blood Libel
                     of 1840. Zion, 10:83-108. (Hebrew and
                     English abstract).

————
1945-46   Avaq Derakhim. Tel Aviv: Hebrew.
Cohen, H. J.
1971   Picciotto. Encyclopedia Judaica, 13:498.

————
1973   The Jews of the Middle East 1860-1972.
                     Jerusalem: Israel University Press.
Coon, C.
1951   Caravan. New York: Henry Holt & Co.
Davison, Roderic H.
1963   Reform in the Ottoman Empire, 1856-1876.
                     Princeton: Princeton University Press.
Dayan, A.
1849/50 (5610)   Holekh Tamim Ufo'el Ṣedeq. Livorno.
Dayan, I.
1902/03 (5663)   Imre No'am. Aleppo.
Dothan, A.
1957   On the History of the Ancient Synagogue in
                     Aleppo. Sefunot:I:25-61. Jerusalem: Ben Zvi
                     Institute. (Hebrew; English abstract).
Dwek, J. S.
1913/14 (5674)   Derekh Emunah. Aleppo.
Dwek, S. E.
1909/10 (5670)   Emet Meereṣ. Jerusalem.
Fischel, W. J.
1944   The Jews of Kurdistan 100 Years Ago. Jewish
                     Social Studies 6:195-226.
Franco, M., and R. Gottheil
1903   Damascus, Jewish Encyclopedia. New York,
                     Vol. IV:415-421.
Galante, M.
1808/09 (5569)   Berekh Moshe. Livorno.
Gibb, H. A. R., and H. Bowen
1950   Islamic Society and the West. Part I.
                     Oxford University Press.

————
1957   Islamic Society and the West. Part II.
                     Oxford University Press.
Gidney, W. T.
1897   Sites and Scenes: Descriptions of Oriental
                     Missions. London.

Gidney, W. T.
1908   A History of the London Society for Promoting
                Christianity Amongst the Jews, 1808-1908.
                London.
Goitein, S. D.
1955   Jews and Arabs. New York: Schocken.
Goodblatt, M.
1952   Jewish Life in Turkey. New York: Jewish
                Theological Seminary of America.
Gulick, John
1976   The Middle East: An Anthropological Per-
                spective. Pacific Palisades, Calif.:
                Goodyear.
Haddad, Robert M.
1970   Syrian Christians in Muslim Society.
                Princeton: Princeton University Press.
Himadieh, S. (ed.)
1936   The Economic Organization of Syria. Beirut.
Hitti, P.
1924   Syrians in America. New York: Doran.
Karpat, Kemal H.
1978   Ottoman Population Records and Census of
                1881/2-1893. International Journal of
                Middle Eastern Studies 9:237-274.
Kassin, Jacob
1924/5 (5685)   Sefer Or Ha-Levanah U Sefer Pri-es-Hagan.
                Jerusalem
Katz, Ruth
1970   Mannerism and Culture Change. Current
                Anthropology 11:465-475.
Krikorian, M. F.
1977   Armenians in the Service of the Ottoman
                Empire, 1860-1908. London and Boston:
                Routledge and Kegan Paul.
Laniado, D.
1951/52 (5712) La Qedoshim Asher Ba-ares. Jerusalem.
Laniado, S.
1774/75 (5535) Bet Dino shel Shlomo. Constantinople.
Lutzky, A. (Dothan)
1940   The Francos and the Effects of the
                Capitulations on the Jews of Aleppo. Zion
                6:46-79. (Hebrew)
Malachi, A. R.
1934/5   Ha yehudim beHitkommemut ha Druzim. Horev I:
                105-116.
Maoz, Moshe
1968   Ottoman Reform in Syria and Palestine. London:
                Oxford University Press.
Marx, E.
1967   Bedouin of the Negev. Manchester: Manchester
                University Press.

Naaneh, R.
1960/61   Osar HaMa'asiyot.   Part 5.   Jerusalem.
Nehmad, M.
1943   The Family of Ha Dayan, Hamishor, 26.2.33.
                 (Ben Zvi Archives) (Hebrew).
Neeman, P.
1927 (5687)   Jewish Communities: Beirut (12 Av);
                 Sidon (3 Av); Damascus (10 Elul); Aram Sobah
                 (Aleppo) (24 Elul); Ha Aretz (Tel Aviv).
Patai, Raphael
1965   Cousin Right in Middle Eastern Marriage.
                 Southwestern Journal of Anthropology 11:371-
                 90.
Paton, Andrew Archibald
1844   The Modern Syrians, or Native Society in
                 Damascus, Aleppo and the Mountains of the
                 Druse.   London: Brown, Green and Longmans.
Rabi, Moshe
1966   Bizekhut Hatsalat Nefashot.   B'Ma'arakhah
                 6:8 (No. 68), 14-15.
Russell, A.
1794   The Natural History of Aleppo.   London
                 (2nd Ed., 2 Vols.).
Sauvaget, J.
1941   Alep: Essai sur le Development d'une Grande
                 Ville Syrienne.   Paris: Haut Commission
                 de l'etat Francase en Syrie et Liban.
Schechtman, J. B.
1961   On Wings of Eagles.   New York: Thomas
                 Yoseloff.
Segall, J.
1910   Travels Through Northern Syria.   London:
                 Society for Promoting Christianity Amongst
                 the Jews.
Shama' HaLevi, Elijah
1820/21 (5581)   Qorban Ishah.   Livorno.
Shiloah, Amnon
1971   Farhi.   Encyclopedia Judaica.   Jerusalem.
                 Vol. 6:1182-3.

————————
1971   Bakkashah.   Encyclopedia Judaica.   Jerusalem.
                 Vol. 3.
Sutton, Joseph A. D.
1979   Magic Carpet: Aleppo-in-Flatbush.   Brooklyn,
                 New York: Thayer-Jacoby.
Taoutel, F.
1960   Contributions a'la Histoire d'Alep.   Beirut:
                 Imprimiere Catholique Textes et Etudes 9.

Wehr, H. (J. W. Cowan, Eng. ed.)
1961   A Dictionary of Modern Written Arabic.
               Wiesbaden: Harrowitz.
Wood, Alfred C.
1935   A History of the Levant Company. Oxford.
Zenner, Walter P.
1965a   Syrian Jewish Identification in Israel.
               (Ph.D. Thesis in Anthropology, Columbia
               University.) Ann Arbor: University
               Microfilm Order No. 66-8536.

1965b   Saints and Piecemeal Supernaturalism Among
               the Jerusalem Sephardim. Anthropological
               Quarterly 38:201-217.

1970   Ethnic Stereotyping in Arabic Proverbs.
               Journal of American Folklore. 83 (No. 350):
               417-429.

1972   Some Aspects of Ethnic Stereotype Content in
               the Galilee: A Trial Formulation. Middle
               Eastern Studies 8:405-416.

1980   Censorship and Syncretism: Some Anthro-
               pological Approaches to the Study of Middle
               Eastern Jews. In Studies in Jewish Folklore
               (F. Talmage, ed.). Cambridge, Mass.:
               Association for Jewish Studies, 377-394.

CHAPTER 10

THE SOCIAL STRUCTURE OF JEWISH EDUCATION IN YEMEN

S. D. GOITEIN

> More than any other Middle Eastern community,
> Yemenite Jewry has captured the imagination of
> both scholars and visitors to Israel. One rea-
> son for this is the combination of traits that
> Yemenites have exhibited until recently: pas-
> sionate attachment to the Jewish literary tra-
> dition and the background of an exotic, closed
> country untouched by Westernization. In this
> pioneer treatment, S. D. Goitein, professor
> emeritus of Middle Eastern Studies at the
> Institute of Advanced Studies at Princeton,
> discusses one aspect of this combination. This
> chapter is an abbreviated version of a much
> longer article which was published in the early
> 1950's on the basis of Goitein's numerous con-
> tacts with Yemenite immigrants freshly arrived
> in Israel.

In order to assess correctly the educational
activities of the Yemenites we should take into
account two demographic factors: firstly, the small
size of the population, and secondly its distribution
over an immense area. In Israel today there are
perhaps 80,000 Yemenite Jews. During the past two
generations the number of Yemenites in their own
country did not exceed 100,000. The 48,000 Yemenite
immigrants who have entered Israel since the inception
of the Jewish State - not all of whom could be asked
to furnish particulars about themselves - had lived
scattered over more than 1,000 different settlements
in Yemen prior to their migration. This means that
the size of Jewish communities in Yemen was extremely
small. If we add to this the fact that communities
in the actual sense of the term did not exist in Yemen
but that Jewish life centered round the synagogue, it
becomes clear how limited the organizing power of
Yemenite Jewry was.

SOURCE: Reprinted and abridged from Jewish Education
in Yemen as an Archetype of Traditional Jewish
Education. From C. Frankenstein (ed.) Between Past
and Present, pp. 109-146. By permission of the
Henrietta Szold Foundation for Child and Youth Welfare.
ⓒCopyright 1953.

The dispersion of the Jewish population over the whole of Yemen was somewhat weakened in its effects by another characteristic feature of their lives, their constant migrations within that territory. This led to the intermixing of Jews resident in different zones and, together with the predominance of the Jewish community of the capital Sana'a - which has been on the decline only during the last few decades - to a certain degree of unity. Nevertheless, the fact that the Jews of Yemen were split into divisions and sub-divisions differing greatly among themselves, should make us wary of generalizations. About 80 percent of the Yemenite Jewish population lived in villages or townlets whereas all investigations into their mode of life refer solely to urban areas. During the past year I have given my attention mainly to the rural population, but the scope of my research is very limited and this publication can only be considered as preliminary. As regards the details given below they stand open to correction and supplementation.

The Negative Attitude of the Yemenites to Childhood

Many educationalists are inclined to regard their conceptions of the child's place in society as axiomatic and to believe that they were held to be valid throughout all ages and among all nations. Nothing, of course, is further from the truth. Our evaluation of childhood, and our views on the rights of the child and his natural independence have only been evolved during the last few generations. If we want to appreciate and understand the methods of education in force among a people of different culture, such as the Yemenite Jews - then we must put aside all our modern prejudices and ask ourselves what theory of education prevailed in that civilization and was consciously or unconsciously applied in the upbringing of children in its various stages.

Throughout the civilization of the Middle East during the Middle Ages the view prevailed that the state of childhood had no intrinsic value and no rights of its own. It was merely the state of a person who was not yet complete, a phase through which one should pass as quickly as possible. In the colloquial language of the Inhabitants of Yemen a child was called "Jahil", meaning not only "ignorant" but also "one who does not want to know", for "the impulses of man are evil from childhood".

It is this spirit which pervaded and determined every phase of Jewish education in Yemen. No one doubted that the evil spirit must be driven out of the child's mind by the use of the rod and the strap; that its strength must be sapped by the study of the Torah and that the evil spirits must be conquered, although, it must be noted, extreme cruelty on the part of the teacher was not tolerated in Yemen and could lead to the teacher's dismissal. Even the child's loving, devoted and gentle mother did not refrain from using the stick on her little son to prevent him from committing evil deeds, such as quarrelling with his playmates, although, as he grew up, she was frequently moved to save him from the greater severity of his father. When she brought her child to the teacher for the first time, she would say to the latter: "I have brought you flesh, return bones to me," which meant, "don't spare him." She did this out of the conviction that only the discipline of the Torah and the chastisements of his teacher could make a man of her little boy. It was the aim of parents and children alike that the boy should become a man and that he should leave the state of ignorance as soon as possible. The good child was the one who behaved like an adult, who sat quietly without moving, "like a cup of arrack" i.e. a cup which stands firm and without motion, although the wine bubbles and foams. The manner of dressing was an expression of the same attitude. Nowadays when even adults wear shorts and open-necked shirts, go bareheaded and in sandals, and generally adopt a mode of dress which a generation ago was permissible only to street urchins - the little Yemenite boys and girls in their long clothes seem like dolls masquerading as adults; so that we often have to admit the aim of likening the child to the adult has been achieved with considerable success. Even in Israel today - where the influence of environment pulls in the opposite direction - we can still see small boys, sitting next to their elders in the synagogues, silent for hours on end.

No Bar-Mitzvah Ceremony

The negative attitude of the Yemenites towards the state of childhood as a state in its own right is also reflected in the fact that, as far as our information goes, there is no ceremony by which the boy enters adult society, such as the Bar-Mitzvah ceremony of the Sephardi or the Ashkenazi Jews. Such an "initiation" ceremony is given great prominence by many nations. Yet it is completely lacking among Yemenite Jewry, just as it was non-existent in Israel during the Talmudic era, although it is true that the age of thirteen is sometimes mentioned in Talmudic literature as the age when the youth must begin to observe the commandments. The expression "Praise be to the Lord who has freed me of the punishment which might be meted out to this child," usually uttered by the father on the day of his son's Bar-Mitzvah, is also of Talmudic origin, but a Bar-Mitzvah ceremony for every boy was evolved only much later. The lack of a correct Hebrew name for the ceremony as well as the marked difference between the Ashkenazi and the Sephardi customs are significant. (The former stress the reading from the Torah and the Prophets on the Sabbath, the latter the ceremonial putting on of phylacteries on a weekday, sometimes to the accompaniment of music.) The Yemenites, however, have no fixed age for putting on of phylacteries or for reading from the Torah. Some Yemenite boys start putting on phylacteries at the age of 10 or even 8 and others wait until they are thirteen or fourteen. One finds village boys aged fifteen who have not yet started putting on phylacteries. The reading from the Torah in the presence of the congregation is not restricted to the age group which is obliged to keep the commandments, for with the Yemenites, according to the Mishnah (Megila 4.6 and 4.5), "the little ones may read in the Torah and may translate from it," and they may also read from the Prophets (Maphtir). On the Sabbath young boys are given the honour of being called to the Torah in the sixth place. Thus neither the putting-on of phylacteries nor the first calling to the Torah is celebrated by a meal or any other form of festivity.

The Synagogue as the Principal Centre of Child Education in Yemen

It can be said that in the main the education of Jewish boys in Yemen was carried out <u>within</u> the synagogue, <u>by</u> the synagogue and <u>for</u> the synagogue.

From a very early age the child spent many hours at synagogue, especially on the Sabbath and holidays. He rose before daybreak - and often several hours before it - and sat in the synagogue with his father from the beginning of the service until the very end. As mentioned above, this custom still prevails in Israel today and anyone visiting a Yemenite synagogue will be impressed by the deafening "Amen" coming from the mouths of the smallest children. How natural then that in a country with a high infant mortality rate, the father should be anxious to ensure a place for his son in the world to come as early as possible. On weekdays, it is true, schoolboys prayed in the place where they studied, but since they studied for a few years only, especially in villages, we find that the synagogue was the only communal centre for the education of adolescents. There were many children who received their entire education in the synagogue. To this category belonged orphans, children of poor parents, children who had run or been driven away from home, and thus had not studied with a teacher for over a year or longer. It seems that the brighter and more alert among them profited more from their participation in the studies of their elders than from the instruction of their teachers.

Moreover, all the details of the syllabus of the Yemenite school were arranged so as to ensure the child's participation in the life of the synagogue as early as possible. The syllabus and the school had one aim, namely to teach the child prayers, the reading from the Torah, the appropriate passages from the Prophets and their translation and the Oral Law so as to enable the boys to follow the discourses which were a regular feature in Yemenite synagogues. They learnt nothing which had no direct bearing on the life of the synagogue. The fact that the school was of secondary importance as compared with the synagogue, can also be inferred from the fact that it had no name of its own. In those parts of Yemen where the synagogue was called "Kenees", the school was likewise called "Kenees", and in those districts where the synagogue was called "Ma'alama," i.e. the house of study, the school was called by the same name.

In its educational influence, too, the Yemenite school could not compete with the synagogue. Neither the school-room, nor the teacher, nor yet the system

215

of instruction was of a type likely to instill feelings
of love and respect in the children. The synagogue,
however, though often housed in a small and most
primitive building, inspired deep feelings. Anyone
who has ever joined Yemenites in villages in their
prayers, must have become aware that, in some measure,
the conduct of the people transformed the most primitive
place into a sanctuary. The old men and other adults
usually sat along the walls, on hassocks or fur-skins.
At their feet or in the centre of the synagogue the
boys were grouped, the supervision of whom was the
duty not only of their fathers, but also of all the
adult members of the congregation. The fact that he
spent hours amidst a congregation whose members were
studying and praying, implanted in the child a firm
feeling of belonging to the community of Jews as a
whole, which his community, no matter how small it
might be, represented to him. The joint recital, or
more correctly, the joint shouting of prayers was a
form particularly suitable for children because of
their natural bent towards activity; and it strengthened still more the boy's feeling that he was a
member of a strong and closely-knit community. When
the prayer "Shmoneth Esreh" was recited, so complete
a silence reigned in the synagogue that one could
hear a pin drop. The recital of this prayer, repeated
three times daily, made a deep impression even on the
small boy and aroused in him the feeling of God's
omnipresence and of the reality of spiritual existence.
What is perhaps even more important: the regular
and constant study in the synagogue (which, of course,
varied greatly, according to conditions of time and
place) awakened in the boy the desire to emulate
the adults and he was given a constant opportunity of
doing so.

The Subordinate Position of the School as Compared to the Home

The Yemenite School was subordinate not only to
the synagogue as a channel of education but also to
the parental home. Many of us may find it difficult
to understand such a value system, since we (in
Israel, eds.) are wont to accord to the home the third
place, at most, as a formative factor in the boy's
education, the first two places being held by the
school and the youth movement; and even this third we
are ready to concede to the home only because we

recognize it as a source of moral influence and appreciate the part it plays in teaching the child the rules of conduct. We do not think of it, however, as a source of learning and education. In order to understand the position in Yemen, we must always bear in mind the fact that in this, as in all other spheres of life, the Yemenite obeyed the Jewish law literally: it is the father's duty to instruct his son in the Torah, a duty of which he cannot absolve himself by paying a fee for his son's instruction. The teacher in Yemen was only a "Makrei Dardekei", i.e. one who teaches small boys to read aloud. Thus he was also called derisively in the Yemenite colloquial tongue, "Megarri". But he was not an educator whose task it was to teach the child the meaning and importance of the text he was required to memorize. This applied not only to the initial stages of study (prayers, the Bible and the Aramaic translation), but also to those subjects the study of which implied a comprehension of their meaning, such as the Mishna. As far as these books were studied at all, the children were taught to read them aloud with the correct intonation, but the teacher did not consider it his task to elucidate their contents. Sometimes, but very seldom, a teacher could be found who "explained" as well as "read". This was in conformity with the view prevailing in Oriental schools, viz. that memorizing, or at least reading aloud, should precede explanation and understanding. There was a widespread belief to the effect that explanation before reading was harmful to the child's mind.

To sum up: The Yemenite school generally resembled the Eastern-European "heder" insofar as the system prevailing in it was to teach by memorization. It appears, however, that the system of education differed in that the Yemenite gave pride of place to the parental home in the instruction of the child. The child acquired his real understanding of things, as far as he attained it at all, from his father and not from his teacher. The father considered this an ancient tradition and a holy duty. He did not content himself with explaining difficult points to the child when the latter repeated to him the text he had learnt at school. Even after the boy had left school he continued to benefit from his father's instruction and it was from his father that he acquired all the higher and more profound knowledge, such as the laws of ritual slaughter, which can be considered a sort of "secondary school education" for the Yemenites and

217

which, of course, were also studied under special
teachers. This custom applied to sons of ordinary
artisans as well as to sons of educated men. A man
from Saada told me that after he had left school at
the age of thirteen, he sat for two years in his
father's workshop and learnt the Scriptures. While
the father carried on with his work, the son read to
him from the sources and received the necessary
explanations. A man from Goran told me that at
school the children used to read various religious
texts without any explanation. In the evening, the
boys of the family, i.e. my informant, his brothers
and a cousin, used to sit together with his father,
his uncle, his grandfather and his grandfather's
brother. The grownups would carry on with their work
while the children were examined in what they had
learnt at school, and together read the book "Reshit
Hokhma," a highly mystical commentary on the
Pentateuch receiving adequate explanations whenever
the text was not clear to them.

It is obvious that a system which entrusts to the
family the imparting of learning and education can
only succeed where education is restricted to the
knowledge and understanding of a certain number of
holy books which every adult and every pater familias
can know. Moreover, children of the poor who were
wholly preoccupied with the task of making a living,
or children of uneducated parents and especially
orphans, grew up without any education at all unless
they had the initiative and the luck to find a teacher
among the men who regularly attended synagogue. On
the other hand, the system was based on a noble
conception of the relationship between the generations:
the father who begot the son has the duty of intro-
ducing him to the lofty sphere of intellectual life.
Here lies the source of the honour accorded to the
father which is carried to such lengths in a good
Yemenite family.

The Maturing Influence of Adult Society

The synagogue and the parental home thus determined the life of the Yemenite child much more than
did the school. The boy was drawn into the life of
adult society from the day he began to think and,
perhaps, we might say, even a little sooner. We must
remember that life in a Yemenite home was crowded.

Apart from the parents a considerable number of other adults - grandfathers, uncles, grown-up brothers - frequently already married - all lived in it together. Moreover, Yemenites in general are a very sociable people and festive gatherings as well as mourning ceremonies are numerous and long drawn out. The children join the adults in the prescribed meals, such as wedding celebrations lasting a whole week or celebrations of circumcision, or meals arranged for the consolation of mourners etc. Our children would be preoccupied with their own interests on such occasions, and would not pay the slightest attention to what was being said or done by the adults. The Yemenite child, however, has been trained not to raise his voice in the company of his seniors. It is amazing to see the restraint of which these small children are capable for hours on end. But the time is not wasted: the child is all eyes and ears. He absorbs the adults' conversation and quickly learns to understand hints and allusions. It can be said that while modern education now tends to prolong the age of childhood artifically, the Yemenites shortened it to a minimum which appears to us unnatural. An Arabic proverb which has also gained currency among Yemenite Jews says: "When your son grows up make him your brother." Yemenite Jews, however, do not wait until he grows up, but accustom him at an early age to consider himself responsible for his actions.

According to the Halakha, the father is not obliged to feed his sons after they have reached the age of six; at the same time he is urged not to be cruel to his small children. This outlook prevailed in Yemen until recently, although, as we shall see later, there existed a very effective system of exerting public pressure towards keeping small children at school. If the family lacked sufficient means of subsistence, neither the father nor the son considered it was incumbent on the father alone to bear the burden of earning a living. Even a boy of eight or nine was ready to shoulder the task of supporting himself and to contribute to the family income. (In certain cases he might run away from home to lead an independent life). The negative attitude of Yemenite society towards the state of childhood made the child strive to leave this state as soon as possible, even when there was no economic necessity for it. A Yemenite boy of fourteen compared with one of our children makes the impression of an adult.

Duality in the Attitude of the Yemenite Father Towards His Son

To all appearances, there is a contradiction
between the inclination of the Yemenite father to
grant independence to his son at an early age and even
to encourage it, and his task of "instructing him in
the Torah" which entailed years of supervision and
guidance; and, indeed, there was a strange duality
in the relationship of the Yemenite father to his
son - as far as it is possible to make any general
statements on a subject where so much depends on
proper evaluation of the temperament and character
traits of the individual. On the one hand, we find
the father's constant endeavour (often entailing
the use of severe corporal punishment and other
means of evoking fear) to guide his son in the paths
of righteousness, and to ensure his becoming a perfect
Jew. On the other hand, there is a certain indifference which often comes close to deliberate
renunciation of any attempt to exert influence. I
have frequently heard bitter complaints from orthodox
youth leaders that Yemenite fathers are quite un-
perturbed when their children are taken to non-religious
or even anti-religious educational institutions. Then
again, there are sons who would not lift a finger without asking their father's opinion beforehand, even when
they are already grownup, while at the same time their
younger brothers pay no attention at all to the desires
and opinions of the father who raises no objection
whatsoever. Infant nurses are often taken aback by
similar inconsistencies in the attitude of the Yemenite
mother. On the one hand, she shows the most devoted
love, almost beyond reason, and on the other, when a
sick child dies, she is likely to accept this as an
act of fate, with an apathy which seems quite heartless.
The outside observer must be careful lest he mistake
deliberate self-control for indifference. The Yemenite
father does not usually show his son excessive signs
of affection, especially after he has reached the stage
of education - for he is his teacher and "you should
fear your teacher as you fear Heaven." I once met a
Yemenite in a ma'abara whose eyes expressed deep
sorrow. From some of his neighbours I learnt that
nine of his sons had died. In his tent I saw a sweet
little girl and a charming boy of about six whose
brightness was amazing. The father smiled briefly at
the girl - since she was the daughter - but his
attitude toward his son was very reserved, although

one can easily imagine how dear to him was his only
remaining son.

The Grandmother as the Mistress of the House

   The person who plays an important part in the
childhood memories of any Yemenite and whose picture
will always be before his eyes, is his paternal
grandmother. This seems natural enough. The young
couple generally lived in the house of the bridegroom's father. When the Yemenite woman gave birth
to her first children she was usually very young and
inexperienced, and the care of the baby and its upbringing thus devolved to a large extent upon the
mistress of the house, i.e. the grandmother. A
Yemenite proverb says: "The mother has the joy and
the grandmother has the mess" (since it was the
grandmother who washed the child and laundered his
linen). The grandmother often took her grandson or
granddaughter to one of the many festivities which
were so characteristic a feature of Yemenite life, and
tried on such occasions, not always successfully, to
teach him or her good manners. It seems that the
grandmother was accorded this status not only for the
practical reasons mentioned above, but also because
she occupied the position of the mistress of the
house, i.e. the position accorded in all ancient
Eastern households to the husband's mother. The
author of the "Travels of Habshush" describes such a
grandmother. Round her neck she wears an iron chain
to which all the keys of the house are attached, and
whatever is done in the house is decided by her, even
though her son may have two or three wives. It need
hardly be mentioned that the part played by the grandmother in the child's upbringing often gave rise to
quarrels between her and the young wife. Nevertheless,
it seems that the supervision of the upbringing of
small children by a mature woman with her greater
experience of life could be counted as a blessing,
and years later she was remembered with affection.

The Role of the Yemenite Woman in the Education and Upbringing of Children

   There is a mistaken belief that illiteracy is
identical with lack of culture. It must be conceded
that throughout the length and breadth of the country,

in the urban as well as the rural areas, the Yemenite woman was completely illiterate. A famous proverb says: "He who reads alouds to his mother will never make a mistake." Moreover, no woman knew the prayers, a fact which is certainly surprising in the Yemenites, though not at all uncommon in other groups, for the Yemenites pay meticulous attention to the letter of the Law and are so exact in its observation, and it is specifically laid down in the Mishna and by Maimonides that women are obliged to pray. On the other hand, there were in Yemen, again in accordance with Jewish law, women acting as slaughterers of animals.

Without entering into a discussion of the position of women within the Jewish community in general, it seems evident that their position in Yemen was determined by an excessive emphasis on laws dealing with uncleanliness and purity (which was also the reason for the exemplary cleanliness of Yemenites in urban areas, stressed by all those who have visited the country). For fear that she might attend services during the periods of her menstruation, woman were excluded from all communal prayers. Thus women did not recite the Hewbrew prayers, not even the grace after meals, since there was no point in teaching it to someone who did not know the principal prayers. Although "the wife of a scholar is like a scholar herself", it is evident that the Yemenite woman was incapable of giving her children religious education, the only type of education recognized in Yemen. In fact the secular education of Yemenite women was also extremely limited. She knew innumerable proverbs; her songs were very beautiful and distinguished by great emotional power and splendid imagery, but the subject matter was restricted to a few themes.

As a result, we find that the influence of the Yemenite woman on her children was far greater than could be expected considering her scanty education. It is not correct to say that her educational tasks ended with the child's admission to school, and that she was only in charge of his physical well-being and care, teaching him, for instance, habits of personal cleanliness. As a Yemenite boy has put it in an essay: "At noon the children go home in order to eat and talk to their mothers." The father's duty, like that of the teacher, was to be strict, for he taught the child, but the mother could talk to her son like one human being to another. From her he could

receive what an adult can give to a young person. We
also have to consider the big sister, who took her
brothers to school and often sat with them for hours
looking after them. It would be worthwhile investi-
gating the mother's influence on her sons, after they
had left childhood behind them and even after their
marriage. The bitter complaints of the aging
mother - which we meet in proverbs and songs - that her
son has betrayed her and delivered himself body and
soul to his young wife, is indicative of what was
considered the normal state of affairs in these matters.
If a man was successful in his life, it was said that
"his mother has prayed for him," or "happy is she
that bore him." On the blessing of his mother rather
than on the discipline imposed on him by his father
depended man's fortune in life. The central point of
a Yemenite wedding was the solemn moment when the door
leading from the room of the women to the hall of the
men was opened and the bridegroom walked up to his
mother and kissed her knee, asking her forgiveness   for
all his sins in word or deed against her. For the son
belonged first and foremost to the one who "suffered
and toiled for him and who watched over him during the
night." In critical moments he turned to her first,
"all the boy's comings and goings center round his
mother," and when a man was cursed in Yemen, the evil-
wisher prayed that he should be in distress without
his mother's knowing about it.

The allocation of educational tasks in the Yemenite
home can be easily discerned from the expression of the
parents' faces. The father's face was, as a rule, stern
and set, whereas the mother's smiles testified to her
cheerfulness and practical wisdom, which were a blessing
to those around her.

Our knowledge of the woman's part in Yemenite
education and child care is scanty as yet. It is clear,
however, that we must revise our previous conceptions
and explore new sources of information, such as proverbs
and popular sayings illustrating various situations in
the relationship between the mother and her sons. We
should collect direct evidence from the women themselves and also from the objects of education. As
regards the human problem, it can be said that the
part played by woman in Yemenite education and the upbringing of children is of much greater interest than
the part played by man, for the Yemenite father transmitted to his child texts which came to him ready and
prepared, whereas the Yemenite mother, notwithstanding

223

all the tradition at her disposal, had to rely on her
own resources. An illiterate educator within a
community of which one-half read books written in a
language which was not the vernacular, is a fascinating
and unique subject of research.

The Education and Upbringing of Girls

As stated above, there is not enough information
at our disposal regarding the part played by Yemenite
women in the education and upbringing of their children.
It is equally true that what has been written hitherto
on the upbringing and education of Yemenite girls
cannot give us an adequate picture of the real position.

Firstly, it is not correct to say that the girl
grew up without any religious teaching. From her
earliest childhood her mother taught her to recite
the short prayers to which she herself was accustomed.
On various occasions during the year, for instance before the grinding of the flour for the unleavened
bread of Passover, the women recited short prayers;
they were generally in the habit of addressing themselves to the Lord of Creation, or, as a little girl
put it: "Mother tells God whatever she likes," in
contrast, of course, to the father who could only say
what was written in the book. However, the fact that
the whole religious education in Yemen was fed
exclusively on classical sources which were mainly
Hebrew, set up a barrier between the girls and
religious teaching. Substitutes in colloquial Arabic
did not occupy an important place. Nearly all
instructors who have taught daughters of Yemenite
immigrants confirmed the fact that these girls had
very little knowledge of Biblical stories. A clear
proof that the stories of the Scriptures were not very
familiar to Yemenite women is the surprising fact that
Biblical names of women were hardly to be found among
them. Only the regulations for women concerning impurity
and a few of the Passover laws, as well as the stories
about Hanna and her seven sons and similar material,
were specially edited in a language they understood.

It is therefore all the more surprising to note
the profound Jewishness, the mental alertness and the
strong character of these little girls who have now
come to us in their thousands. This applies in
particular to those who were born and bred in places
where there was a Jewish community of some size. The

upbringing of girls in Yemen proves that the home atmosphere was of paramount importance as an educational factor and that all educational activities occupy a secondary position only. The home atmosphere provided the child with a living example of a strong faith in absolute values and their realization in daily life.

The girls did not attend synagogue on the Sabbath. At most they sat in the courtyard of the synagoguge in the afternoon, all dressed up, not in order to listen to the "learning" or recital of prayers but to chat and to listen to the talk of grown-up women. They could not take part in the religious discourses at the family table, but the Sabbath was a day of rest for them. While for the boy it was a day of study with the adults, to the girl it afforded an opportunity for friendly social contacts. Yet the girls, too, observed the Sabbath strictly. The Yemenite woman was brought up to be a Jewess even though she did not enjoy systematic instruction in the tenets of Judaism.

It is not quite correct, however, to say the Yemenite girl lacked all "formal" education. As far as I could gather from my conversations with girls from all parts of Yemen, the Yemenite woman had a special system for the gradual introduction of girls to the fields of domestic work, to matters concerning conduct and to vocational training. Training for needle work meant for the girl what admission to school meant for the boy. A small town girl told me: "When I began to learn embroidery I ceased to play." Up to the age of five she used to play in the street, such games as "five stones" for instance. When she began to learn embroidery she stayed at home. A similar story was told by a girl from Sana'a when she explained the course of her vocational training. At first one made a Khirkah, a simple kerchief, worn over the skull-cap of the Arab woman, and then the Tarjulah, simple embroidery on the trousers of Moslem girls. At the age of eight the girl was capable of making two Tarjulas weekly. She would bring her work to the Jewish merchant at the market, who sold it to Moslems. For her work she received one-quarter of a rial per Tarjulah, or half a rial per week - while for her brother's studies a sum of one-eighth rial was paid every week. At the age of nine she thus managed to take her place in the life of the community, just as did her brother if he showed promise in his studies, in which case he could put on phylacteries already at that age.

I have heard of isolated instances of fathers who
had no sons giving instruction to their daughters and
of the daughters having become very learned. There
is the case of Sham'ah, the famous daughter of Shalom
Shabazi and Miriam, the daughter of Benayah the scribe,
who wrote a scroll of the Pentateuch while still
nursing a child.

The Transition from the Home to the Mori

The subject of the education of boys lends itself
more readily to a systematic presentation than that of
the upbringing of girls, for it was closely linked
with definite stages of mastering the books which
formed part of the syllabus.

The transition from education in the home to the
school was not sudden, for, in accordance with Jewish
law, the father taught his son from the day he was
capable of absorbing such instruction, i.e. from the
age of three upwards; (I was told by many that they
began learning the blessings over food and also some
of the letters at the age of two). From that age
the child is taken to synagogue services and to the
prescribed festive meals. Thus his ear becomes
accustomed to the sound of the Hebrew tongue from
his earliest youth. Small boys joined their elder
brothers for some lessons (for which they were
exempted from paying a fee), and some fathers also
started a more systematic instruction. A boy from the
town of Rada', the second largest Jewish community in
the country, gave a vivid description of this early
instruction. In the morning between 10 and 11 he used
to go to his father's workshop, and after an hour's
instruction would receive a "Ja'alah", i.e. a portion
of roasted beans and fruit, a typical Yemenite dish.
In the afternoon he returned to his father's shop for
another hour's tuition, after which he was given the
"Ghavaath", i.e. the meal of the afternoon, consisting
of bread and a thick pea-soup. In this way he was
made to like his instruction. At the same time he
also learnt the long grace after meals. Another boy
related that he acquired his first instruction from
his grandfather who used to teach him for one hour
in the morning, at sunrise, and one hour in the
evening, at sunset, at the time he fed the cows.
There was also a very significant emotional preparation
for school. The naughty boy was threatened with
"mori," his teacher, who was used as a scarecrow, to

226

inspire fear, a function which is carred out in other countries by the policeman. In the memories of many a Yemenite the first day at school is associated with fear and trembling, which the mother did not attempt to alleviate.

The "Mori" (Rabbi)

The word "mori" is derived from "mar," i.e. the Aramaic equivalent of master, whereas "Rav" is an Assyrian word which has been incorporated into the Hebrew tongue. The teacher or spiritual guide was called "Master," for the relationship between him and his pupil was like that between a master and his servant. The law prescribes that a pupil should do for his teacher all the work that a servant is supposed to do for his master, except for the "untying of his boots" (Ketubboth 96.1) and this precept was valid in Yemenite schools too, although there were not many opportunities for its application. The world "Mori," i.e. "my master" thus had the formal meaning of "Rabbi" or "Monsieur".

Since the state of childhood had no value of its own, it stands to reason that the man dealing with children could not be accorded an important position. Since the teacher's task was merely that of making children memorize texts for use at the synagogue and at home, it obviously required little expert knowledge. As a rule, only those who had either no talent for, or success in, other, more remunerative types of work, turned to the teaching profession. It is particularly surprising that in scores and perhaps hundreds of places in Yemen boys, some of them very young ones, aged nine or ten, served as teachers. More than once the villagers presented a young lad to me, mentioning with pride that since he was an orphan, they had provided for him by making him an infant-teacher. It was not difficult for a clever Yemenite boy who had run away from home to find refuge as an infant-teacher in one of the small towns, or, since such boys were fond of wandering, in several small towns in succession. Boys whom we would still consider children wrote down for me in minute detail the outlines of the syllabus according to which they taught and the conditions of work at every place in which they had been employed as "megarriein." This phenomenon can perhaps best be explained by the fact that in Yemenite schools, where

227

as a rule several groups of children learnt together, young boys were given opportunities to serve as infant-teachers and the step from infant-teacher to real teacher was not very big. At the other end of the scale there were very old men who on reaching the retiring age, had taken up teaching. As in Yemen, so in the times of our forefathers, young lads and very old scholars were often employed together as teachers. Neither was suitable, but it would seem that a very old teacher was preferable to one who was an immature boy.

I shall conclude with a characteristic detail. Up till now I have heard of only one case of willful murder committed by a Jew against another. This took place in the town of Sana'a. After the murderer had spent many years in prison he was reprieved and appointed as an infant-teacher. Taken aback, I exclaimed: "Teacher?!" My informants replied, equally astonished: "Why, of course. What else could he have done?"

There were, however, also professional teachers in Yemen who learned their calling from their fathers, as was the rule followed in all trades in Yemen, and who continued studying and teaching all their lives. Such teachers were usually to be found in the cities, but if they lived in the villages they also served as Rabbis, i.e. performed marriages and granted divorces and might also serve as the head of the synagogue or as the local slaughterer. Sometimes they were strangers to the place and its foremost intellectuals. Usually there were one or two additional teachers and the boys passed from one to the other, though no definite arrangement was adhered to.

There was no teaching certificate; anyone so desiring could become a teacher. In the towns this was a question of free competition. In villages the local inhabitants usually agreed on the appointment of a particular teacher, the latter not often staying long in one place. Whereas no one could be a ritual slaughterer, let alone a minister of religion without an authorization - and as a rule this letter of authorization had to be renewed by a recognized rabbi at set times - I have never yet seen a teacher's letter of authorization, and it need hardly be mentioned that there was no teachers' training college. It is most significant that even in Sana'a, where in recent years there were some twenty teachers, and in other towns where there were between three and six, it occurred to no one that they might join forces and found an institution comprising several forms. There were, of course, marked differences in the standards of instruction between the various teachers, but there was no system of promotion. Some boys "read" with several teachers, others received instruction from the same teacher throughout the years. It was not before the beginning of this century that, as a result of outside influence, a school was organized but even this experiment was short-lived.

The Care of the Community for the Education of Boys. The Status of Tuition and Its Economic Basis.

The Yemenite community laid great stress on the education of boys. Public opinion brought very strong pressure to bear upon every father to give his son a certain amount of instruction in Jewish subjects. If he failed to do so, the shochet (the ritual slaughterer) would refuse to serve him and he would remain without meat. (Yemenites ate meat almost every day); he would not be allowed to join in the prayers. In the villages of the Sana'a district, where since the last generation there has been compulsory attendance of religious schools for all Moslems, the police were called in if the father persisted in not sending his son to school. As a result we find that almost every boy who comes to Israel from Yemen has had some schooling even if he has spent only some months under the teacher's care and has or has not continued his studies elsewhere, as in the case of orphans and waifs. There are, however, also boys who have never had any instruction from a teacher and who have received their entire education at home from their fathers, grandfathers or an uncle, and as far as I could see, these were by no means the most ignorant ones. In little villages in which the number of Jewish households was small - and there were hundreds of such villages in Yemen - the teacher was usually a boy unless the sons were sent to the house of a relative in the next city. The enthusiasm of the French Jewish tourist, Joseph Halevy, who visited Yemen eighty years ago, was justified on the whole. He remarked on the fact that in a country most of whose inhabitants were illiterate, it was precisely the most ostracized and lowest of all classes that took care to provide a widespread education.

The amount of schoolroom space allotted shows how much interest was taken in the education of boys. In hundreds of localities there was a schoolroom next to the synagogue. These schoolrooms, as well as the synagogues, were built by and maintained either through the joint efforts of the residents or by the donation of a single person as in the Talmudic era. The trustee of the synagogue - either a member of the donor's family or a man elected by the congregation - appointed a teacher who then used the schoolroom without paying rent. It is interesting to note that originally the schoolrooms served throughout also as hostels for poor wayfarers. This custom prevailed until about a generation ago, and it was only after it was noticed that the boys had been infected with diseases by the wayfarers that in some places a special "midrash" (literally "school") was founded to give shelter to the poor.

Here it should be mentioned that the link between the school and the duty of hospitality existed to the last in all parts of Yemen. When a poor man came to a place where there was a Jewish congregation he would turn to the school as a matter of course, for there he would always find someone, whereas the householder might be busy with his work. The teacher would send one or more pupils home to fetch food for the wayfarers. Thus the children learned to dispense charity from their earliest youth.

However, not everywhere a schoolroom next to the synagogue could be found. When a man wanted to practice charity he threw open the door of one of his basement-rooms for the use of a teacher. Only a minority of schoolrooms, however, belonged to this category, although, contrary to what might have been expected, they were more frequent in towns than in villages. Since teaching in Yemen was a private or, more correctly, a semi-private occupation, there were also teachers who rented rooms for themselves and others who taught in their own houses or even adapted their houses to the requirements of teaching.

The furniture and equipment of the schoolroom was very simple. The children sat on mats or on fur-skins on the floor, and used bricks or small wooded props brought from their homes for their books. For the mats or fur-skins every member of the synagogue paid a certain sum. The teacher had a special raised seat, and woe to the child who dared to sit on it, even in jest.

As a rule, the books belonged to the boy's parents, and indeed the love for books was one of the outstanding characteristics of the Yemenites, even of those living in villages. The Yemenites clung to the ancient custom of teaching the child to read sideways and upside-down, apart from reading in the normal way, even in such places where there was no shortage of books. In order to avoid the wear and tear on books, the children used a small stick with which they pointed to the passage being read without touching the book itself. Essential parts of the equipment were a whip and a stick.

The maintenance of teachers fell decidedly into the category of charity. The underlying idea was that the work of the teacher is not actually the type of work by which a man should earn a living. Some teachers never collected the tuition fees due to them. When the father did not send or bring the money, the teacher would not claim it. Yet the system worked. Generally speaking, not even the poorest evaded their duty. But if the parents could not find the means for the fee, the teacher would not bar the child from attending school. Of course, not all teachers con-formed to this custom, and there were children who after the death of their father or after his economic ruin could not continue to study. In addition to the fee, the boys after their lunch brought a "Mitzvah" in the form of a loaf of bread for the teacher's household (or for sale).

As indicated above, and as we also find elsewhere, there were teachers who pursued some other occupation while they taught. Here we must distinguish clearly between two different types of teachers. On the one hand there was the teacher who had come down in life, whose main work consisted of teaching and who supple-mented his meagre income by pursuing some other occupation of a despised type, such as spinning or the manufacture of show-fringes. On the other, there was the respected craftsman, such as a silversmith who (especially in the small towns) taught as a sideline, in addition to his main work. He usually gathered together only a small number of pupils around himself, among them the members of his own family. It would seem that the best-qualified professional teachers

231

were to be found in the larger cities although there
were also many miserable "moris," whereas in the small
townlets the general status of the teacher was much
higher.

The Youth ("Bachelors") Age Group

Just as the entry into school took place only
after prolonged preparation, so also the leaving of
school was not an abrupt process. The boy continued
his studies, apart from the discourses in the synagogues, in which he had participated from the time
he had joined the advanced class in his school. He
learnt from his father, either while receiving
instruction in a trade or at another time. Furthermore, it was widely accepted that a boy did not work
full time upon leaving school. After breakfast he
would return to one of the synagogues for two or three
hours of study. This arrangement did not place a great
burden upon the father, for the son usually took up
his father's trade and worked in his house.

"It seems," says Israel Yeshaya, "that in Yemen
there is no youth in the full sense of the word. The
young people have no special interests of their own.
They are not organized in groups or societies of their
own. They participate in all the activities of the
older generation, are identified with it and completely
absorbed by it." This statement is, of course, on the
whole correct, for, as we have already noted, childhood was considered only as a preliminary stage subordinate to adulthood, and the child lived within the
adult society from the day he started his conscious
life. In spite of this, it seems to me that this
particular age group was more united and marked off
from other age groups. It had a distinct character
within Yemenite society. In Sana'a there was an
ancient custom, preserved up till the time of the
Exodus from Yemen, according to which the bachelors
of the town assembled on Friday night, shortly after
midnight, in the synagogue of the Great Alsheikh. The
older men would leave the synagogue that night and
the young men would chant their special prayers, the
songs and customary "Tikkunim" and psalms. They also
prayed for a good and beautiful wife. Occasionally
the young men held special gatherings outside the
precincts of the synagogue, such as a special party
on the seventh day of Hanukkah.

232

In short, the organization of youth into groups of their own within the framework of the Jewish community in Yemen, though less marked in comparison with other communities, did exist.

CHAPTER 11

THE AUTHORITY OF THE COMMUNITY OF
SAN'AA IN YEMENITE JEWRY

YOSEF TOBI

> Jewish communities throughout the world
> face the problems of how to maintain unity
> and adherence to a common code of practice,
> despite dispersion. In this essay, Yosef
> Tobi, Lecturer in Jewish History at Haifa
> University, shows how this was tackled in
> Yemen during the past two hundred years.
> Unlike most of the contributors to this
> volume, Tobi is a professional historian,
> and his work shows how historians utilize
> documents to reconstruct social and polit-
> ical relationships. He infers ways in which
> the ancestry, personality and scholarly
> reputation of the rabbinic leader helped his
> acceptance as an authority against the back-
> ground of external forces which shaped iner-
> communal relations.

The community of the Jews of Şan'aa, the capital
of Yemen, has for long been regarded as the spiritual
center for that country's Jews, and its religious
courts and Rabbis were regarded as the supreme authority by all the Jewish communities of Yemen.[1] In the
first part of this chapter, we review general data of
the last 200 years concerning the authority of the
San'aa community. In the second part, we examine a
series of particular documents dealing with the topic.

The period of the last 200 years was chosen for
several reasons. In the middle of the 17th century,
an important event took place that caused great changes
in Yemenite Jewry, the temporary expulsion in 1679 to
the littoral desert. Thereafter Jews were subjected
to intensified degradation, and engaged, more than
previously, in Messianic activities (Ratzabi 1972).

SOURCE: Original contribution for this volume.

After the 17th century, Yemenite Jewry lost much of its cultural richness and ancient traditions. However, ties with the world-at-large expanded. Scholar-travellers, such as Christian Niebuhr, and emissaries from Eretz-Israel came in considerable numbers. Trade movement, both from the Persian Gulf and from the Red Sea, increased. There was also the missionary activities of Joseph Wolf and Aharon Stern, and in the second half of the 19th century the conquest of Yemen by the Turks. As a result of all these developments, information about the Jews of Yemen increased, and we now possess a considerable number of historical sources (see Tobi 1976).

The authority of the Ṣan'aa community is not something to be taken for granted. There was a time during which leadership passed from this community to another community, that of Aden. The period alluded to covers the 11th-13th centuries, when there was much international trade that proceeded from India via Aden to Egypt and Europe, and in which Jews played a significant role. The letters of the Gaon of Babylonia in the 10th century reflect the supremacy of the Ṣan'aa community. In the three centuries that follow, however, we find that the negidim of Aden, and the Aden community generally, enjoyed authority and power recognized by all the communities of Yemen (Goitein 1967). The standing of the Ṣan'aa community was also diminished during that period, because in the middle of the 12th century approximately, the Royal Court of Yemen was transferred to the town of Jiblah in the south, and Jews also moved from Ṣan'aa to Jiblah (Goitein 1953:48). It would seem that in the 14th century Ṣan'aa once more regained its previous eminence, but it was not an undisputed position, since the Rabbis of the Ṣa'dah community, in the north of the country, did not accept the decision of the Rabbis of Ṣan'aa against the allegorical interpretation of the Torah and only after excommunication was pronounced by Ṣan'aa sages did they consent to submit the matter to sages from Eretz-Israel, and to accept their judgment (Qafih 1951). However, from this time on it appears that the authority of the Ṣan'aa community was accepted without question.

In the middle of the 18th century, we hear of the activities of two distinguished personalities in Ṣan'aa, the results of whose work were felt right up until the great emigration of our times, Rabbi Shalom

ben Aharon Ha-Kohen (known also as 'Iraaqii) and Rabbi
Yihyaa ben Yosef Ṣaaliḥ who officiated in the parallel
functions of head of the community (Sheikh) and Head
of the Rabbinical Court (Bet-Din). Rabbi Shalom
'Iraaqii was from a family that came to Yemen from
Egypt in the 16th century, and was prominent in the
public life of Yemenite Jewry. In the 18th century
the 'Iraaqii family produced community leaders and
royal counsellors and ministers. During the lifetime
of Rabbi Shalom ben Aharon the 'Iraaqii family attained its greatest renown. The standing of the family
was practically uncontested, both at the court and
among the Jews, and Rabbi Shalom's renown reached even
the Jews of Eretz-Israel. Upon his father's death,
Rabbi Shalom inherited his position as royal adviser
and served two Imams; over a period of thirty years
(1731-1761).[2] There can be no doubt that the
eminence of Rabbi Shalom in the royal court strengthened his status as leader of Jewry. This we may
learn, for example, from his order to arrest in "royal
custody" anyone cutting his hair during the days of
the 'Omer, in opposition to the custom of those Yemenite Jews who did not accept this prohibition, and in
accordance with the practice of most Jewish communities
(Ṣaaliḥ 1964 II:57-66).

Rabbi Shalom was active on behalf of the members
of his community, both in the royal court as well as
within the community itself (teaching Torah, aiding
the needy, building synagogues and ritual baths), so
that he became known by the title "Sayyedna al-Shaikh
Saalim" (our Master the Head Shalom) as well as by that
of al-'Ustaa (the master craftsman), a name bestowed
on him apparently by the Imam. He also expanded his
charitable activities to include other communities
such as Dhamaar, 'Ibb and Mochaa. The attitude of the
Jews of his community towards Rabbi Shalom was, however, ambivalent, and some of his actions aroused
opposition. Rabbi Shalom attempted to introduce to
Yemen the form of prayer of Eretz-Israel. This action
was apparently aimed at increasing his stature in the
community (for it may be assumed that his family,
which originally came from Egypt, did not worship
according to the Yemenite rite but according to that
of Eretz-Israel), and it engendered controversy.
Ultimately, Rabbi Shalom admitted that he failed in
that dispute. Another reported controversial act was
the destruction of the genealogical records of the
Jewish families of Ṣan'aa because of their having

refused to give a daughter to Rabbi Shalom's son in marriage; claiming that his family had come from Egypt and had no genealogical record. But it is probable that this is legend (Sappir 1866:100-102).

It would seem at all events that Rabbi Shalom 'Iraaqii was the outstanding secular leader of Yemeni Jewry of recent centuries. No such figure emerged under Turkish rule, when communal institutions were more formally organized by the authorities (Tobi 1976b: 104-117). Rabbi Shalom's activities undoubtedly enhanced the standing of the San'aa community and particularly the status of the Bet-Din of San'aa. That body was headed by the second half of the 18th century by Rabbi Yihyaa Saalih. Rabbi Yihyaa was elected by the Bet-Din of San'aa in 1758 when still a young man, and from then until his death in 1805 he presided over the religious leadership of San'aa Jewry and of the Jews of Yemen as a whole. Rabbi Yihyaa was the outstanding religious figure of recent centuries in Yemen, and was regarded as the "ultimate" authority. His treatises were so highly considered that everything that followed was based on his work. This is the case with the form of prayer, since the Tiklaal (prayerbook) that he drafted together with his exegesis is the accepted text used by the Yemenite Jews, and all subsequent prayer-books are derived from it. And so too for the reading of the Bible, since it was his treatise "Heleq ha-Diqduq" which determined the form accepted among the Jews of Yemen, and to which they adhere to this day. The same is true in the area of Halakha, for his work of Responsa, entitled "Pe'ulat Saddiq", together with three other works on laws of slaughtering and ritual purity, are considered to be the ultimate of religious judgment among Yemenite Jews. Rabbi Yihyaa's status was acknowledged throughout the Yemen, and in his work we discover that he was approached for decisions by many communities there. Even the sages of the communities of Aden and Habban, far from San'aa, base themselves to a great extent on his treatises. He was also renowned outside Yemen, and maintained ties of correspondence with the communities of Israel in Egypt, India and Salonika (Ratzabi 1967:248-277; Greidi 1938:134-137).[3]

However, there remain questions concerning the nature of the secular and religious authority that was exercised by the San'aa community over other communities. From the information we possess, it is clear

that until the end of the 19th century this authority
was of a moral nature only; it depended upon the
personalities of the leaders involved.[4] It seems that
only with the conquest of Yemen by the Turks in 1872
was the Head of the community appointed and officially
recognized by the ruling powers, and thus we find that
Rabbi Shelomo Qaarah was that same year appointed
Ḥakham Baashii, a title conferred by the Ottomans on
the Chief Rabbi appointed in the conquered country
(Tobi 1976b:104-117; 239-245). From this time on
there is increasing information concerning intervention by the authorities, first by the Turks and
later by the local Yemenites, in the appointing of
leaders of the community (Nahshon 1972).

    We do not possess the document confirming the
appointment of Rabbi Shelomo Qaarah as Ḥakham Baashii.
However, deducing from "the Royal Decree" given to
the first Hakham Baashii in Jerusalem, Rabbi Abraham
Hayyiim Gagen (Luntz 1891:203-208), it would appear
that his powers were extensive, and that he was
supported by the authorities. We find support for
the assumption, that the leadership of the Yemenite
community was organized in Turkish times according to
the manner prevalent in other parts of the Empire, in
the form of the signatures of the leaders of the
community in those days. The stamp of Saalem ben
Yiḥyaa Jamaal, who officiated as Ḥakham Baashii in
the years 1897-1899, reads in translation: "The Chief
Rabbi of Ṣan'aa and environs and the (Jewish) community of the Yemen." The seal of the sages of the
Ṣan'aani academy reads: "The scholars of the academy
of the Holy Community of Ṣan'aa (May the Lord find it
well), the spiritual Committee" (Ratzabi 1970). From
these formulae it appears that the Turkish authorities appointed, as they did elsewhere in the Empire,
two committees, one for religious matters and one for
material affairs, and that the authority of the Ḥakham
Baashii encompassed all Jews of the country.

    During the 20th century, however, it seems that
the head of the Ṣan'aa community was not entrusted
with officially recognized authority over all Jews of
Yemen. This may be learnt from at least two documents.
One of these, from the year 1905, when the Imam
Yaḥyaa succeeded in forcing the Turks out of Ṣan'aa
for a brief period, is a "Religious Regulations for
the Jew" given to the Jews by the Imam (Hibshush 1937:
220-223). This document constituted an abrogation of

rights granted to the Jews by the Turks, and regulated
the relations of the government with the Jews on the
basis of the traditional view, that the Jews were
strangers under protection. One of the interesting
features of the document is that it concerns the Jews
of Ṣan'aa, and nothing is said of other communities.
Also, in another document, of the year 1932, appointing Rabbi Yiḥyaa ben Shalom 'Abyaḍ as Head of the
community and issued on behalf of the Imam Yaḥyaa, it
is clearly indicated that he is chosen as Ḥakham of
the Jews of Ṣan'aa and nothing is said of other
communities (Qorah 1954:76-77). The Imam thus abolished the function of Ḥakham Baashii, perhaps because he did not desire an official who might act on
behalf of the whole of Yemenite Jewry. As a result
of this policy, the Head of the Ṣan'aa community dealt
with the collection of the poll-tax of his community
only, and not with that of other communities. The
Imam appointed the heads of individual communities,
and these were responsible for the collecting of the
poll-tax (Tobi 1976:65-111).

A formal change did not, however, cause a radical
change in the actual position of the Ṣan'aa community.
Thus Rabbi Yiḥyaa Yiṣḥak Halevi, who was Ḥakham Baashii
under the Turks and who continued to serve as Head of
the Bet-Din in the time of Imam Yaḥyaa, was active
among the communities outside Ṣan'aa. He appointed
an emissary on behalf of the Bet-Din of Ṣan'aa, who
visited various communities in order to ascertain,
that ritual slaughterers and the officials at marriages
did their work properly and were qualified to do so
(Qorah 1954:45). Rabbi Yahya Yiṣḥak Halevi also cer-
tified, on behalf of a Moslem ruler in a provincial
town, a permit to slaughter, which had previously been
given to a Jew of that town (Goitein 1953:52, also
Tobi 1976b:111-115).

In the second part of the chapter we now examine
a series of new documents that throw light on the
nature of the relations between the community of
Ṣan'aa and other communities. The original sources
have been published in Tobi (1976a:191-209).

I. Memorandum of the Bet Din of Ṣan'aa to the commu-
    nity of 'Arjaaz concerning the safeguarding of
    morality, 1809 (?). (Ms. Adler Geniza 2561,
    photograph Ben Zvi Institute, file 417).

The document is a rather stern appeal to the members of the 'Arjaaz community, concerning the slackening of morality and religion, and the need to abide by the courts of the Moslems. The document refers in particular to the apparel of women, and complains about the lack of modesty when women leave the Jewish quarter and enter Moslem neighborhoods. The authors of the memorandum dwell at length on the importance of modesty, and of the dangers implicit in the lack of this virtue:

> And one more observation concerning women when there is no difference between those of Israel and the heathen, for not only do they add to their sinfulness by adorning themselves with all kinds of ornaments and parade among the nations without any trepidation and the Gentiles mock at us, but they also behave in a lewd manner.

Moslems used to set their eyes upon Jewish women, particularly on Sabbaths and holydays, and therefore the Rabbis of Ṣan'aa ordained that women be prohibited from wearing jewelry except on the Sabbaths and holydays, and then only in the privacy of the Jewish quarters. Men too were prohibited from wearing white garments except on Sabbaths, in order not to attract the attention of Moslems. The writers of the document threaten all who do not heed them with excommunication, and bestow upon the leaders of the 'Argaaz community power to excommunicate, besides refraining from providing ritual services, such as ritual slaughtering and circumcision.

The document is torn at the margins so we do not know the names of the signatories or of their community. But it may be assumed that the signatories were members of the Ṣan'aa Bet-Din, for we cannot conceive of such forceful language being that of any other figures. If our hypothesis is correct, and the Rabbis of Ṣan'aa were the authors of the memorandum, then we may learn from here that the Ṣan'aa Bet-Din saw, as its duty, to ensure the preservation of proper social and ethical standards among all Jews, even though this authority was not granted to it by the government of the country. This will emerge more clearly from a scrutiny of the documents that follow.

II. A letter of rebuke from Rabbi David ben Abraham
Ṣaaliḥ to the community of Ḍaale' concerning the
sale of wine to Moslems (before 1839). (Ms.
Ben-Zvi Institute 1118, pp. 111b-112a)

Rabbi David Ṣaaliḥ, grandson of Rabbi Yiḥyaa
Ṣaaliḥ, was a judge in the Ṣan'aa community during
the years 1827-1839, headed at the time by the Judge
Yosef Qarah. Rabbi David rebukes members of the Ḍaale'
community for having sold wine to Moslems. In the 19th
century Ḍaale' was outside the area ruled over by the
Imams; it came under the jurisdiction of independent
sultanates. In spite of this, the Rabbis of Ḍaale' saw
fit to inform Rabbi David that some Jews in the community were selling wine to Moslems, which was prohibited
by general Islamic law and by the regulations of the
local Jewish community. It appears that Rabbi David's
letter of rebuke was penned in response to a request
of the local rabbi. So, although Ḍaale' did not belong politically to Yemen, its Jews regarded themselves as subject to the Rabbis of Ṣan'aa. Also, in
the days of Rabbi Ṣaaliḥ, the Rabbis of this community
had come to him for advice on a point of custom (Ṣaaliḥ
1946 I:3). But it is unclear why Rabbi David wrote
this letter of rebuke, and not the greatest of the
Rabbis of Ṣan'aa and the permanent Head of its Bet-Din
at the time, Rabbi Yosef Qaarah. Possibly the Rabbis
of Ḍaale' addressed themselves to Rabbi David, as the
grandson of the reverend Rabbi Yiḥyaa Ṣaaliḥ.

The structure and style of the letter are of interest. The first part deals with the state of Jews
in the Diaspora and their relationship with God, and
the need for repentance in order to bring closer the
divine redemption. The letter was written in the month
of Ellul, and constitutes an exhortation connected with
the High Holy Days. Rabbi David goes on to speak of
the Tabernacles Festival following the High Holy Days,
when one is enjoined to make merry with wine and song,
and he reminds the community of Ḍaale' of the regulation not to sell wine to the Moslems. Only after that
lengthy introduction does the writer come to the point.
Moreover, the author repeats that he does not come to
rebuke, but only to remind that dire consequences are
likely to follow transgression, both from the Almighty
(the postponement of Redemption), and from the Moslem
rulers. The letter is written in a moderate style,
probably because a mildly-worded reprimand was more
likely thought to be effective, but also because Rabbi

David possibly lacked the authority that his ancestor, Rabbi Yiḥyaa Ṣaaliḥ had possessed. We learn here of the moral authority of the Rabbis of Ṣan'aa over other communities.

III. Letter of rebuke from the Ṣan'aa Bet-Din to the members of the Jabal 'Amr community concerning moral decline (1853). (Ms. of Mr. Y. Daḥuuḥ, Tel Aviv)

From this letter we learn of the intervention of the Rabbis of Ṣan'aa in the lives of other communities, at least those not too distant from Ṣan'aa. Here is the background of events: in the latter months of 1852 tribal fighting took place north of Ṣan'aa. It appears that as a result of this the inhabitants of Jabal 'Amr[5] were obliged to leave their homes. After the disturbances had abated, people began to return to their hometown, but their religious and moral life had deteriorated. Also, personal relations among people were disturbed to the extent that they used to address themselves to the Moslem town-governor over trivial issues. As the letter puts it, "one sin brings a more grievous sin in its wake, since every person who quarrels with his fellow even over a trivial matter is responsible before the governor of the town, and through this quarrelling they transgress our Holy law". Jews on the whole opposed at all times having to resort to common law courts, but here apparently the leaders of the community were busy with their own affairs, and did not devote themselves effectively to the reorganization of communal life. When rumors about this state of affairs reached the Ṣan'aa Bet-Din they addressed themselves to the heads of the Jabal 'Amr community, the brothers Rabbi Ṣaalim and Rabbi 'Awaaḍ, the sons of Yosef Yiṣḥaḳ, warning them that, as leaders of the community, they were duty-bound to strive for the restoration of orderly communal life. The brothers replied to the Bet-Din in Ṣan'aa that, due to the extent of the suffering and their preoccupation with their families and households, they had no choice but to act as they did, and as the Rabbis of Ṣan'aa recount in their letter, "their words are words of truth, but the hour was one of pressing need." Rabbi David ben Ṣaalim Daḥuuḥ, sent by the leaders of Jabal 'Amr to the Bet-Din in Ṣan'aa, told the Rabbis of Ṣan'aa that the heads of the local community were not neglecting their duty, and that they were doing all in their power to restore orderly life. In spite of this

the Rabbis of Ṣan'aa appointed Rabbi David on behalf
of the Ṣan'aa Bet-Din to be head of the Jabal 'Amr
community, and to run local affairs assisted by the
brothers, Rabbi Ṣaalim and Rabbi 'Awaad Yisḥak. The
punishment with which they threatened anyone who disobeyed Rabbi David was moral and not material, since
they did not have authority to the latter. The
signatories are the members of the Ṣan'aa Bet-Din -
the Head Rabbi Suliimaan ben Yosef Qaarah (died 1889),
his brother Rabbi Yiḥyaa (died 1887), Rabbi Yiḥyaa ben
Shalom Ha-Kohen (died 1867), Rabbi Yiḥyaa ben Ya'aqov
Saalih (died 1859), and Rabbi Yosef ben David Manzilii
(died 1899). The date is September 1853. Once again
we learn that the authority of the Ṣan'aa community
was essentially a moral one, conditional upon the consent of the Jews of other communities. In the days
of such a forceful and respected Head of Court as
Rabbi Suliimaan Qaarah, the Ṣan'aa Bet-Din could man-
ifestly intervene in the life of another Yemeni
community, and even appoint on its behalf and as it
saw fit, a man to watch over local affairs.

IV. The verdict of the emissaries of the Bet Din of
     Ṣan'aa with regard to the dispute between the
     members of the community of Ḥufaash and the local
     Rabbi, 1885. (Ms. Sassoon 973, pp. 99-100,
     photograph Ben-Zvi Institute, file 296).

     Rabbi Yiḥyaa ben Ḥayyim al-Shaikh and Rabbi
Ḥayyim ben Rabbi Ṣaalim Ḥabshuush were sent on behalf
of the Ṣan'aa Bet Din to other communities of the Yemen,
in order to inspect affairs in these communities. On
their arrival in the town of Ḥufaash, which lies some
three days distance to the west of Ṣan'aa, they found
themselves confronted with a dispute "over authority
in the synagogue and ritual slaughtering, and all
sections of the community assembled before us for
judgment, including their leaders and dignitaries, and
we heard all their testimony with regard to their
quarrel with their rabbi, Sa'iid Suwailum." The
emissaries decided in favor of the congregation, and
the rabbi accepted the judgment and agreed to abide by
it. As emerges from the document, the affair came to
the knowledge of Shaikh Yiḥyaa Muusaa, he was apprised
of the judgment and added his signature beside that of
the above-mentioned emissaries. The document is dated
May 1885. We learn that at that time the Bet Din of
Ṣan'aa did not take action only when asked to do so,
but also took the initiative in supervising communities.

244

Furthermore, the authority of the Bet-Din of that
particular time was great, and its decisions were
uncontested. The Head of the Bet-Din was Rabbi
Shelomo Qaarah, considered as the Rosh Galuta (Head
of the Diaspora), and his Court was known as the Bet-
Din Ha-Gadol (Supreme Court).

The wording at the beginning of the document is as
follows:

> ...(W)e the undersigned being sent on
> a devine mission by the Rosh Galuta of
> the Bet Din of Ṣan'aa (may the Lord
> find it well), in order to inspect the
> affairs of the Jews outside the city
> of Ṣan'aa, in such matters as the
> slaughterers and inspectors and
> religious laws and disputes, and whatever
> greatly requires the powers invested
> in us by the Supreme Bet Din
> of Ṣan'aa.

The activity of the Bet-Din of Ṣan'aa has to be viewed
against the background of the comparative quiet that
prevailed in that period under Turkish rule, and stems
from the fact that the Bet-Din enjoyed official
recognition of the authorities. Another point worthy
of comment is that the emissaries of the Bet-Din
associate the local shaikh with their decision, he
being the secular leader of the community. In small
communities, where there were not always great rabbis
or religious guidance, the standing of the shaikh was
frequently superior to that of the local rabbi.

V.   The appeal of Yosef ben Shukr of the town of
     Mahwiit to the Bet Din in Jerusalem against the
     judgment of the Rabbis of Ṣan'aa, 1890.
     (Elyachar 1891:60a-63a).

An important document that reveals an interesting
episode in the relations between the Ṣan'aa community
and other communities is a Responsa by the late-19th-
century Chief Rabbi of Jerusalem, Rabbi Ya'aqov Sha'ul
Elyachar. Yosef ben Shukr Busaanii, from the town of
Mahwiit to the northwest of Ṣan'aa, addressed himself
in writing to the Bet Din of Ṣan'aa, requesting the
annulment of a divorce granted to his wife, on the
grounds that, as he claimed, he had been compelled to
give it against his free will. The husband claimed
that his wife had rebelled against him because, so

she argued, he was afflicted with boils, and had left
him. The husband recounted that there had been a great
dispute between him and his wife's relatives in the
town; therefore, the case was transferred to the Bet
Din of another town, and that Bet Din had decreed that
the husband grant his wife a divorce and also pay a
fine. The husband had not accepted the verdict. Then
the Shaikh, possessing secular authority within the
Jewish community, intervened and ordered him to accept
the verdict. He also decreed that, if the husband
disobeyed now, he would have to pay a monetary fine
to the Muslim authorities. Finally, the Shaikh
threatened to imprison the husband unless he granted
the divorce. The husband writes:

> At that time they caused me to become
> depressed by telling me that if I dis-
> obeyed...I would suffer torture at the
> hands of the authorities, and would in
> spite of myself be compelled to divorce.

The husband addressed himself to the Rabbis of Ṣan'aa
after he had gone from town to town in order to win
support for his cause, but had failed to find supporters. The Bet Din of Ṣan'aa addressed itself to the
local Bet Din that had reached the first verdict,
received a full report, and gathered new testimony.
After deliberations, and basing themselves on the
codex of Maimonides, the Rabbis of Ṣan'aa ruled that
the divorce was valid. The husband did not give up;
he appealed to the Rabbis of various communities,
and eventually obtained opinions, against the judgment
of the Rabbis of Ṣan'aa, that the divorce was invalid.
These other Rabbis expressed the opinion that the
decision should have been reached according to the
codex of Rabbi Yosef Karo, and not that of Maimonides,
because judgment in the communities outside Ṣan'aa
customarily followed the school of the former and
not that of the latter.[6] The husband returned to
Ṣan'aa and came before the Bet Din, to whom he presented the answers of the Rabbis of the communities
outside Ṣan'aa. The reaction of the Ṣan'aa Rabbis
was predictably sharp, and they rejected the arguments
of the other Rabbis, particularly that which stated
that the Maimonidean school was not to be followed.
The husband appealed once more to one of the other
Rabbis, who reacted in a manner not respectful towards
the Rabbis of Ṣan'aa, and advised the husband to turn
now to the Rabbis of Jerusalem. The latter finally

ruled that the divorce was valid, and that the judgment of the Ṣan'aa Rabbis was correct.

We learn from this case that there was tension between the Rabbis of the Bet Din of Ṣan'aa and the Rabbis of the other communities, mainly, it would seem, because in those communities judgments were not reached following the Maimonidean school of thought but according to that of Rabbi Yosef Karo. In Ṣan'aa, Maimonides was considered the authoritative source, but the Rabbis of the provincial communities did not abandon their views. The ruling of the Rabbis of San'aa is stamped with a sense of superiority, but that was neither absolute nor final, since the authority of the Rabbis of Jerusalem was still greater. In the modern period, with the entry of Yemen into the sphere of the Ottoman Empire, we find the Rabbis of various Yemenite communities addressing themselves to the Rabbis of Jerusalem without just having recourse to the Ṣan'aa Bet Din (Tobi 1973:286-291). We also learn that the power of the local Shaikh was considerable, for he could impose prison sentences and fines. That was obviously due to the support of the authorities, for revenues from the fines he threatened to impose were earmarked for them.

In conclusion, we have presented here a survey of the authority wielded by the community of Ṣan'aa in relation to other communities of Yemen, over the last two hundred years, while they adapted themselves to the changing political conditions of the period. Undoubtedly our knowledge is incomplete, in particular due to the limited sources which do not afford us a full picture. Frequently we have been compelled to make assumptions on the basis of fragmentary data. With a steady uncovering of new sources, future research will hopefully fill in the gaps in our information.

NOTES

[1]See Goitein (1953, especially 50-53). Nahshon (1972: 45-49) devotes a chapter to the power and influence of the community of Ṣan'aa. See also Tobi (1981:12-18, 204-211). On the Jewish community of Ṣan'aa in general see Qaafiḥ (1968) and Goitein (1953:48).

[2]Towards the end of his life Rabbi Shalom fell from royal favor. He was imprisoned and heavily fined, and the Imam decreed the locking of all the synagogues in the Jewish Quarter of Ṣan'aa. They remained so for thirty years.

[3]Many poems, mostly still in manuscript, were written in eulogy of Rabbi Shalom, both during his lifetime and afterwards. One is published in Tobi (1974:268-269).

[4]The important and comprehensive correspondence between the Jewish courts of Aden and Ṣan'aa in the years 1812-1834, concerning the issue of the Ṣan'aa court's authority over that of Aden demonstrates this point. See Nahum (1981:75-107).

[5]This town is close to the larger town of Hajjah, which lies to the northwest of Ṣan'aa. For a note about this community see Daḥuuḥ (1964:7). This is an opportunity to express my gratitude to Mr. Daḥuuḥ for having made available the document discussed here.

[6]Maimonides (12th century) was accepted by the Jews of Yemen as supreme Rabbinic authority. He was contested from the 17th century on by the Rabbi Yosef Karo Codex of religious law. The dispute between these two rabbinical schools lasted through to the last days of the Jews in Yemen, in our times.

REFERENCES

Daḥuuḥ, Y.
    1964   Ha-yehudim lo hit'arvu bo-goyim. Da'at,
                    Tel Aviv, No. 8 (1964), 7.

Elyachar, Y. S.
    1891   Ma'ase Ish, Jerusalem.

Goitein, S. D.
    1953   'Al ha-hayyim ha-tzibburiyyim shel ha-
                    yehudim be-eretz-teman. In Jubilee Volume
                    for M. Kaplan. Hebrew Section, New York,
                    1953, 43-61.

    1967   Negide eretz teman. In Bo'i Teman, edited
                    by Yehuda Ratzabi, Tel Aviv 1964, 15-25.

Greidi, S.
    1938   Kavvim le-toldot yehude teman ba-me'ah ha-
                    yod-het (1700-1800). In Mi-teman Le-tzion,
                    edited by Shimon Greidi and Israel Yesha'yahu,
                    Tel Aviv, 1938, 106-138.

Hibshush, S.
1937   Eshkelot Merorot Va-Halikhot Sheva, edited
                by S. D. Goitein, Kovetz 'Al Yad II (1937),
                197-230.

Luntz, A. M.
1894   Yerushalayim IV.
Nahshon, Y.
1972   Demutah shel Ha-Hanhagah Ha-yehudit Be-Teman
                (mimeographed) M.A. Thesis, Bar Ilan Univer-
                sity, Ramat Gan.

Nahum, Y. L.
1981   Mi-Yetzirot Sifrutiot Mi-Teman, edited by
                Yosef Tobi, Holon.

Qaafiḥ, Y.
1951   Ketav haganah mi-teman 'al ha-shitta ha-
                alegorit be-ferush ha-mikra. Kovetz Al Yad
                V, 39-63.

1968   Kehillat San'a shebe-teman. Mahanayim 119,
                36-45.

Qaarah, A.
1954   Sa'arat Teman, edited by Shimon Greidi,
                Jerusalem.

Ratzabi, Y.
1967   Mahritz u-veto. In Bo'i Teman, edited by
                Yehuda Ratzabi, Tel Aviv 1964, 248-277.

1970   Kehillat San'aa bi-shnot 5659-5673 (1899-
                1913). Sinai LXVII, 202-218.

1972   Gerush mawza' le-or mekorot hadashim. Zion
                XXXVII, 197-215.

Ṣaaliḥ, Y.S.
1946-1964   Pe'ullat Tzaddik, Tel Aviv, 2 vols.
Sappir, Y.
1866   Even Sappir, Vol. I, Lyck.
Tobi, Y.
1973   Yediot 'al yehude teman mi-tokh she'elot
                u-tshuvot. Shevet Va-Am VII, 272-291.

1974   Peniyyat pekide kushta el ribbi shalom
                iraqi nesi yehude teman be-shnot 5502
                (1742). Shalem I, 257-269.

1976   Yehude Teman Ba-Me'ah Ha-Yod-Tet. Tel Aviv.

1976   Ha-kehilla ha-yehudit be-teman. In Moreshet
                Yehude Teman, edited by Yosef Tobi, Jerusalem,
                65-117.

1981   Ha-merkazim ha-yehudiyyim be-asya.   In
            Toldot Ha-Yehudim Be-Artzot Ha-Islam by
            Yosef Tobi, Ya'aqov Barna'i and Shalom Bar-
            Asher, edited by Shemu'el Ettinger, Jerusalem,
            3-70, 197-244.

CHAPTER 12

ASPECTS OF THE SOCIAL LIFE OF KURDISH JEWS

DINA FEITELSON

The following reconstruction of social life
in Kurdistan is an outcome of research on the
domestic life and childbearing of Kurdish Jews
in Israel by Dina Feitelson, professor of
education at Haifa University. We hear of the
positive attitude to physical labor, the love
of the open-air, and of the character of Kurdish
men, self-assured, taciturn, and concerned with
personal honor. Such characterizations, stemming from the Culture and Personality school of
the 1950's, are least common in anthropological
writing today and this is the only paper repre-
senting that approach in our selection of
Middle Eastern Jewish ethnographies.

For the past forty years a constant stream of
immigrants from the Kurdish mountains of Iraq has been
reaching what is now Israel. The mass exodus of 1951
finally transferred the whole group known as "Kurdish
Jews" to Israel.[1] This paper is a reconstruction of
what once was and is no more.

The fieldwork which served as the main basis for
this reconstruction was undertaken in Israel in 1953-4,
only two to three years after the families observed
moved to Israel. At that time, the impact of new
surroundings and institutions had as yet left intact
many of the usages practised in Iraq. Furthermore,
the remembrance of the "old" ways of life was still
very vivid and could be elicited in interviews.
Naturally, information obtained in this way had to be
checked and rechecked, and needed to be compared with
the scant literary sources available.

SOURCE: Jewish Journal of Sociology, I (1959):2:
201-216. ©Copyright 1959 by the Jewish Journal of
Sociology. Reprinted by permission of the Editor of
the Jewish Journal of Sociology and the author.

THE COMMUNITY

(1) Physical Surroundings

After the First World War, the main area in which
the Kurdish tribes lived was divided between Turkey,
Iraq, and Iran, smaller parts falling to Syria and the
U.S.S.R. The Jews of this region had been settled
mainly in the area of Mosul, so that the majority of
them found themselves in Iraq, while lesser groups
were in Turkey and Iran. This paper deals only with
those Kurdish Jews who came to Israel from Iraq.

The area in question was very diversified.
Politically it belonged to the young nationalist Arab
state of Iraq. The language of the Government and its
officials was Arabic.

But, in fact, centralized forms of government had
not caused basic changes in an area ruled for generations by Kurdish trival chiefs. The main bulk of the
population was made up of Kurds whose first loyalty
was to their chiefs and local interests, a fact wit-
nessed by the numerous uprisings by the Kurds of Iraq
and the neighbouring states against their respective
governments. The Kurdish area was not a clearly defined unit, and, on its fringes, Kurdish settlements
were interspersed fairly closely with Arab villages.

The Jews in this region formed the second largest
minority. The Nestorians outnumbered them by far and
were a politically recognized group.

The Kurdish Jews lived in the northeastern part
of Iraq, not far from the Persian border. This
mountainous and remote area, traversed by deep gorges
and ravines, was, until very recently, largely cut off
from outside influences. Very little change seems to
have occurred throughout the generations. Travellers
who reached the communities of Kurdish Jews in the
thirteenth century mention by name many of the
communities surviving until 1951, and described a way
of life reminiscent of the one which will be depicted
in the following pages. Life in the Kurdish mountains
was hard. The winter was very cold, the summer
extremely hot. Travel, on foot or horseback, was
difficult. Water was plentiful, the settlements often
sited near a stream. Fields could be watered and the
area was fertile.

The Kurdish Jews lived mainly in small towns in which they formed communities with institutions of their own. A smaller number lived in villages. There existed a few completely Jewish villages, one, Sandur, which is mentioned repeatedly in travellers' reports of all ages; it had a Jewish headman of its own. In other villages, the Jews were a minority, sometimes only a family or two to a village.

(2) Occupation

The Kurdish Jews differed from most other Jewish communities in the Diaspora in that many did hard manual labour and in their close affinity to the soil and its products.

As already mentioned, some Jews lived in villages. But even the families who practised a non-agricultural way of life seem to have owned at least some livestock for their personal needs and to have kept a sort of kitchen garden. Skilled artisans were rather rare, and most occupations were pursued in the household. People built their own houses, sewed their own clothing, preserved their own food for winter, spun their own wool. As far as it is possible to ascertain, typical Jewish occupations seem to have been dyeing, weaving, and goldsmithing. Jews were often peddlers travelling among the remote Kurdish villages. As non-participants in the recurrent hostilities between rival Kurdish tribes and villages, they seem to have been especially suited to this profession.

(3) Jews and Their Neighbours

It is rather difficult to establish exactly the relations between the Kurdish Jews and their neighbours. These relations must have been subject to change with political upheavals. It is clear that the Jews were much closer to their Muslim neighbours than the other religious minority group, the Nestorians. The latter, more numerous than the Jews, formed a politically recognized minority living in isolation, while the Jews were bound by social and economic ties to the Kurdish lords of the land. Though as a matter of their own choice, the Jews lived in separate quarters in the small towns; these quarters were adjacent to those of the Muslims. Quite often Muslims lived there too and even in Jewish households, either as lodgers or as workers who performed the necessary tasks on the

Sabbath. Jews were employed by Muslims and vice versa.
Nowadays the Jews like to exult in the memory of the
social ties which existed between the two groups. It
seems clear that mutual visiting took place, and,
while the Muslims are said to have adored the kasher
food, the Jews also ate in Muslim houses, abstaining
on these occasions from meat and sometimes preparing
part of their meal themselves.

On the other hand, an element of mutual distrust
seems to have underlain many of these relationships.
Though the Jews were usually under the protection of
the Agha[2] and no pogroms occurred, the rise of Arab
nationalism seems to have given scope to open hostility, and there were even instances of the murder of
individual Jews. Even before that, Jewish girls were
sometimes kidnapped, and, in general, the Jews suffered
the fate of the stranger "not of the faith" in a
predominantly Muslim society. Perhaps we could sum up
the situation in the words of one of my informants,
"Heaven be praised there are only Jews in Israel. But
some of the 'Heaven be praised Jews' here are much
worse than the 'Heaven forbid Arabs' in Iraq."

But more interesting than the problem of the
relationship of the Jews to their neighbours, is the
extent to which the Jews were similar in their
attitudes and way of life to the Kurds. At work they
hummed Kurdish songs dealing with the themes of love,
honour, and violence so dear to the Kurds. Even at
weddings most of the songs chanted were Kurdish. These
songs were only an external sign of the acceptance of
Kurdish values. (It is not clear whether the Jews
were in a position to live up to these values; probably
not; but then neither did the Kurds). The ideal of the
manly male, quick to anger, jealously guarding his
honour and that of his family, stubbornly standing by
his word once it is uttered, also became their ideal.

The close cultural proximity between Jew and
Muslim cannot be stressed enough. Jews consulted non-
Jewish "wise men", and Muslims and Christians asked
the help of Jewish ones. Both Jews and Muslims revered
the same holy graves and undertook pilgrimages to them
on feast days or in fulfilment of vows.

CULTURE

(1) Language

The Kurdish Jews spoke an Aramaic dialect called Targum[3] which varied slightly from place to place. According to the location of the town, Arabic, Kurdish, Persian, or Turkish elements also penetrated ordinary speech. It is of interest that Targum is rather similar to the language used by the other ethnic minority group, the Nestorians. It might thus be said that the Jews lived in the orbit of the "Modern Syriac" language circle.[4] Targum, as well as the foreign words it contains, was written in Rashi script.

Fischel ascribes special significance to the linguistic isolation of the Kurdish Jews from their Muslim neighbours. He maintains that, living in a tribal society, in which each tribe has a dialect of its own, the Jews scattered among the various tribes would have been hopelessly divided. Their Aramaic dialect served as a unifying bond and was a most reliable and characteristic way of recognizing a "Kurdish Jew".[5]

It should be noted that most Kurdish Jews, especially the men, were able to speak and understand the dialect of the Kurdish tribe among whom they lived, as well as the other local language, Arabic in the case of the Kurdish Jews originating from Iraq.

(2) Religion

A. General. Religion formed an integral and indivisible part of everyday life. Actually, only the Bible was known. Knowledge of the Mishnah, even among the "wise men," was scarce, and the Talmud and most later religious writings were virtually unknown.

But the laws of the Sabbath, Kashrut, and Purity were observed most strictly by everyone. As among the Muslims, devoutness was revered[6] and was generally one of the attributes of the respected members of the community. Learning or devoutness itself did not lead to the attainment of high status; it was, rather, that the wealthy member of the community, after having obtained his position, made a great show of his devoutness.

Daily life was hedged in by an endless variety of usages aimed at warding off the evil eye, spirits, etc. All these were, as far as the individual was concerned, part and parcel of the all-embracing concept "religion."

There was no clear understanding of the difference between the official Jewish doctrine and the customs developed locally. Such an understanding could hardly be expected when the Chacham was the foremost practitioner of the occult arts. He prescribed "mystic" cures, performed spells, wrote amulets, and expounded dreams. He himself saw all these as part of his Jewish heritage and would explain blandly that thus it was written in the Bible. I myself sent one of them off on a vain hunt through his scripture in search of the law which forbids one to set chickens to hatch.

It should be noted here that in general the beliefs held were common to Jews and their neighbours, and that the usages practised were similar.

B. Feasts. The Kurdish Jews have a great zest for enjoying life. Festive occasions, religious as well as personal, were made much of and led to pro-longed and joyful celebrations. The leisurely course of everyday activities was punctuated by the seasons and the great religious feasts. Weeks of preparation preceded each of them. Passover might be deemed the foremost; on this occasion, houses were repaired and whitewashed and all the members of the household clothed anew. The same suits of clothes were worn throughout the following year.

No work was undertaken during all the days of Chol Hamoed, and one of the oft-repeated grievances of Kurdish immigrants is that the pace of life in Israel forces them to forgo this habit. In general, feast days were used in order to visit relatives and for pilgrimages to holy places. The Kurdish Jews had a great affinity for outdoor life and one of the accepted ways of celebrating religious festivals was to picnic in the countryside.

The feasts marking the rites de passage in the life cycle of individuals were no less drawn out. The wedding may serve as a good example; we shall touch on some of the others more briefly in the follow-ing paragraphs. Actually it might be said that all of the weeks which intervened between the engagement

and the wedding itself were a time of joyful antici-
pation and heightened activities in the households
concerned. The engagement, called more commonly the
"signing of conditions," was a grave affair in which
the fathers of the young couple concerned reached an
agreement going into minute details of the provisions
to be made by each side, after much initial bargaining
and without any concern for the feelings of the young
people themselves. However, once the agreement was
signed, the time for joyful celebrations had come.
These culminated in two big parties on the eve of the
wedding, one in the house of the groom and one in that
of the bride. After prolonged dancing and singing,
henna was put on the hair of the perspective bride
and her mates, as well as on the hands and feet of the
groom.

The next day, the wedding was celebrated in the
house of the bride's family. A brand new praying shawl
belonging to the groom served as <u>Chuppah</u>. After the
ceremony, the bride was conveyed in a procession,
usually on horseback, accompanied by music and dancing
to the house of the groom, where the wedding meal was
held. At this meal, the young couple broke their fast,
and morsels of their food were snatched up wildly as
tokens of good luck. Only on this one occasion, when
she was a bride, was a girl allowed to sit down with
the celebrating males. On all other occasions her
place would be in another room or serving the refresh-
ments, as at this very moment were her mother-in-law
and related womenfolk, none of whom took part in the
meal.

During the following week, the celebrations continued, constant visiting and entertaining taking
place. The young couple was not supposed to leave the
house unaccompanied or do any work, and every effort
was made to divert them. One cannot end this description without noting that the nuptial chamber, its walls
decorated with carpets and its bed covered with embroidered sheets and pillows, was well in evidence during
the celebrations. The time of the consummation of the
marriage was well known, and a throng of relatives from
both sides used to wait for the sheet to be brought out
immediately afterwards as evidence of the bride's
chastity. Only thereafter were the couple considered
properly married. A lapse discovered at such time
would have had the most serious consequences.

C. The Synagogue. The synagogue was the chief
formal institution of the Kurdish Jews. Here every
male member of the community was to be found on the
Sabbath and feast days. On work-days only the old men
visited the synagogue which they regarded mainly as a
place for social gathering. Women among Kurdish Jews
did not go to the synagogue.

Usually the synagogues owned large sums of money,
as the "ascents to the Torah" used to be auctioned
off, occasions used by the more affluent members of
the community to increase their prestige by the offer
of staggering sums. These funds were rarely used, the
buildings themselves, according to Fischel, being
neglected and in disrepair. There was no organized
charity or other cultural or religious activity by
the community as such.

Usually the wealthiest and most influential
members of the community were elected as Gabaim and
charged with the whole responsibility for the upkeep
and functioning of the synagogue. No accounts whatsoever were kept, and it seems highly probable that the
funds mentioned were often mismanaged though perhaps
not always intentionally.

Furthermore, it must be remembered that mis-
appropriation of public funds, as well as susceptibility to bribery, were traditionally expected of all
holders of public office.

D. The Chacham. In the typical Jewish community,
one person carried out all the official religious
functions. Usually the Chacham (wise man) also served
as cantor, circumciser, teacher, and slaughterer, as
well as scribe. This last "person" was among the most
important, as he wrote the charms which brought help
in times of illness or preserved one from evil when
all was well. The smaller villages had no Chacham of
their own and were served by an itinerant who reached
them about twice a year.

As the Chacham also served as the teacher, it will
be understood that in many cases the boys growing up
in these villages remained uneducated and even illiterate. A Chacham told me of an experience he had when,
as a young man, he was sent to such a village to
celebrate the Seder. Next morning a minyan was
organized, but everybody kept looking at him and

258

copying his actions, as most of those present did not know how to pray. Naturally this story may, to some extent, be exaggerated and tinged by the town dweller's contempt for villagers, but it is certainly true that in contrast to other Jewish ethnic groups there were illiterate adult males among the Kurdish Jews. As will be seen further on, even the town dwellers who did in fact study under a <u>Chacham</u> reached only a very low standard of learning as compared with other Jewish communities.

Thus religion is again a field in which the great similarity between the Kurdish Jews and their Muslim neighbours is apparent. The role allotted to religion in both groups is rather similar, but its way and means are different. While the content of the official doctrines differ, both are freely interspersed with local customs, labelled Jewish in one instance and Muslim in the other.

THE HOUSEHOLD

(1) The Dwelling

In the typical community, building land was without commercial value, and each family owned the building in which it lived. As there were no rules concerning building, rooms could be added to each dwelling according to the needs of the household. The house could be extended to accommodate all - both people and livestock.

In its construction and equipment, the Jewish house seems to have been rather similar to that of the non-Jews. Detailed descriptions can be found in Barth, Leach, and Brauer.[7]

Agricultural land had commercial value, and it seems that the Jews in the villages were sharecropping tenants of the Agha (although, when questioned, they maintain stoutly that they themselves "owned" the soil).

The Kurdish Jews liked the open-air life, and much of daily activity took place out of doors. Most of the women's tasks were performed in the yard attached to each house, and in summer the rooftops served for sleeping.

259

Each nuclear family of the household had a room
to itself in which parents and children slept all
together. Usually livestock and food stores were also
kept in the house.

(2) The Extended Family

As amongst their Muslim neighbours, the extended
family was a basic social unit. The principle of co-
residence was patrilocal, married sons remaining in
their father's household. Thus a typical household
consisted of the parents, their unmarried sons and
daughters, as well as their married sons with their
wives and children. In many cases, this unit continued
to exist after the death of the head of the household,
becoming a fraternal joint household. This unit would
later break up, each brother forming a household of
his own.

The household was the economic and political unit
of the community. Usually all the males worked together in one occupation. The income was shared, as
were the expenses. No accounts of the income and
expenses of the various nuclear families of the household were kept. Meals were prepared in common, stocks
laid in for the whole household, clothing prepared for
all members of it, and so on.

In general, the Kurdish Jews lived a frugal life.
Food was cheap and, though eaten in huge quantities,
not expensive. Clothing was simple. Furnishings
barely existed. The main luxuries were tea, coffee,
sugar, and tobacco. Surplus income was invested in
"gold," mainly in the form of ornaments for the womenfolk.

(3) The Cohesion of the Extended Family

But, while the extended family functioned as a
corporate group as far as economic activities were
concerned, its social bonds were less tight. Although
it was the household as a whole which was allied with
various factions in the constant overt and covert
struggle for position and honour in the community, and
though it was the household which either participated
or withheld participation in various gatherings, which
travelled on a pilgrimage or stayed at home, yet, in
fact, even while acting as a corporate unit, it broke
up into smaller groups. Thus, at any rite de passage,

be it joyful or sad, a wedding or a death, the household, as one, was triggered into action in accordance
with its degree of involvement in the event. The
household, as a whole, would act differently according
to whether, for example, the deceased was the brother
of its head, or only a second cousin. But in this
general policy of "participation to a certain degree"
special members of the household would be activated
in a special way according to long established and
well known patterns. At the wedding of a young man,
it might be his mother and his aunt who for days had
been preparing the feast, the preparation serving as
a joyful occasion for all the related womenfolk. But,
at the wedding meal, it would be the husbands of these
women who, uninvolved till then, would sit down to the
meal and who, at its end, would donoate their share
of the wedding presents.

At the time of the consummation, these diversions
no longer existed, and men, women, and children would
all be united in a joyful throng awaiting the event.
This group would be made up mainly of the direct
members of the households concerned, the other relatives, whatever their degree of involvement during the
preparatory stages, having retired to their respective
homes.

But aside from this patterned way of differentiated participation by the various sub-groups of the
household in events affecting it, there were also
possibilities of under-currents of feeling and even
activity by sub-groups directed "against" the official
interests of the household. For instance, the
surreptitious help rendered a pair of young lovers by
the women of the households concerned, while they were
being hunted hotly by the men; help that, if discovered,
would have incurred hard retribution.

(4) The Men

Authority in the household of the Kurdish Jews
was lodged absolutely in its male head. He was the
one to decide on every issue and none dared question
him. Actually, he and the other adult males of the
household lived a life of their own, remote and
unapproachable by women and the children. They generally spent much of their time outside their homes at
work, prayer, or social gatherings. On their return
home, silence descended. None dared speak in their

261

presence. Nor could the womenfolk sit with them, but kept apart, guessing at their wishes. The ideal was that of the strong silent man who would not change his mind once it was made up - a man to command respect from women and children. Such an ideal was well in keeping with a community in which every transaction depended on drawn-out bargaining. Only the individual known for his stubborn endurance was likely to succeed, while giving way in any instance was only the prelude to future compromises. In this connection, it is interesting to note that it was not necessarily the eldest son who succeeded his father as head of the family, but, rather, the one with the strongest personality. Naturally a man tried to live up to this image, at least in his own family circle, and woe betide any of his immediate kin who dared contradict or was not circumspect enough in word or gesture.

The strongest motivating force of such a man was his personal honour. His concern for the welfare of his family stemmed, not from his warm emotional ties with any of its members, but, rather, from a mechanism which we might call, in William James's wake, "ego extension." Thus all his household was felt to be part of himself and any affront was felt as a personal insult and acted upon immediately. An example of the functioning of this mechanism will suffice. When Mrs. Levi was married out into a family two houses down the path, the marriage contract stipulated that a special kitchen should be erected for her by her husband's family.[8] This part of the contract was never fulfilled, and her father severed relations with her husband's family, the reason being (as she herself pointed out) that a contract signed by him had not been honoured. As by this time she was of her husband's household, her father included her in his ostracism, and she dared slip home for a chat with her mother only when he was known to be out. We see that it was not concern for the welfare of his daughter which triggered off the father's reactions, but a very strong sense of having been personally slighted by the offence done her.

(5) Womanhood and Its Tasks

While men ranged afar, women were confined to the compound. Up to marriage, her father's and, from then on, her husband's yard made up the woman's world.

Only the fetching of water and family occasions were causes for going out. In the compound, work proceeded unceasingly, directed by the mother-in-law and carried out willingly by her daughter-in-law. Since the women were generally of a very industrious disposition, no problems seem to have arisen in the allocation of work. On the contrary, the atmosphere of the women's work group was usually relaxed and carefree with incessant small talk accompanying the effort. As the young woman usually got her final training in the tasks of the household only after her marriage, her teacher being her mother-in-law, there was no divergence of opinion as to how a given task should be performed and no frictions arose on that account. Work was never urgent, as food was always ready to be served to the home-coming males or any guest; work could proceed at a leisurely pace, performed by the group as a whole, without responsibility weighing heavily on anyone.

Might it not be that the great gulf between the men's world and that of the women and a way of life which did not allow intimacy between spouses to evolve, made for a drawing together and warm relations in the women's group even though it was composed mainly of affines? Such a group would not normally show great intimacy in a Western society.

THE LIFE CYCLE OF THE INDIVIDUAL

(1) Marriage

Marriage is but another field in which it seems that the Jews accepted, at least nominally, the values dominant in the Muslim society in which they lived. The preferential marriage among the Muslim Kurds, namely with the father's brother's daughter, is attributed by Leach mainly to economic factors[9] and said to serve to perpetuate the extended family. Barth, on the other hand, emphasizes the "political" significance of this type of marriage. By giving a daughter to this kind of marriage and foregoing the accepted bride price, a man gains the political support of his nephews. While he can usually depend on his own sons and brothers, the relationship with his brother's sons is more critical and in order to maintain lineage solidarity, ties with them should be reinforced.[10]

Though political power in the Jewish community did not depend on the number of riflemen an individual could muster,"[11] it is certainly true that success in the more subtle struggle for power depended to a large extent on the size of the cohesive family group ranged behind one. Thus it was in the interest of any individual to head a family group as large and as stable as possible. Naturally more could be expected of a kinswoman in this respect than of a complete stranger. It should be noted that, though in general marriage tended to take place within the kin group, and as a general rule the bride and groom were related even if only remotely, actual father's brother's daughter marriages were much less common than one would be led to assume by the generally expressed sentiment in their favour. This would be in keeping with the facts reported by Granqvist[12] and tends to support Barth's view that there is a smaller incidence of this type of marriage when the lineage group has less political significance.

In general, it seems that the Jewish parents, when seeking a suitable bride for their son, considered, among other things, their own personal future. A girl from the family of one of them was sure to be more loving and willing in her attentions when they themselves would be old and in need of her services. Thus, quite often, the bride chosen was related to the mother of the groom, a type of marriage which, although it occurred, was less usual among the Muslim Kurds.

In the household of her husband's father, the young bride was usually considered as a stranger "not of our blood." Should any issue arise, her husband would always side with his family against her. The fact of her marriage also weakened her ties with her family of origin, and one might say that the fate of the young wife was not an especially happy one.

Among the Kurdish Jews single people were virtually unknown. Widowers and widows tended to remarry after a short time. Divorces were rare and caused mainly by barrenness; usually both parties would remarry at once. Polygamy occurred, and might even have been more widespread than is generally assumed.

(2) The Baby

Every new member of the household was eagerly awaited, and the unborn baby would soon be one of the main topics for talk among the circle of women. Naturally there was a great many beliefs and usages concerning the pregnant woman, the act of birth, and the care of both mother and infant. The joy of the household would be boundless if the new-born was a son, especially the first of his father. Not only was he an additional bearer of the family name, but also, and mainly, a potential contributor to the earning capacity of the family. He would stay in his family of origin and take an active part in its upkeep. The father of many sons had many pairs of hands for work, a fact which assured his prosperity. He might look forward to an old age when he would be well provided for and revered as the head of a large and prosperous household. Since in these communities wealth and not learning was the criterion for social status, such a man would play a leading role in the affairs of his community.

Furthermore, there were instances in which conflicts in the community were settled by a show of force, each side enlisting as much active support as it could muster. Naturally it was at such times that the actual strength of each household, i.e. the number of its adult males, counted most. Thus the more adult males a household included, the more affluent it was and the more sought after would its head be as a potential wielder of influence. The wife of its head would be revered as the mother of many sons and could look forward to a time when she would rule a large household and direct many daughters-in-law in their daily tasks.

Not so happy by far was the lot of a father of daughters. After being fed and cared for during their early years, they would marry out just upon reaching the age when they were strong enough for work. Strangers would profit by their working power, and their sons would be born into other households. The father himself would be forsaken in his old age and his material fortune decline. Thus we may well understand the great disappointment felt when the child eagerly awaited was but a daughter. The disappointment was expressed quite openly. As the saying goes: "A son builds up the house; a daughter destroys it."

Generally a child was named after a relative, even if the latter was still living. Very often a firstborn son was called after his paternal grandfather. Usually the personal qualities of the person after whom he was named were attributed to the child, and the great resemblance in looks and deeds remarked on constantly. In the case where the relative after whom the child was named was especially loved or honoured, the child was accorded special privileges. The children knew about this special attitude which was expressed quite openly. A man might say: "I do love this girl; she is my mother."

Sometimes, when the day of a birth has any special significance, a child will be named accordingly. Thus a boy born on Purim would be named Mordechai, a girl Esther, etc. The circumcision is performed at home by the Mohel. Every community has a special stool upon which the child is laid.

During his early months the baby is made much of. In the case of a son, even the men of the household will stop to fondle it and play with it. As the women's work is done collectively, there is always a pair of hands to spare to take him up, fondle him, nurse him, or rock him to sleep. It would be quite unthinkable to allow a baby to cry any length of time. He is nursed whenever he is restless. He is rocked to sleep, swaddled in a special small wooden cradle or in a hammock hung from the ceiling.

(3) The Toddler

The child suffers a great change in these loving and warm relations when, as it reaches the age of a year or two, a new baby is born. Now he watches as another baby is fondled, made much of and fed, while he is thrust aside quite harshly. Nobody takes much interest in him and he is left to his own devices. When he is hungry, he has to be very persistent in his demands in order to arouse his mother from her conversation with the other women. He soon learns that the more insistent and aggressive his behaviour, the quicker she will be in her response to his demands. All outward signs of effect, such as throwing oneself to the floor, shrieking, crying and hitting one's head against something, prove useful in this respect.

The mother's attitude in these cases may perhaps be clarified by the following example. A 5 year-old boy snatched an old cigarette box from his 2 year-old brother who had been handling it contentedly for quite a while. Both burst into shrieks. Without much ado, the mother (who already had a new baby) took the box

and placed it firmly into the hands of the older boy.
Called upon to explain, she said simply that the
smaller one would forget the matter soon, while if she
had crossed the older one he would have continued to
shriek "for half an hour."

Though it is, of course, not our intention to show
a cause-effect relationship, it is worth while to
remember at this point the educational ideal of the
Kurdish Jews, which has been described above, namely,
that of an aggressive and stubborn man.

One will remember as part of this description that
women and children fall silent upon the husband's
approach. This silence typifies the behaviour of the
toddler always and everywhere. He is a silent participant in everything that happens in the household.
Never is he sent away as being too small. At birth,
death, wedding, circumcision, slaughter, always he is
there to observe, watch, and learn. But he must never
disturb. Even the women chatting while they work will
not stand for any noise or running about. Thus he
lives on the fringes of adult society, always present,
quietly observant, and completely passive.

(4) Boy Becomes Man

At about the age of 5 a new phase was reached in
the education of the boy. Except for the families who
lived in small villages without a Jewish Chacham, the
boy now went daily to the Knista where he learned with
the other boys of the community. Since, among these
practical people, all the other roles of the Chacham
were deemed more important than his educational one,
he was frequently called away from supervising their
studies. Furthermore, the teaching methods were
rather inefficient, so that the sum total of learning
gained was meagre indeed. Usually a boy needed a long
time in order to master the reading skill. He was set
to read the whole Pentateuch as a reading exercise
without any understanding of what was read. Only after
finishing this task, which took several years, did he
start to read the Pentateuch again aided by an older
boy who translated to him. But many quit before ever
reaching this stage. There were no holidays, and,
except for festivals, the boys spent the greater part
of each day in the Knista.

This was part and parcel of the attitude prevalent
among the Kurdish Jews towards the Knista and educa-

267

tion in general. There was very little belief in the possibilities of education as such. According to the Kurdish Jews, there is no way of training a child to refrain from the forbidden. With opportunity, the unwanted act is sure to occur. The Knista, then, is viewed not so much as an institution which imparts learning, as a place where the boy is kept under supervision and thus out of mischief. The long hours are to be viewed as a safety measure rather than as an effort at imparting knowledge.

In most cases, the teacher was not employed by the community but paid directly by the parents concerned according to an agreement reached individually in each case. As the teacher was the agent paid for educating the boy, he was considered the proper address for dealing with complaints about the boys' behaviour at all times. Thus, even misdemeanors committed in the home circle were often reported to him in order that he might punish the offender. The father, busy with gainful employment, thought it only right that the educational authority should be wielded by the one paid to do so.

In the small communities, where the ways of life were greatly similar and the value system was shared by all, the process of being educated was relatively simple. One had but to accept the prevalent normal values and behaviour which one well knew, since one had participated from early childhood in all that went on in the community.

At each stage of his development, the young boy knew what would be expected of him. If he acted accordingly, approval was sure to follow. If he did not, any adult member of the community was sure to point his error out to him. Education was not patterned to form an individual able to reach autonomous decisions of his own, but one willing to accept the supremacy of public opinion.

The stage looked forward to most eagerly by everyone concerned was that when, at long last, the son would join his father in work and turn into an earner. For the father, this was the attainment of his hopes, for now he had another pair of hands to work for his household and was one step nearer his ultimate goal of rising into the ranks of the secure and wealthy.

For the boy, the start of gainful employment meant a change of status from that of a child to that of a man. From now on his place would be among the men of the household, and he would be revered and served as such by women and children, although among the men he would remain for years to come the last and the lowest.

Last, but not least, even the Chacham saw in the early participation of the boy in the work of his father's household a practical solution to the dilemma which might arise if, after protracted studies, he were to become a contender for the position of his own sons as future Chachamim. Small wonder that Knista leaving age was low, and especially so in the case of the first born.

Also the Bar Mitzvah did not furnish any added motive for the continuance of study. Usually it consisted only of a morning visit by the boy and the male members of his immediate family to the synagogue where he put on the Teffilin for the first time. Occasionally a festive meal was held in the evening, at which time the boy was supposed to hold a Derasha. Generally each Chacham had a prepared one, which was declaimed by heart in turn by the various boys of the community. Furthermore, it was quite acceptable for the Chacham to take the place of his pupil should the latter have difficulties in mastering his task. Moreover it should be remembered that in these communities where learned men were scarce, gifted boys were called upon to read the Torah in synagogue, if they were able to do so, even before their Bar Mitzvah. Thus the Bar Mitzvah rite did not mark the attainment of any special skill or status, and did not furnish an incentive for special efforts.

(5) Girl Grows Into Woman

With the boy's leaving the compound for the Knista, there begins the separation of the sexes so typical of Kurdish Jews. From now on his way of life will differ radically from that of his sisters, and the opportunities for contact between them will be limited. For the girl, on the other hand, the identification with the group of working women becomes more pronounced. No longer will she be a completely passive observer of the goings on, but she will herself become a part of these happenings, though at first in a limited way only.

269

A young girl hovering on the fringes of the women's group will be used as a messenger by all her elders, being sent to and fro incessantly at their bidding. Nobody will bother to fetch anything if such a girl is at hand. As a further step she will be asked to perform simple tasks by herself such as carrying, cleaning floors, and minding small children, but no intricate tasks will be demanded of her until she reaches marriageable age. Cooking and the simple embroidery practised are deemed complicated and difficult. Might it not be that such an attitude prepares the young bride to accept eagerly her mother-in-law's instructions and facilitates a respectful attention to the woman who is so well versed in these tasks? These are sentiments which surely make for the harmony of the women's group.

Actually such an aim was never expressed, and might even seem preposterous to the Kurdish Jews, as the overt aim of the girl's education is completely to break any signs of self-will. A Kurdish woman ought not to have any will of her own but be only a tool of her husband. In the education of the girl and the attitude towards the young bride, this point is stressed again and again. One of the mothers exemplified it best when she raised her foot as if it were to crush her daughter's head beneath it. Thus should all will be crushed out of the young girl.

As the Kurdish Jews did not believe in the possibility of training children to refrain from the forbidden, the girl had to be confined most strictly to the compound as, given an opportunity, she was sure to err. Actually cases of misbehaviour did occur which ended mostly in the acceptance of Islam by the girl concerned.

In a society in which single people were virtually unknown, which allowed polygamy, in which widowers and widows remarried, and in which interest in sex was predominant, one must not wonder at the easy susceptibility of the young girl. After all, sex and love were the main themes of talk among the women, and to this talk she had been an avid listener for years.

NOTES

[1] Some Kurdish Jews still live in Iran.

[2] The landlord of the village. For a detailed discussion of his functions and scope of influence, see E. R. Leach, 1940.

[3] Targum forms the theme of prolonged and extended studies by Profs. Polotsky and Rivlin, the former to whom I am indebted for the information contained in this paragraph (Polotsky 1961).

[4] This language, also called Modern East Aramaic, has been studied repeatedly. The work of Lidzbarski and MacLean ought especially to be mentioned (see MacLean 1895).

[5] W. Fischel, 1949, 557.

[6] See Leach, op. cit.

[7] F. Barth, 1953. E. R. Leach, op. cit. E. Brauer, 1947.

[8] In this case the families concerned were "old timers."

[9] E. R. Leach, op. cit., 21.

[10] F. Barth, 1954, 168.

[11] Jews were forbidden to carry firearms.

[12] H. Granqvist, 1931.

BIBLIOGRAPHY

Barth, F.
1953   Principles of Social Organization in Southern
              Kurdistan. Oslo: Universitetets Etnografiske
              Museums Bulletin No. 7.

Brauer, Erich
1947   The Jews of Kurdistan (Hebrew). Jerusalem:
              The Palestine Institute of Folklore and
              Ethnology.

Fischel, Walter
1944   The Jews of Kurdistan. Commentary, 8:554-559.

Granqvist, Hilma
1931   Marriage Conditions in a Palestinian Village.
              Helsingfors: Societas Scientiarum Fennica.
              Commentationes Humanarum, III:8.

Leach, E. R.
  1940   Social and Economic Organization of the
                      Rowanduz Kurds. London: London School of
                      Economics and Political Science: Monographs
                      on Anthropology, No. 3.

MacLean, Arthur John
  1895   Grammar of the Dialects of Vernacular Syriac
                      as Spoken by Eastern Syrians of Kurdistan,
                      Northwestern Persia, and the Plain of Mosul.
                      Cambridge at the University Press.

Polotsky, H.
  1961   Studies in Modern Syriac. Journal of
                      Semitic Studies, 6:16-32.

Sara, Solomon
  1974   A Description of Modern Chaldean. The Hague:
                      Mouton.

CHAPTER 13

FAMILY CONFLICT AND COOPERATION IN
FOLKSONGS OF KURDISH JEWS

DONNA SHAI

> The author, who lectures in Middle Eastern
> Jewish folklore at the University of Penn-
> sylvania, amplifies our knowledge of Kurdish
> Jews by making use of their folksongs as
> texts for understanding their social world.
> Like many anthropologists, Shai assumes that
> words recited at important rites of passage
> like weddings and funerals reflect under-
> lying tensions which exist in the society.
> She is particularly concerned with the role
> of women among the Jews of Kurdistan. Con-
> trary to certain stereotypes, she finds that
> women could exercise considerable authority
> in certain spheres of activity, such as mate
> selection, and, like Feitelson, Shai's work
> shows the heterogeneous nature of the Kurdish
> region.

Folksongs of the Jews of Kurdistan appear in a
number of collections and studies. Brauer (1947) in
an ethnological study offers texts associated with
customs; Rivlin (1959) treats the songs from historical and literary aspects. In this article I
present folksongs in a discussion of some aspects of
social relations among Kurdish Jews in order to show
that such an approach can contribute to a fuller understanding of both the songs and the social world of
which they are a part. The texts included here were
collected from traditional singers of the Kurdish Jewish population in Israel, and were recorded in the
original languages, Neo-Aramaic and Kurmanji (Kurdish).[1]
The data on the social life of Kurdish Jews are based
on interviews and on field work carried out in Israel
during 1969-1970.

For the purposes of this paper, "cooperation"
refers to the mutual help which kinsmen extend to one

SOURCE: Original contribution for this volume.

another on family occasions and at times of need, and "conflict" to clashes of interest among kinsmen. "Family" is used here in the sense both of the extended family unit and families related by, or in the process of becoming related by, marriage. In order to examine the relationship between these concepts and the folksongs, I first describe the social setting: the Jewish community in Zakho, Kurdistan, and the social context of folksinging. I then discuss local cooperation and conflict which form the themes of many of these songs, and finally, I relate the role of the Kurdish Jewish woman in family conflict and cooperation to her image as it emerges in the folksongs.

The town of Zakho in the Mosul province of Iraqi Kurdistan was the location of an important Jewish community. Prior to immigration to Israel in the 1950's there was a Jewish population of 5,000 in the town. The household was comprised of the extended family unit of which the head was the father or, in his absence, the eldest son. As each son married he brought his bride into the family household where she would work together with the other daughters-in-law under the supervision of the mother. The age of marriage for girls was between thirteen and sixteen, while that of boys was between fifteen and twenty-two. There were polygamous marriages in the Zakho community including the practice of the <u>levirate</u>.[2] Marriages with up to three women were cited. The preferred marriage partner was the patrilineal parallel cousin, the most general form found in the Middle East. Unlike many Islamic cultures, however, the preferred cousin had no clearcut rights to a particular bride. Sons usually followed their father's trade and worked together as a family. The majority of Jewish men in Zakho engaged in various forms of commerce including merchants, spice dealers, peddlers, and artisans, particularly goldsmiths and weavers.[3]

The Jews of Zakho spoke a dialect of Neo-Aramaic which includes Turkish, Persian, Arabic and Hebrew words. Other languages which were used in Zakho included Hebrew, for the liturgical music of the synagogue, Arabic for secular songs taken over from popular urban music, and <u>Kurmanji</u> (Kurdish) for heroic epics, ballads and country dances.[4] The great majority of Kurdish Jews were illiterate and as an ethnic group they possessed no written literature of their own, neither religious nor secular. There was never a

Hebrew press in Kurdistan and no book had ever been printed in Neo-Aramaic or Targum. Very few hand-written works in Neo-Aramaic have ever been found.[5] No doubt related to this lack of written tradition is the fact that the oral tradition was very highly developed and the Kurdish Jews possess an oral literature which is remarkable in its abundance and high quality.

Among the Kurdish Jews, folksingers were specialists who were invited to perform on family and ritual occasions such as weddings, housewarming ceremonies and funerals. Much folksinging was done in a situation of communality, as on the evening when the roof was added to a new house; the work was done with singing, dancing and a communal feast which lasted until midnight.[6] It was especially at communal meals that secular and heroic songs were sung, many of which are related to ceremonies of engagement and wedding. The majority of these were in Kurmanji with very few in Neo-Aramaic. With the exception of the brit millah, very few Hebrew songs were sung at such gatherings.[7]

A striking feature of these songs is the recurrence of themes of family conflict and cooperation. Solidarity and mutual cooperation among kinsmen is one of the basic ideals among Kurdish Jews. This mutuality is fundamental to social life which is characterized by cooperative work, daily visiting, communal feasts and large gatherings of kinsmen at family ceremonials. Cooperation among kinsmen includes contributions to the expenses of a family wedding, and assistance, both preparatorial and ceremonial, for a family ritual function (see Shai 1970, Chapter Two). When a young man married in Zakho, his father and brothers worked jointly to finance the occasion including a substantial payment of brideprice to the bride's parents and obligatory gifts of gold jewelry to the bride. When his brother married in turn he would contribute to the expenses. This system of cooperation which permeated daily life is basic to the understanding of social relations among Kurdish Jews.

Social relations were open to conflict on various levels of interaction, conflicts which are inherent in constant interaction in a relatively limited group. Failure to fulfill obligations resulted in estrangement ranging from a temporary avoidance to a public display of aggression. Aggressiveness, although

275

considered reprehensible, is in fact regarded as
one of man's natural expressions. Feitelson (1959)
has described the educational ideal of the Kurdish
Jews as that of the aggressive and stubborn man.

One of the occasions on which family conflict and
cooperation are of particular significance is in the
preparations for and the carrying out of wedding rituals. Marriages in Zakho were arranged by the parents
of the prospective bride and groom. The father of the
groom made the formal request for the bride's hand,
and preliminary discussions were held between the
respective fathers to determine the brideprice. As
in many societies, brideprice was closely related to
matters of status; the payments increased with the
wealth and prestige of the bride's family. Included
in the brideprice were a specified amount of money and
gold in the form of traditional pieces of jewelry.
The engagement period lasted from six months to several
years depending on the time needed by the groom's
family to accumulate the brideprice. The bride's
parents, in turn, used the money to purchase the
bride's dowry which consisted of clothing, furniture
and household items. In the following song, traditionally sung by the groom's mother at sheekla-daveh
("beginning of the wedding") parties, the themes of
cooperation and joint effort come out clearly:

A s ng of the bridegroom
I will marry off my son
I will put henna on my hair
I am joyful
I am the mother of the bridegroom

I tell his father
Father, build a room
Make all the flowers roses
We are making a marriage
For our son

We say to the elder brother
Don't be joyful on the side
Today is the day of presents
That is your brother
Bring a present and come

I say to the second brother
Roll up your trousers
Go and bring the trousseau of the bride

> Today is our day of happiness
> Don't be joyful on the side
>
> They go, one brings the trousseau
> One goes and brings gifts
> One builds a room
> Father, sons, family, relatives
> All come and everyone does something else
>
> I am the mother of the bridegroom
> I henna my hair and dress every day in a
>   new suit
> Dance, and all the family is with me
> I am the mother of the groom
> I dance first and everyone else after me

It is interesting to note that in the song, as well as in social life, the groom's mother exercised a certain amount of authority <u>vis-a-vis</u> the men of the extended family. Also, the song emphasizes the differentiation of tasks and specific roles expected from each family member. The recurring phrase, "Don't be joyful on the side," suggests that while it was normative for the family members to work jointly and cooperatively on family occasions, nevertheless some coordination and direction was necessary to ensure that everyone did his share, and it would seem likely from the songs that this role belonged to the groom's mother. According to informants, in Kurdistan the wife of the household head decided matters concerning housework arrangements and her authority went unchallenged even by the men of the household.

The theme of mutuality among family members is expressed in other folksongs as well. In "A Dirge for Myself" the theme is that devotion among siblings should transcend death:

> When I die put my grave
> Next to my parents' house
> When my brothers will pass by
> In the morning and in the afternoon
> May they tell me, "rest in your grave,
> So you will be righteous in your grave,
> Our sister, a thousand times
> There will be rest for you in the grave"
> If I will dress in clothes
> And pass the house of my parents
> My brothers will see me and say

277

"What a sister we had--a pity that she died"
They will see me as I was,
And as I am dead
All day they will speak of me
My brothers loved me
All day they pass my grave

Mutuality was obligatory not only among brothers,
but also among kinsmen related by marriage, who were
expected to lend money to each other, to participate in
joint business ventures, and to help finance family
ritual occasions. Since an alliance through marriage
initiated a lifetime relationship of reciprocity and
implied equality in social status, the refusal to
marry a particular partner who was suitable from social
and economic aspects often engendered ill-feelings
between the families involved. In such a situation,
underlying tensions and conflicts of interest are
expressed, as in the following song usually sung at
the betrothal ceremony:

I am going to ask for a bride for my son
If they will give her
I will put her in the car and bring her
If they won't give her
With force and fighting
I will take her for my son
Why won't they give her to my son?
Do they want her to throw herself into
    the sea
Or isn't it better to give her my son?
I will go and ask for her from her parents
So that they won't cause difficulties
We are a family--the same as they
They are not better than us
We are better than they
The families are suitable
The boy and the girl suit each other
Do they want her to throw herself into
    the sea
Because of my boy, my child?
Let them marry so that we can have peace.

In Kurdistan, as in the Middle East generally, a
bride was absorbed into the household of the groom's
extended family so that in a certain sense she married
not only her husband but also his entire family. The
breaking of ties with her parents and the transfer of
loyalties to the groom's family were abrupt and com-

plete. In ceremony the groom, together with his kinsmen and friends, came to the bride's house in procession. The bride was brought out and placed on a
white mare amidst wailing by herself and her family.
The procession continued to the groom's house, porters
following behind bearing the bride's dowry. The
bride's parents did not accompany her to the groom's
house and took no part in the last wedding evening's
festivities. They remained at home where they dined
with notables from the Jewish community. The ambivalence of the bride at this abrupt separation is
expressed in a number of wedding songs, such as the
following:

> Why does the girl go hide
> Alone beneath the rock?
> Why is she shy?
> She should come
> We are all relatives now
> Her parents are no longer her relatives
> The groom's parents are her relatives
> She should not be shy
> Go Mother of the groom and bring her

and in another wedding song:

> You will cry enough, sleep more tonight
> Tomorrow you are going
> Say good-bye to your sister-in-law
> And your three brothers
> As much as you cry, it won't help you
> You are going
> Why are you running to the mountains?
> The bridegroom's parents are taking you
> Don't hide yourself, it won't help you
> To hide yourself in the mountains
> Come and go, it is best for you
> Why are you standing against the wall
>   crying?
> Go with the parents of the groom
> That will be best for you
> They take her and go

Reluctance to make the changes which the wedding
necessitated was also recognized as likely on the part
of the bride's parents, for on the way to the bride's
house to carry out the henna[8] ceremony, the women of
the groom's family sang:

> It is already late
> Father of the bride
> It is already late for us
> Let us take our bride
> And we will be on our way
> It is already the evening
> We are in a hurry
> Don't you want to give her to us?
> Quick, give her to us
> We are in a hurry
> We are going--it's getting dark

From the above songs we have seen that the role of the woman in ceremonies of cooperation and conflict is an important one. Many of the ceremonies which established relationships of mutual obligations between families, or which stressed conflicts of interests, were carried out by women. During the engagement period the groom's mother brought frequent gifts of food to the bride after the presentation of which both mothers danced before the assembled relatives. When the marriage certificate, or ketuba, was signed, the two mothers bargained to determine which pieces of jewelry were the bride's personal property and therefore to be listed in the ketuba as returnable in the event of divorce, and which pieces were to be excluded from the ketuba as the property of the groom's family. The inspection of the blood-stained marital sheet and its display before witnesses, a matter which affected family honor, was carried out by the women of the two families.

In ethnological sources the Kurdish Jewish woman is usually portrayed as being entirely subordinate to her husband's authority and living a life of unrelieved drudgery. For example, according to Brauer (1947):

> Even though occasionally there is
> among young girls an Eastern beauty,
> among women an attractive image is
> rarely found. The hard work, harsh
> treatment, multiple pregnancies, and
> conditions of primitive life detract
> early in a woman's life all charm
> and pleasantness. There remain the
> heavy lines of the typical farmer's
> wife. The Kurdish Jewess is not a
> delicate creature; in her feelings
> and emotions she doesn't display much

> of what we call feminine tender-
> ness...the wife is treated (by her
> husband) as a governor treats his
> subjects...

Contrary to the above view, it can be substanti-
ated both from field study among Kurdish immigrants
and from an analysis of their folklore that within
limited but important social spheres, women exercised
a considerable authority and that the image which
emerges from the folksongs is that of a strong and
dynamic personality. In Kurdistan the mother of the
family was responsible for settling quarrels within
the household and was regarded as a dominant figure
whose decisions were rarely challenged in this context.
Even in matters traditionally in the male realm among
Kurdish Jews such as the selection of marriage partners
for the sons, women could apply pressure against a
contemplated match through the use of interpersonal
techniques such as creating strain by quarreling with
the prospective in-laws. The breaking up of the
extended family and the division of family property
were usually attributed to quarrels among the women.
In folksongs we also find the woman portrayed as a
dynamic personality. There is a sense of intensity
in her actions, such as in the lines:

> I am going to ask for a bride for my son.
> If they will give her
> I will put her in the car and bring her
> If they won't give her
> With force and fighting
> I will take her for my son...

and:

> I am the mother of the groom
> I dance first and everyone else after me...

In the ballad, "Nemo Delale" (Nemo the Precious)
a young woman helps her father-in-law to build a
bridge by gathering huge stones and bringing them on
her back. When the bridge collapses time and again,
it is decided that the first living thing to step on
the bridge will be sacrificed. Nemo, who brings her
father-in-law his noontime meal every day, is the
first and is subsequently buried in the foundation of
the bridge. Thereafter, the bridge remains standing.[10]
According to tradition, this song is sung by her
family at her death:

Nemo came from the mountains
A stone on her back...
...
Nemo will bring stones
A stone on her back
And on her hand bracelets and jewelry
A stone on her back
Nemo is done with boyfriend and girlfriend
A stone on her back
And they cut off her hand
A stone on her back
She came from the fields and they killed her
A stone on her back
In the middle of the road she was abandoned
A stone on her back
Without boyfriend and girlfriend
A stone on her back
Her friends remain; a bracelet on her hand
A stone on her back...

Here we find the ideal of the woman as strong, beautiful, bejeweled, food-bearing and dutiful as a daughter-in-law, in short, an image which is eminently social. Nemo Delale is considered a heroine by Kurdish Jews who sing this ballad when a kinswoman dies young, substituting "Her children remain" for "Her friends remain". Again the emotions expressed bear little resemblance to the stereotype of the Kurdish Jewish woman as devoid of charm, tenderness and emotionality.

One of the conclusions which might be drawn concerning the subject of family conflict and cooperation in Kurdish Jewish folksongs is that while mutuality usually takes places in a social situation stressing generosity, warmth and gifts freely given, nevertheless these exchanges are not only obligatory but also highly defined. This is evident from the folksongs which enumerate specific roles accorded to particular family members as in "The Song of the Bridegroom" (supra). The folksongs express the underlying tensions inherent in a systematic exchange of services within a fairly limited group and where marriage is a part of this system, the tensions of rejected suitors, unwilling brides and reluctant parents.

The image of the groom's mother as it is expressed in folksongs sheds light not only on her social role in the coordination of family tasks, but also shows that contrary to stereotype, the Kurdish Jewish

282

woman was not completely subordinate to her husband but was authoritative in matters concerned with cooperation and conflict within and between families. Similarly, in the folksong "Nemo Delale," we find the woman described in positive, even herioc, terms. The image which predominates is that of a social order in which one's relationship with others is reckoned by participation in common interests and by the zealous guarding of one's own interests in an intricate set of social interactions. In conclusion, the songs are an inextoicable part of the society which produced them and they are of interest to folklorists not only as artistic creations but also for what they reveal about the way of life of a unique Jewish community.

NOTES

[1] The folksongs included here were recorded at the Kurdish Seminar held at the Mercaz l'Nafesh, Ya'ar Yerushalaim, January 14-24, 1973.

[2] Levirate: the custom of marrying a woman to her deceased husband's brother in order to procreate children "in the name of" the dead man. See Fox, 1967: 235.

[3] See Ben-Jacob, 1961: 15-20.

[4] See Encyclopedia Judaica, "Kurdistan": 1299-1300.

[5] Rivlin, 1959: 67-68.

[6] Brauer, 1947: 59.

[7] Rivlin, 1959: 71.

[8] Henna is widely used in the Muslim world as a prophylactic against the evil eye. Almost everywhere in that cultural sphere, one finds that one of the days before the marriage's consummation "is set aside for the ritual dyeing of the bride's hands and feet" with this reddish dye. (Encyclopedia of Islam, 3:461).

[9] Brauer, 1947: 150.

[10] For a discussion of the legend and ballad of "Nemo Delale" see Shai, 1976.

REFERENCES

Ben-Jacob, A.
1961

Kurdistan Jewish Communities. Jerusalem: The Ben-Zvi Institute, The Hebrew University. (In Hebrew).

Brauer, E.
1947

The Jews of Kurdistan: An Ethnological Study, (edited and translated by R. Patai). Jerusalem: The Palestine Institute of Folklore and Ethnology. (In Hebrew).

Feitelson, D.
1959

"Social Life of Kurdish Jews." Jewish Journal of Sociology 1:201-6 (in this collection).

Fox, R.
1967

Kindship and Marriage: An Anthropological Perspective. Harmondsworth, Middlesex: Penguin Books, Inc.

Nikitine, B.
1956

Les Kurdes: Etude Sociologique et Historique. Paris: Imprimerie Nationale.

Rivlin, Y.
1959

Shirat Yehudei Hatargum. Jerusalem: Bialik Institute. (In Hebrew).

Shai, D.
1970

Neighborhood Relations in an Immigrant Quarter: A Social-Anthropological Study. Jerusalem: Szold Institute.

_____
1974

Wedding Customs Among Kurdish Jews in (Zakho) Kurdistan and (Jerusalem) Israel. In Studies in Marriage Customs, I. Ben Ami, ed. Folklore Research Center Studies Iv. Jerusalem: Hebrew University.

_____
1976

A Kurdish Jewish Variant of the Ballad of "The Bridge of Arta". Association for Jewish Studies Review 1:303-310.

CHAPTER 14

PRESTIGE AND PIETY IN THE IRANIAN SYNAGOGUE[1]

LAURENCE D. LOEB

The author, associate professor of anthropology at the University of Utah, did fieldwork in Shiraz, Iran, in the late 1960's.
Conditions at that time do not, of course,
reflect traditional times, which terminated
with Pahlavi rule in the 1920's. In a provincial city like Shiraz, however, the pace
of change was slow. Loeb shows that besides
the religious aspects of the Persian synagogue, it was a major arena for status
juggling. Much social skill was needed to
participate successfully. This chapter is
valuable in providing us with a picture of
traditional Persian Jewish etiquette, a
subject that has hardly been touched by
other scholars.

Despite the frequent assertion by sociologists and
social historians that the synagogue is the central
institution in traditional Jewish society, there is a
remarkable dearth of competent description or analysis
of synagogue behavior. Most of the available material
is limited to a discussion of the synagogue's physical
structure and the ideal mechanics of its organization
and operation, but little has been said about process-
ural matters, although there is considerable insightful
fiction dealing with the American synagogue (Deshen
1969, 1970, 1972, 1974; Heilman 1975, 1976).

This article focuses on certain procedures of the
synagogues of Shiraz, a provincial city in southern
Iran, observed during 1967 and 1968.[2] Much of the
accompanying analysis is somewhat applicable to
behavioral patterns observed in other oriental as well
as some occidental synagogues. The procedures
described also supplement the literature currently
available on the formal mechanisms of Middle Eastern
face-to-face interaction and presents a perspective

SOURCE: Anthropological Quarterly 51 (1978): 155-161.
© Copyright 1978: Catholic University of America
Press. Reprinted by permission of Catholic University
of America Press.

on their function which differs somewhat from those
proposed by Bourdieu (1966) and Abou-Zeid (1966),
among others.

The Setting

Jews first settled in Iran during the 6th Century
B.C.E., and have probably been in the southwestern
province of Fars ever since. They constituted part of
the founding population of Islamic Shiraz in the 7th
Century C.E., where they have been an important
component of the urban population (15+%) until
recently (now less than 3%).

The Jews of Shiraz have been more harassed and
intimidated than most Iranian Jews and their lives
less secure than in many other places Jews have lived.
One result of frequent persecution has been the
inhibition of free social development, marked, for
example, by a lack of visible political structures
(Loeb 1977). Jews treated political power with
ambivalence, fearing involvement with the authorities.

The only social institution in which the entire
Jewish community participates is the knisa,
"synagogue,"[3] of which there are a considerable number
in the city. Here, largely concealed from the outside
world, men can vie for a measure of influence in
procedural decision making. The decision making
process culminates in a consensus only after the issues
have been disputed and factions formed to support the
contending personalities. The weight of communal
opinion depends primarily on the relative religious
and secular prestige of the protagonists. The main
"bone of contention" in Shirazi Jewish social life is
prestige; the elite (top ranked) have it and wish to
deny it to others. Everyone else wants a greater share.

Although Shirazi Jewish society is clearly not
egalitarian, neither can it be sharply demarcated
into bounded classes nor strata. Rather a ranking
system is operative, whose composite scale is the
product of several prestige scales. Prestige
(influence) is measured by indices of kin, affluence,
occupation, religious knowledge, piety and education.
Like Stirling (1965: 233), I am unable to derive the
precise rank of all Shirazis since: a) it is difficult
to evaluate the relative weight given the various

indices in each particular case, and b) prestige
fluctuates through accrual or loss of honor.

In the past, social mobility among Shirazi Jews
was very limited. Kinship, perhaps the most important
single factor in rank, is not subject to major alteration. Great wealth always guaranteed acceptance into
the elite, but wealth was unavailable to most potential
social climbers. Bettering one's occupation might
enhance one's prestige, but this alone did not
guarantee acceptance into the elite. Today, some can
circumvent the tedious struggle to achieve higher rank
by use of a shortcut, i.e., by becoming college-
trained professionals (doctors or engineers) or by
becoming high-level government employees. But for
most potential social climbers, only traditional
means are available.

Two traditional mechanisms which simultaneously
serve to: a) reinforce rank differences, and b) allow
social mobility are: ta'arof (the Persian code of
formal behavior) and the auctioning of kvodot (ritual
honors). Each of these is a procedure dealing with
transactions involving honor and will be considered
shortly.

Honor

Honor is understood to be a value associated with
relative prestige which may be exchanged in face-to-
face situations. It is also a valuation, composed of
two factors:
   1.   an individual's self-estimation
        (pride), i.e. his claim to rank;
   2.   society's acknowledgement of this
        claim (deference, respect) confirming
        his right to rank.

In Iran, as throughout the Middle East and circum-
Mediterranian, honor is the critical factor in social
relations (cf. Peristiany 1966). The Jew considered
devoid of honor as publicly insulted and forced to
suffer various indignities by the population at large.
Nevertheless, within Jewish community life, honor
with its traditional Persian ramifications, became an
essential complex in the Jewish value system. Despite
the Shirazi Jew's preoccupation with physical
survival--perhaps because real wealth and security

were unattainable goals--honor became as much sought
after as wealth.

Honor can be acquired, added to, saved, exchanged
and even spent (e.g. in exchange for loans, political
power, etc.). It is suggested that the whole system
of honor exchange could be fruitfully analyzed in
economic terms, but that is not the subject of this
paper.

The loss of honor (shame), no matter how slight,
is a very serious matter. The offended withdraws,
becomes sullen and often sulks by himself. He avoids
the offender at all costs. If amends are not made,
the offended individual may attempt to enlist support
and has been known to spread rumors about the
offender. Defense of one's honor is almost always
verbal. When, infrequently, outright anger ensues,
it is always contained before it reaches the point
of violence.

In this presentation, the concern is with personal
honor, which, in most situations among Shirazi Jews,
outweighs other kinds (e.g. family honor).

Ta'arof

Ta'arof refers to the Persian system of polite
formal behavior, verbal and non-verbal, by which means
honor exchanges are transacted in face-to-face
situations. Descriptions of ta'arof are found in
Chardin (1923: 188), Waring (1807: 101-3), Bishop
(1891, 1: 196-7) and Wills (1883: 28-32), among others.
It used to be most strictly observed by the elite to
reinforce rank differentiation, and it was considered
the model of proper behavior, much imitated by the
rest of the population.

Among the Jews of Shiraz, the elite is now affecting Western manners and less frequently initiates
ta'arof exchanges. In its pristine form, ta'arof is
best preserved among society's more conservative
elements: the aged, religious and poor. Shirazis have
maintained ta'arof to a degree rarely observed elsewhere in Iran.

The fundamental meaning of ta'arof, "offer,"
gives a clue to its most important process. The offer

may, for example, be in the street, when acquaintances meet: "befarmayid!"..."please" (come along, be my guest, etc.), by which the speaker implies that the other should accompany him to his house. Such offers are never accepted, nor are they meant to be.

A variety of offers are made in guest situations.[4] The guest is offered a seat of honor, bala, "up front," away from the entrance. He may then be offered (the order varies) the water pipe, tea, nuts, raisins, fruit and perhaps a meal. At the meal, the guest is offered the choice portions of food to the point of satiation and beyond, for the host may finally resort to placing the food in the protesting guest's mouth. The guest, on the other hand, no matter how hungry he is and no matter how little food he is given, must leave food on the plate to demonstrate that the host has been overly generous. Should a chance remark slip from the guest's mouth that some item belonging to the host pleases him, the latter will press the guest to accept it as a gift, for the host will declare: "manzel-e-man, khod-e-tun"--"my house is your own."

The target of the offer is expected to politely refuse it. Repeated offers are declined and great power of persuasion may be necessary to force their acceptance. If more than one guest is present, the initial target of the offers must attempt to defer the honor of acceptance to the others. Eventually, each person present will accept the offer in rank order, from highest to lowest. Should someone accept out of turn, everyone else who considers himself to have been slighted, with adamantly refuse to accept at all.

Ta'arof in Knisa

Ta'arof is the foundation of the traditional code of synagogue behavior. Thus, with regard to seating: the most prestigious sit nearest the western wall (in which the Tora scrolls are kept), away from the entrance. Synagogue "guests" are asked to sit bala and they accept a place befitting their rank.

The ta'arof mechanism is of central importance in one of the synagogue's critical procedures: the selection of the shaliah zibbur. The shaliah zibbur leads the congregation in worship. Each knisa has one

chief shaliah zibbur and several regular substitutes.
At some time or other, nearly every male, literate in
Hebrew, acts in this role. The chief shaliah zibbur,
who ranks high on indices of piety and learning, is
considered among the knisa's elite, although usually
not being wealthy, he ranks considerably lower in the
community's overall ranking. The opportunity to
perform as shaliah zibbur is eagerly sought after (as
it is among Jews all over the world), since it
identifies one as pious and learned, qualities highly
respected in Shiraz.

If the chief shaliah zibbur is present, he usually
begins by offering the honor of leading worship to
someone else, with the words: "aghaye so-and-so,
bakhavod"--"Mr. so-and-so, with the honor" (using the
Hebrew terms for honor). Mr. so-and-so declines the
offer and offers it back, or, less often, defers to
someone else. The chief shaliah zibbur may now offer
the honor to someone else, to several others, perhaps
returning to his original choice, or he may persist
immediately with his first choice. On Sabbaths and
holidays, the chief shaliah zibbur is expected to lead
the worship and the offers are then made performa,
since no one would accept the honor on these occasions.

This kavod (honor) is first offered to the
substitute shlihey zibbur. Next it is offered to
others in order of general rank, with somewhat more
weight given to knowledge of Judaica and piety than
in secular ta'arof situations. One need not wait to
be offered a kavod, but may take the initiative in
offering it to others at any time, providing one is
literate.

Such ta'arof is a game, albeit a serious one.
Its object is for the individual to accrue as much
honor as possible. One "scores" by: (1) accepting
the offer after much protestation, (2) deferring the
honor upward to the individual who accepts it, (3)
magnanimously bestowing it on someone lower in rank,
(4) pressing it on a near equal. All participants in
these exchanges gain honor, though in different
measure depending on their rank, posture during the
exchange, and other variables. Non-participants
suffer relative loss however slight. Because
illiterate congregants cannot participate in these
exchanges, the prestige gap between them and literate
congregants would be everwidening were there no
countering mechanisms in operation here, in knisa.

Things being equal, it is best to accept the honor offered (after appropriate refusal). One should not, however, accept an honor offered by someone very much higher in rank, should he make the mistake of offering it. He would appear to be mocking the recipient and this is frowned upon, both parties sharing a consequent loss of honor. The proper strategy is to defer the honor elsewhere, preferably upward, to avoid embarrassment. One may accept an honor offered from below, since such is one's due.

The ta'arof exchange for selecting a shaliah zibbur usually lasts 2 or 3 minutes. Only 8 to 10 men, out of a much larger congregation, participate in the selection. Men can inject themselves into the transaction at any point and do so. After the first exchanges, the participants usually sense who is eventually going to accept the kavod. The signs are subtle. The recipient's attempts at deferring are quieter and less convincing than those of the others. Instead of gesturing with the offer and looking toward the potential recipient, he will studiously look at the floor. Even if initial offers are not directed at him, he will initiate his own offers. In terms of total number, the eventual recipient tends to make more frequent offers than anyone else. In this way, he covertly proclaims that he wants the kavod, while he overtly demonstrates his modesty, apparently only accepting the honor because everyone is deferring to him.

One who has yerze'it, "memorial day," or is in mourning, may feel that he has a priority claim to this honor on a given day, without regard to rank. He may seize the honor without even perfunctory deferral, usually without loss of honor. Honor-gaining strategies also depend on mood. One may simply not want to act as shaliah zibbur and will instead accept a lesser honor by deferring. One of high rank may defer to one of lower rank who is more pious or learned or has a better voice. The elite need not participate at all, without penalty, since as Julian Pitt-Rivers (1966:37) put it, "Just as capital assures credit, so the possession of honor guarantees against dishonour."

Sometimes, one of low rank may cut through the ta'arof and seize the honor of leading the worship. Such mavericks lose more honor than they gain, since this is in violation of the rules. The ultimate loss of honor faces those who frequently resort to such tactics. They may be stopped by the ḥazzan, "overseer," of the knisa and asked to desist.

The Purchase of Kvodot

This is the second mechanism being considered. Kvodot (sing. kavod-lit. honor) are certain ritual acts and objects which are auctioned off in the knisa. These include: the opening of the ark and removal of the Tora, the various aliyot (being called to "go up" to the reading of the Tora), "ownership" of various parts of the knisa for specified periods (e.g. the eternal light), the right to lead certain prayers and (rarely) to act as shaliah zibbur.

The various kvodot are of unequal merit. Thus among aliyot the last, haftara, is the most important, followed by mashlim (next to last), shlishi (3rd), samukh (3rd from end), the 4th, 5th, etc. Some are restricted, e.g. the first one belongs to the kohanim, "priests," and rarely will a non-priest purchase it since he cannot make use of it himself. The absolute value of the kvodot varies with the occasion. On Yom Kippur, the Day of Atonement, they are worth most, on Sabbaths and holidays less, and during the week, least. In order to purchase and use a kavod, one need not be literate in Hebrew. Since during the weekday worship, the bidding is well within reach of the poor, this mechanism tends to be less exclusive than ta'arof.

The purchaser of a kavod demonstrates his wealth. This is the only traditional example of conspicuous consumption among Shirazi Jews. In the past, Jews were not permitted to own real property; household items, carpets, etc. were kept to a minimum, for fear that these would be seized by the Muslim population. Only within the confines of the knisa, through auctioning of kvodot, could one demonstrate relative wealth. The elite, who need not support their claim to honor, but fear to express lack of piety (as would be assumed if they totally abstained), try to purchase kvodot at low prices. The rest of the congregation competes to keep the bidding up, thus justifying claims to position on this most important "wealth" prestige scale.

The purchaser of kvodot demonstrates reverence for the knisa and Tora - important markers of piety - since the high bidder's money goes for synagogue maintenance and improvement. During mourning expecially, when the merit of these purchases accrues also to the decreased (at the same time protecting the purchaser from neshamot, "spirits," one buys many kvodot, thus testifying to one's respect for the dead.

The Social Climber in Knisa

Since the knisa is Shiraz' only public Jewish forum, the social climber exhibits a marked interest in synagogue problems. He becomes the vigorous defender of synagogue improvement. His attendance becomes more regular, if it has been erratic in the past. He tries to be friendly with those who sit bala. At weekday services, he gradually moves balatar (further from the entrance), often at the insistence of his new friends who ta'arof him to do so. He may eventually establish himself up front. He may also leave the Muhalleh (ghetto) knisa of his family and join a more prestigious one out on the main streets.

The social climber endeavors to call attention to himself for the "right" reasons. He enters knisa a few minutes late, puts on his zizit, "prayer shawl," and tfillin, "phalacteries," while loudly reciting the appropriate blessings. Worship is momentarily suspended as everyone replies "amen!" After receiving an "aliya" to the Tora, he like everyone else, waves the fringe of his zizit over the congregation and wishes them, "kulkhem tihya brukhim" - "may you all be blessed." Afterwards, he goes to the elders of the congregation, touches the fringe of their heads and kisses it, personally giving them this blessing.

The social climber must verify his claim to higher rank by demonstrating increased wealth. To solidify this ranking, he must prove his piety and by participating in synagogue ta'arof, constantly bettering his image and increasing his prestige.

The social climber participates frequently in the auction of kvodot. His bids are conspicuous and mostly directed to the more meritorious honors. He must have the audacity to challenge the very wealthy in the bidding. By outbidding the elite or forcing them to bid much higher than they would normally, he gains great honor. Another honor-gaining strategy is to outbid someone and then, after some ta'arof, bestow the honor on the opponent. The social climber gives evidence of benevolence by purchasing the honor for someone who cannot afford to bid for it. These last two strategies pay the added dividend of obligating the target of such generosity to reciprocate in some way.

The social climber clinches his claim to higher rank by showing that he is considered a near-equal by the elite, through participation in ta'arof exchanges with them in public.[5] A common vehicle for this exchange is the selection of the shaliah zibbur, previously described.

At first, no offers are made to him. The social climber must himself take the initiative by offering the honor to others. His moves must be subtle, to avoid appearing brazen. If he can establish himself as a respected shaliah zibbur, so much the better; but he should at least act the role on occasion. His aim is not so much being shaliah zibbur, as it is to regularly participate in the selection process, thereby benefiting from the continual (though lesser) honor of deferral. On occasion, by acting as shaliah zibbur, he can convince the congregation of his learning and piety, as he demonstrates his acceptance by the elite through direct ta'arof exchanges.

The underlying assumptions of the social climber is, by constantly adding small increments of honor, he can enhance his prestige and subsequently his rank: Accumulated honor → Increased prestige (influence) → Higher rank.

Conclusion

The manipulation of the appearance of piety by the social climber serves to both validate the primacy of piety within the hierarchy of Shirazi values, while maintaining the importance of rank distinctions within Jewish society. Since some indices of prestige are not with the province of personal control (e.g. family, wealth, etc.), individuals seeking to maintain or better their position within the community are often compelled to resort of the manipulation of prestige through pious behavior. This should not be cynically misconstrued to suggest that all public manifestation of piety is insincere, not that piety alone could suffice to raise one to high rank. Rather, for most Shirazis, because status (and all that accrues to it) is subject to upward and downward fluctuation and the most important public forum, the synagogue, is the nexus of community consent or dissent over its members' relative self-estimation, synagogue practice itself sets the parameters by which Shirazi Jewish men may be judged.

NOTES

[1] An earlier draft of this paper was presented at the annual meeting of the American Anthropological Association, 1969.

[2] The field work, upon which this article is based, was conducted in Iran from August 1967 to November 1968. Financial support was provided by the Memorial Foundation for Jewish Culture, the Cantors Assembly of America and the State of New York.

During a brief return visit to Shiraz in October, 1977, I observed that the formal behavior described here has diminished somewhat as the older generation dies out and younger generations assume responsibility for the synagogues. The relative ranking of my main informants seems to have changed little.

The data herein derives from participant observation and interviews of informants during the research period. At the time, Fredrik Barth's Models of Social Organization (1966) was not available to me, consequently, the application of "trans-actional-analysis" was not attempted in the field. I have been nevertheless highly stimulated by Barth and his critics, especially Paine (1974), in analyzing the procedures presented here.

[3] All of the foreign terms used in the article are utilized by the Shirazi Jews themselves. With the exception of Hebrew terms centering on ritual and the synagogue, the words are of Persian origin (see Loeb 1977:301-306).

[4]Among Shirazi Jews, the guest-house or guest-room is
not institutionalized. Guests are invited or come for particular
purposes or at specific occasions.

[5]The parallels between this behavior and potlatching are
duly noted. Even the purposed social ends attainable by both
procedures are similar.

BIBLIOGRAPHY

Abou-Zeid, Ahmed
    1966   Honor and shame among the Bedouins of Egypt. In
            Honor and Shame. J. C. Peristiany, ed.
            Chicago: University of Chicago Press.
Barth, Fredrik
    1966   Models of social organization. Royal Anthropological
            Institute, Occasional Paper No. 23.
Bishop, Isabella
    1891   Journeys in Persia and Kurdistan. London: John
            Murray.
Bourdieu, Pierre
    1966   The sentiment of honour in Kabyle society. In
            Honor and Shame. J. C. Peristiany, ed. Chicago:
            University of Chicago Press.
Chardin, Sir John
    1923   Sir John Chardin's travels in Persia. London:
            Argonaut Press.
Deshen, Shlomo
    1969   The ethnic synagoguge: a pattern of religious
            change in Israel. In The Integration of Immigrants
            from Different Countries of Origin in Israel.
            S. N. Eisenstadt, ed. Jerusalem: Magnes Press.

    1970   Immigrant voters in Israel: parties and congregations
            in a local election campaign. Manchester: Manchester
            University Press.

    1972   Ethnicity and citizenship in the ritual of an Israeli
            Synagoguge. Southwestern Journal of Anthropology
            28:69-82.

    1974   The varieties of abandoment of religious symbols:
            ethnicity and citizenship in the ritual of a
            synagogue of Tunisian immigrants. In The
            Predicament of Homecoming. Sholomo Deshen and
            Moshe Shokeid, eds. Ithaca: Cornell University Press.

296

Heilman, Samuel C.
    1975   The gift of alms: face-to-face almsgiving among
                Orthodox Jews. Urban Life and Culture 3:371-395.

————
    1976   Synagogue life: a study of symbolic interaction.
                Chicago: University of Chicago Press.
Loeb, Laurence D.
    1977   Outcaste: Jewish life in southern Iran. New York:
                Gordon and Breach.
Paine, Robert
    1974   Second thoughts about Barth's models. Royal
                Anthropological Institute, Occasional Paper No. 32.
Peristiany, J. C., editor
    1966   Honor and shame. Chicago: University of Chicago
                Press.
Pitt-Rivers, Julian
    1966   Honour and social status. In Honor and Shame.
                J. C. Peristiany, ed. Chicago: University of
                Chicago Press.
Stirling, Paul
    1965   Turkish village. London: Weidenfeld & Nicolson.
Waring, E. S.
    1807   A tour to Sheeraz. London: T. Cadell and W.
                Davies.
Willis, C. J.
    1883   In the land of the lion and sun, or modern Persia.
                London: Macmillan & Co.

CHAPTER 15

THE DOWRY AS CAPITAL ACCUMULATION AMONG THE SEPHARDIC JEWS OF ISTANBUL, TURKEY

MARK GLAZER

This chapter by Mark Glazer, professor of anthropology at Inter-American University, Edinburg, Texas, is comparable to the one by Loeb. Like Loeb, Glazer bases his contribution on fieldwork done in the 1960's. In the case of Istanbul, we deal with a much more dynamic social environment than Shiraz, so conclusions relative to traditional Turkish Jewry must be made very hesitantly. We, nevertheless, include this chapter because Turkish and Balkan Jewry is a virtual terra incognita for social scientists and, at the very least, this pioneering study will generate ideas for future research. The author dwells on the important function of the dowry in maintaining the cohesion of Istanbul Jews as a community of businessmen.

The dowry is the movement of women and goods in the same direction (Goody 1973:18). Or, as Tambiah puts it, "Wherever dowry is paid, wealth is not transferred in one direction and women in the other, for both wealth and women travel in the same direction" (1973:62). This one-sided exchange is rather curious as one side in the transaction gets all the values while the other seems to give them all away. A person who gives a dowry as a father has once received a dowry as a groom. As a consequence of his once being a receiver he has an obligation to his daughter to be the giver of a dowry. Unlike other types of wife-giving and wife-receiving, in this system it is individuals and not lineages or families who give and receive women. As a consequence alliances between families are not formed.

The giving of a dowry among the Jews of Istanbul serves two purposes: (1) assuring the economic future of one's daughters and (2) maintaining the status

SOURCE: International Journal of Middle Eastern Studies 10:373-380 (1979). © Copyright by Cambridge University Press. Reprinted by permission of Cambridge University Press.

of all the daughters and the giver of the dowry. Both
the important aspects of giving a dowry are stressed
by Goody when he correctly states that "daughters
had to be assured of a marriage that would provide
them with the same (or better) standard of life to
which they were accustomed" (1973:25). A very
important point made by Yalman must be added to this:
that the dowry links the woman's family with a
particularly desirable young man and not with any
young man (1967:175). Or, as Mair puts it, the dowry
"is the price, not of any husband, but of a particular
husband" (1971:70).

The dowry, especially in an urban context, also
becomes a capital accumulating device as it forces
the parents of daughters to accumulate money which is
utilized as capital for their daughters and sons-in-
law. For any community whose main source of income
is commerce this accumulation of capital is of major
importance.

This analysis[1] of the dowry among the Sephardic
Jews of Istanbul, Turkey, aims to shed some light on
the dowry as an institution in an urban setting. The
dowry is prescriptive in this community and a part of
the marriage contract. It is also used as a means
of acquiring capital. The dowry is not paid among
the Muslim Turks of the country; they pay a bride-
price in the rural areas of the country and neither
the dowry nor bride-price in urban areas.

The Jews of Turkey numbered 38,267 in 1965 with
30,831 of them living in Istanbul (Lewis 1974:212-213).
It is estimated that today more than 28,000 are
Sephardic Jews. A large number of them still speak
Ladino. The official estimate is that 9,981 persons
speak Ladino as their mother tongue (ibid., p. 212).
As Lewis points out, young Jews in Turkey speak
Turkish perfectly (ibid., p. 215). It must be pointed
out, however, that until very recently Turkish was a
second language in this community.

The Sephardic Jews of Istanbul are a traditional,
urban society in spite of the modernization that has
been part of recent Turkish history. This community
lives in a few middle-class or well-to-do areas of
the city and not in a ghetto. Unlike peasants or
other groups within a traditional society, this group,
made up mostly of small businessmen, found itself

300

ideally situated to absorb modernization without
change in many major aspects of its traditional life.
Until recently only few changes have taken place in
family life and spoken language. There have, however,
been important developments in the economy of the
community. With the economic development of Turkey
the Jewish small businessmen expanded their businesses
as they found themselves well situated for international trade and for industrialization. The dowry,
an existing tradition, then became a very important
aspect of this economic development, for it provided
the community with three major economic advantages:
(1) the development of a man's business potential,
(2) the security and economic future of daughters,
and (3) a capital-accumulating and -investing device
with sociocultural and traditional roots. It must be
added that among the poorer families the dowry exists
for similar reasons but with modest amounts of money
being exchanged.

The Sephardic Jews of Istanbul traditionally
used the dowry as the bride's share in a family
economy. On the other hand, for a man the dowry is
capital outside his inheritance and to be obtained
as a young man rather than as a middle-aged one.
This aspect of the dowry became even more important
after 1946 when the economic growth of Turkey made
the accumulation of capital necessary for business
expansion. For example, in 1952, a young man of
limited means married a young woman with a small dowry.
Without it he had no chances of becoming a proprietor
or partner in a business. With that small dowry in
a time of business expansion and inflation he was
able to develop a business that is still alive and
doing well. Twenty years or so later he was able to
marry off his daughters, and the dowries his sons-in-
law received were larger than the one he had received
a generation before.

The dowry is closely associated with the socio-
economic structure of the community. Until very
recently the elite were educated in French or other
foreign schools. Better educated, they control the
internal affairs of the community and are
usually economically better off than the rest. Most
of the members of the elite are businessmen or professionals, and in the past few years some industrial-
ists have been added. Well-educated but economically
less well off individuals are also accepted as part

of this class. The next group is composed of very wealthy but not well-educated businessmen. People in this group speak Ladino rather than French. The next class is made up of middle-income businessmen who speak Ladino. The poorer individuals of the community are clerks who work for Jewish businessmen. Marriages usually take place between individuals whose parents have similar amounts of wealth; dowries are therefore proportional to wealth. Most of the poorer families have now emigrated to Israel so that this discussion is mainly about the elite families of the community. Dowries are, however, still given among the remaining poorer families.

A young man who comes from a high-class family that has money expects a large dowry. Or, as they say in Turkey, "Money attracts money." It must be emphasized that a groom's ability in business is also very important in determining the size of the dowry he is to receive. In his analysis of the dowry in India and Ceylon, Tambiah points out that the groom's occupation, not the size of his inheritance, is the decisive factor in the determination of the dowry; the same is true among the Sephardic Jews of Istanbul where businessmen get larger dowries because of their personal ability to make money, not because of their inheritance (Tambiah 1973:63-64).

The dowry, in such cases, functions as an equalizing factor within the community. This may also be regarded as a type of hypergamy for men; it gives a poor man the ability to move from a lower economic strata to a higher one as a consequence of his personal abilities. It does not, however, create the stress on family finance which results from hypergamy among the Indians of Uganda (Morris 1968:96, 194-195). It also serves as a means of social advancement. On the other hand, there are huge dowries which are topics for gossip for a very long time. These are usually given by the nouveau riche who hope to gain status by giving enormous dowries for their daughters. In such cases the merits of the groom are less important than the wealth of his father-in-law. For example, in the early sixties a young man who was regarded by the people who knew him as both a good businessman and a man of good character (he also spoke French fluently, still socially important), married the daughter of a very wealthy businessman. The dowry he obtained was excellent, but he had already proved to the business community that he had the ability to use the money well.

There are a very few marriages where no dowry is involved. They involve rich men over thirty whose parents and relatives are so afraid that their sons will not marry that they forgo the dowry. These men usually marry young women with desirable class affiliation but without a dowry. But even then a minimal dowry has to be put into the marriage contract. A case in point is that of a man of thirty-four (1960) who was well established as the manager of his father's business, but he was not married and his family was desperate. His father felt that obtaining a dowry was of no importance. His married younger sister felt that unless he married soon he would become a burden to his family. He was consequently introduced to an attractive woman in her early twenties who was well educated but whose father had no dowry to give to a prospective son-in-law. After considerable pressure from both families, they were married.

The dowry normally assures the bride a husband of her own socioeconomic and educational background. It also assures her livelihood as she expects to do no work outside her house. In instances of bride-price the labor of the bride is added to the labor force of her husband's family. The bride's father pays a dowry so that his daughter will not have to work out- side the household. He also hopes that she will be able to maintain her accustomed way of life or, hopefully, improve it. As a matter of fact, the father hopes that the groom will make enough money to hire a maid. In other words, the hope is that the bride will not have to be gainfully employed or do many domestic chores. If a woman has no children it can legally be a reason for divorce, but rarely does infertility alone lead to divorce. In the only case of divorce for infertility I know about, the man was the cause, not the woman! To return a dowry and start a business enterprise all over again seem to be too complex and costly for divorce to take place in cases of infertility. The obligation to pay a dowry for one's daughter is found not only here but also in Greece and India (Friedl 1962:53; Mair 1971:72). A man must give the best dowry he can. A man who gives a lesser dowry for his daughter is considered not to have properly fulfilled his obligations toward his family, a situation that leads to loss of status and face.

In a community where businessmen predominate, the accumulation of capital is of crucial economic importance. The Sephardic Jews of Istanbul accumulate capital for their own business, for use as their daughters' dowries, and as capital for their sons-in law. The proper marriage of a daughter is a capital-accumulating motivation in this community. It assures a constant saving of wealth that as a consequence of marriage is used as capital. Without the dowry fathers would have less motivation to accumulate additional capital. The main function of the system is to assure the marriage of daughters. The con-sequence of this motivation is the accumulation of additional capital which is of major importance to a community where commerce is the major occupation. It is also obvious that for many young men this is an opportunity to succeed in business early in their careers.

Marriages among the Sephardic Jews of Istanbul used to be arranged by the family. The amount of the dowry was agreed upon, and, after an engagement period of a year or two, marriage and the payment of the dowry would ensue. This pattern has remained almost the same. The most important change is that arranged marriages have become the exception rather than the rule. Young people now meet each other without the help of their parents or matchmakers.

Young people meet in two types of situations. One is membership in Jewish youth organizations. Although none of these organizations (these include cultural organizations and Jewish welfare organizations) have the marriage of young people as one of their goals, they act as agencies where young people meet. In these organizations friendships and courtships are regularly initiated and many of these result in marriages. The second way young people meet is through the formation of small groups who get together for entertainment (going to movies, Saturday after-noon parties, and occasional picnics in the spring).

Once a young man and a woman meet, their next step is often to see each other to the exclusion of others. This relationship can sometimes become a continuous one, and in such cases it is said that the

parties are in love. The situation is then ready for
engagement proceedings. By this time the young man
knows the family of his probable bride quite well
because he has been in and out of their house in order
to escort their daughter. He has also heard, any
gossip involving his situation from the young woman's
friends and relatives. Through the gossip he finds
out whether or not the girl's parents find him a
suitable match for their daughter. If he is from
approximately the same socioeconomic background and
a promising young businessman or professional, he
knows that if he wants to marry their daughter he will
not have any major obstacles. If he decides in favor
of marriage he declares his intentions and a meeting
between his family and the girl's family is arranged.
This meeting is usually attended by the young man,
his father, and either a close relative or friend of
the family, the girl's father, and a close relative
or friend of the father. The terms of the dowry are
normally dediced during this meeting. It may, however,
take more than one meeting to decide on these terms.
If the parties agree, an engagement ensues. If they
do not, the courting couple usually separates. This
resembles the situation among the Namboodiri Brahmans
of Kerala where unless a dowry can be arranged no
further plans are made for the marriage (Mencher and
Goldberg 1967:98).

The dowry includes some kind of capital for the
young man. It can be money, or a partnership in his
father-in-law's business, or a small manufacturing
enterprise. Quite often a flat, and all its furniture,
in an apartment building are part of the dowry. Among
poorer families, a year or two of rent and furniture
may be part of the arrangement. Sometimes meals at
the bride's parents' house for a year or more are
arranged. The value of these transactions is sometimes
quite large: with money-making capital, a flat, and
furniture, a dowry can come to a few hundred thousand
dollars. On the other hand, a small dowry is around
ten thousand dollars. The dowry arrangements among
the Sephardic Jews are highly complex and obviously
include much more than a lump of money which is the
case among the Namboodiri Brahmans of Kerala (Mencher
and Goldberg 1967:98).

Once the terms of the dowry have been set an
official engagement party is arranged. It usually is
a rather large and elaborate affair with guests from

both families and friends of the couple. The engagement lasts about a year. If the young man has not
served his military service, the engagement lasts for
the duration of his service, which is eighteen months
in Turkey. Marriage closely follows his return to
civilian life.

One example of a rather large dowry is that
between the son and daughter of two well-to-do families
in 1964. The two young people had met in a Jewish
cultural organization and had gone out together as
part of a group of friends. After approximately a
year or so of "flirting" (this is what it is called
by this community) the parents of the couple decided
that it was time to arrange an engagement or break
"the flirtation." The young man, his father, and a
well-respected cousin (a leader in community affairs)
of the young man's mother met with the girl's father
and another respected member of the girl's family.
In this instance it was considered that although the
girl's family was richer, the boy's family was from a
higher class, or socially viewed as such. This young
man, however, had no particular business experience
and the future father-in-law was reluctant to give him
control over large sums of money. The following
arrangements were made: (1) a small radio factory
would be established in the name of the young couple;
(2) the technical aspects of the factory would be
run by a technician while the business arrangements,
including sales, would be managed by the father-in-law
until the groom learned the trade; (3) the groom
would draw a good salary from the business; and (4) the
father-in-law would buy and furnish a condominium for
the young couple. The salary agreed upon was $500.00
a month, the condominium and the furniture cost
approximately $40,000.00, and I estimate the factory
as having cost approximately as much as the condominium.

The engagement period has two important goals.
The young man and woman have to get along well, and
their families must feel relatively certain that the
marriage will not end in divorce. The breaking of an
engagement is accepted by the community, and there is
no stigma attached to it. It is considered that
people are better off if they separate during their
engagement rather than later when they have children
and when they will also have problems with the repay-
ment of the dowry. The second goal of the engagement

period is that it permits the bride's father to fulfill the terms of the dowry. The dowry is paid at the
time of the marriage. This gives the father of the
bride about a year to fulfill his obligations. Some
of the probable items on the dowry may take some time
to buy and prepare. For example, the selection of a
flat in an apartment building and furnishing the flat
obviously takes some time. Furniture is not bought
read-made in Turkey but is specially ordered. The
bride's father tries to have the dowry ready by the
time of marriage. If it becomes clear that he will
not be able to come up with the dowry within the
year the couple is engaged, the engagement may be
broken by the prospective groom or by his father.
This is accepted as a legitimate reason for breaking
an engagement.

The dowry is usually controlled by the husband
as he has the know-how to use the money as capital.
It is not, however, his money as he has to return it
in case of divorce. Divorce has become more common
among the richer Jews of Istanbul in the past ten
years, and there have been cases where the dowry has
not been returned to the father-in-law. Yalman
points out that among the Sinhalese the father-in-law
retains some control over the dowry; much the same is
true of the Sephardic Jews of Istanbul (Yalman 1967:
174). The husband does not always control the dowry;
sometimes the father-in-law makes him a partner,
and in those cases the husband and wife become
dependent on a monthly allowance from her father.
Although a legal partner, the husband may find himself
totally alienated from his work by being delegated to
unimportant business duties. The newlyweds are, however, provided with a livelihood and living arrangements of their own. The capital savings of the wife's
father have made possible a new nuclear and neolocal
family.

Conclusions

The dowry among the Sephardic Jews of Istanbul is
a complex, multifaceted institution. In this Jewish
community women and capital flow from father-in-law
to son-in-law. In exchange for this the bride's
father is assured of (1) the marriage of the daughter
and (2) the continuous financial support of this
woman by her husband. A woman in this community is

not to work and so has to have a husband to support
her. Through the dowry this support is assured. In
the generations to come all men who have daughters
have to pay a dowry themselves. In other words, men
are both receivers and givers of dowries in different
phases of their life cycles. As a consequence of
paying the best dowry, the father of the bride can
maintain his status, and he hopes to maintain that
of his daughter.

In the Sephardic community of Istanbul the dowry
also functions as a means of providing the groom with
capital which he greatly needs in this community of
businessmen. To be able to provide the groom with
capital, money must be saved and accumulated by all
fathers who have daughters which creates a regulated
accumulation of capital in this community whose livelihood is dependent on commerce.

The giving of a dowry in this community has three
goals: (1) the assurance of a woman's livelihood
through marriage, (2) the enhancing of the prestige
of the giver of the dowry, and (3) the providing of
capital to the groom. The consequence of all three
of these goals is the accumulation of capital, an
item of major importance in a community whose existence
is based on commerce.

NOTES

[1]The data utilized in this paper were collected in
Istanbul between March 1963 and March 1965. Contacts with the
Sephardic community were resumed during the summer of 1974 (both
in Turkey and in Israel) and of 1975.

LIST OF REFERENCES

Friedl, E.
    1962   Vasilika. New York: Rinehart and Winston.
Goody, J.
    1973   Bridewealth and Dowry in Africa and Eurasia.
                  In J. Goody and S. J. Tambiah, eds., Bride-
                  wealth and Dowry. Cambridge: Cambridge
                  University Press.

Lewis, B.
  1974   Modern Turkey. New York: Praeger Publications.

Mair, L.
  1971   Marriage. Harmondsworth, Middlesex, England: Penguin Books.

Mencher, J. D., and Goldberg H.
  1967   Kinship and Marriage Regulations Among the Namboodiri Brahmans of Kerala. Man, 2: 87–106.

Morris, H. S.
  1968   The Indians of Uganda. Chicago: University of Chicago Press.

Tambiah, S. L.
  1973   Dowry and Bridewealth and the Property Rights of Women in South Asia. In J. Goody and S. J. Tambiah, eds., Bridewealth and Dowry. Cambridge: Cambridge University Press.

Yalman, N.
  1967   Under the Bo Tree. Berkeley, Los Angeles, London: University of California Press.

RECOMMENDED READINGS

Those who would like to continue their study of traditional Middle Eastern Jewish communities can find the following items of value. We have stressed works, mostly in English, which follow the lines we have used in selecting articles for this volume, but some other works are included because of their importance in the early study of the area.

I. General Introductions to the Middle East

Eickelman, Dale F.
    1981   The Middle East: An Anthropological Approach. Englewood Cliffs: Prentice-Hall.

Gulick, John
    1976   The Middle East: An Anthropological Perspective. Pacific Palisades: Goodyear.

(Both of these works provide up-to-date overviews of the Middle East as a whole, both over time and space.)

II. General Works on Middle Eastern Jews

Ben-Zvi, Yitzhak
    1957   The Exiled and the Redeemed. Philadelphia: Jewish Publication Society of America.

(The late President Ben-Zvi took an active interest in the study of Jews in Middle Eastern countries and the institute named in his honor has been a center for their study. This book reveals his own outlook on these communities.)

Cohen, H. J.
    1973   The Jews of the Middle East 1860-1972. Jerusalem: Israel University Press.

(A historical account, concentrating on the Fertile Crescent, Turkey, Egypt and Iran.)

Goitein, S. D.
    1955   Jews and Arabs. New York: Schocken (latest edition, 1974).
    1969-   A Mediterranean Society: The Jewish
    1978   Communities of the Arab World as Portrayed in the Documents of the Cairo Geniza. Berkeley & Los Angeles: University of California Press. (Three volumes to date).

(While these works of Goitein concentrate on the early and
middle Islamic periods, they reflect his general overview
of Jews in the Middle East as a whole. A Mediterranean
Society has become the key work in the study of medieval
Jews under Islam and is invaluable.)

Noy, Dov (ed.)
    1963   Folktales of Israel. Chicago: University
                    of Chicago Press.

(A sample of Jewish tales including many from the Middle
East.)

Patai, Raphael
    1971   The Tents of Jacob. Englewood Cliffs:
                    Prentice-Hall.

*See
now
Seeds
of
Abraham*

(Again the work of a pioneer in Jewish ethnography. This
is a general survey of Jewish communities, including those
of the Middle East. His conclusions should be seen as
hypotheses for further study, not as reflections of current
thought.)

Stillman, Norman A.
    1979   The Jews of Arab Lands: A History and
                    Source Book. Philadelphia: Jewish
                    Publication Society.

(Covers the span of Jewish-Arab relations into the 19th
Century. This book provides readings from many sources
in different languages. Many of the 19th Century accounts
are by European observers.)

The Jewish Encyclopedia.
    1903-7   New York: Funk & Wagnalls.

Encyclopedia Judaica
    1971   Jerusalem: Keter Publishing Company.

(These two reference works are, as would be expected,
uneven in quality. Still, one can learn much by looking
up Middle Eastern countries, cities, and individuals.
Much of the material is unavailable in other English
language sources.)

Talmage, Frank (ed.)
    1980   Studies in Jewish Folklore. Cambridge,
                    MA.: Association for Jewish Studies.

(The proceedings of a conference in which leading figures in folklore and ethnology in the United States participated. Some items will be cited further on. The conference included experts on both Europe and the Middle East.)

Tobi, Yosef, Shalom Bar-Asher and Ya'akov Bernai
    1981   The Jews of the Middle East. Jerusalem: Shazar Center.

(A Hebrew textbook dealing with the communities of Yemen, Iraq, Iran, North Africa, Egypt and Turkey in the 18th-19th centuries, including many primary sources.)

Zimmels, H. J.
    1958   Ashkenazim and Sephardim. London: Oxford University Press.

(A general introduction to the relations between Jewish communities emphasizing ritual differences. Stresses the European context.)

Morocco (West of the Maghreb)

Bowie, Leland
    1976   An Aspect of Muslim-Jewish Relations in Late 19th Century Morocco: A European Diplomatic View. International Journal of Middle Eastern Studies 7:1:3-19.

(An account stressing the upper class of Moroccan Jewry in the main cities.)

Brown, Kenneth L.
    1976   The People of Sale: Tradition and Change in a Moroccan City, 1830-1930. Manchester: Manchester University Press.

(While concentrating on the Muslims, gives a good picture of the context in which the Jews existed in urban Morocco.)

Chouraqui, Andre N.
    1973   Between East and West: A History of the Jews in North Africa. Philadelphia: Jewish Publication Society.

(A popular history of North African Jewry as a whole seen from the perspective of a French-educated writer.)

Deshen, S.
    In Press   Individuals and the Community: Jewish
                    Society in 18th-19th Century Morocco.
                    Tel Aviv: Tel Aviv University.

(A Hebrew work based primarily on rabbinical materials.)

Flamand, Pierre
    1959   Diaspora en Terre d'Islam: Les communates
                    Israelite du Sud-Morocain. Casablanca:
                    Presse d'Imprimeres Reunies.

(An account of Jewish life in the Berber hinterland during
the French colonial period.)

Hirschberg, H. Z.
    1974   A History of the Jews in North Africa.
                    Vol. I, Leiden, Brill.

(A synthesis of North African Jewish History. Vol. II
is still only available in Hebrew.)

Rosen, Lawrence
    1972   Muslim-Jewish Relations in a Moroccan City.
                    International Journal of Middle Eastern
                    Studies 3:4:435-449.

Stillman, Norman A.
    1975   Muslims and Jews in Morocco: Perceptions,
                    Images, Stereotypes. Proceedings of the
                    Seminar on Muslim-Jewish Relations in
                    North Africa. New York: World Jewish
                    Congress, pp. 13-39.

(Two sides to the controversy on the character of Jewish-
Muslim relations in North Africa, which was discussed in
Meyers' article above.)

Shokeid, Moshe
    1971   The Dual Heritage. Manchester: Manchester
                    University Press.

(Follows immigrants from the Atlas Mountains to their
adjustment in Israel.)

Willner, Dorothy and Margot Kohls
    1962   Jews in the High Atlas Mountains of
                    Morocco: A Partial Reconstruction.
                    Jewish Journal of Sociology IV:2:207-241.

(An account stressing childbearing and women's roles.)

The Eastern Maghreb (Tunisia and Tripolitania)

(The accounts of Chouraqui and Hirschberg cover much of
this area as well.)

Briggs, L. C. and N. L. Guede
  1964   No More Forever -- A Saharan Jewish Town.
                Cambridge, MA.: Peabody Museum of
                Archaeology and Ethnology. Harvard Univer-
                sity: Papers LV:1.

(A Jewish community studied on the eve of its emigration
from Algeria. Briggs has been a pioneer in Saharan
anthropological research.)

Goldberg, Harvey E.
  1972   Cave Dwellers and Citrus Growers: A
                Jewish Community in Libya and Israel.
                Cambridge: Cambridge University Press.
  1981   Mordecai's Story: Philadelphia: Institute
                for the Study of Human Issues.

(Goldberg's first chapter in the 1972 book gives his first
synthesis of material on the Tripolitanian communities,
while in his translation of Mordecai HaKohen's "native"
ethnography, he gives an account of the state of the art
of Maghrebi Jewish ethnology.)

Memmi, Albert
  1961   Pillar of Salt. New York: Orion Press.

(Memmi's novel gives us a picture of Jewish life in Tunisia
during the 1930's and 1940's when Jews stood between
assimilation to the French way and a nascent Arab nationalism provides an additional perspective.)

Udovich, A. L. and L. Valence
  1980   Identite et communication a Djerba.
                Annales nr. 3-4:764-783.

The Fertile Crescent (Egypt, Syria, Iraq)

Baron, S. W.
  1940   Great Britain and Damascus Jewry, 1860-61.
                Jewish Social Studies 2:179-seq.

(The status of Jews in Damascus at the time of the Lebanese massacres of 1860 is delineated in both local and international terms.)

Ben-Ya'akov, Abraham
1965   A History of the Jews in Iraq. Jerusalem (Hebrew).

(A history of the Jews in that important, albeit understudied, community.)

Kedourie, E.
1971   Jews of Baghdad in 1910. Middle Eastern Studies 7:355-361.

(An account of the Baghdadi community is culled from British diplomatic sources.)

Landau, Jacob
1969   Jews in 19th Century Egypt. New York: New York University Press.

(A Jewish community undergoing incorporation into the modern world, including European immigration.)

Livingston, John W.
1971   Ali Bey al-Kabir and the Jews. Middle Eastern Studies:7:221-228.

(The rivalry of Jews and Greek Catholics in Egypt for some high government jobs during the late 18th Century.)

Sassoon, David Solomon
1949   A History of the Jews in Baghdad. Letchworht. Hertz.

(An old fashioned community history by a member of a distinguished Iraqi Jewish family.)

Shamosh, Amoon
1979   My Sister, the Bride: Stories. Tel Aviv: Massada (English translation).

Sutton, Joseph A. D.
1979   Magic Carpet: Aleppo-in-Flatbush. Brooklyn: Thalyer-Jacoby.

(Both Shamosh and Sutton are Aleppo emigres. The former is a short-story writer living on a kibbutz writing in

Hebrew. The latter is a retired businessman who had
written an account of Aleppo Jews in metropolitan New York
City. Both works contain portraits of how Jews remember
that north-Syrian metropolis.)

Yemen

Goitein, S. D.
1955   Portrait of a Yemenite Weavers' Village.
                Jewish Social Studies 16:3-26.
1980   Research among the Yemenites. In
                Studies in Jewish Folklore (F. Talmage,
                ed.), Cambridge, MA.: Assoication for
                Jewish Studies, 121-136.

(The first piece of an ethnographic reconstruction, based
on interviews with Yemeni immigrants to Israel at the
time of the mass migration in 1949. The second consists
of Goitein's reflections on his Yemeni research during
the 1920's, 1930's, 1940's and 1950's.)

Loeb, Laurence D.
1980   Jewish Life in Habban: A Tentative Re-
                construction. In Studies in Jewish Folk-
                lore (F. Talmage, ed.), Cambridge, MA.:
                Association for Jewish Studies, 201-218.

(This describes life on a South Yemeni oasis, the eastern-
most outlier of Yemeni Jewry on the Arabian peninsula.)

Tobi, Yosef
1976   The Jews of Yemen in the 19th Century.
                Tel Aviv (Hebrew).

(Like several other recent histories cited here, this
one is untranslated.)

Kurdistan

Ben-Ya'akov, Avraham
1961   Kurdish Jewish Communities. Jerusalem:
                Ben Zvi Institute (Hebrew).

(An untranslated account. Much material is presented but
not analyzed.)

Fischel, Walter J.
          The Jews of Kurdistan 100 Years Ago. Jew-
          ish Social Studies 6:196-226.

(A historic account of the "northern tier" of Middle
Eastern Jewry, not just Kurdistan.)

Magnarella, Paul J.
    1969   A Note on Aspects of Social Life among
                the Jewish Kurds of Sanandaj, Iran.
                Jewish Social Studies 11:1:51-58.

(A somewhat naive reconstruction done by an anthropologist,
then a graduate student, on the less-studied Iranian
Kurdish Jews.)

Shai, Donna
    1980   Changes in the Oral Tradition Among the
                Jews of Kurdistan. Contemporary Jewry
                5:1:2-10.

(Traces the social context of the Zakho oral tradition
from Kurdistan to Israel.)

Sabar, Yona
    1978   Multilingual Proverbs in the Neo-Aramaic
                Speech of the Jews of Zakho, Iraqui,
                Kurdistan. International Journal of
                Middle Eastern Studies 9:2:141-274.

(Provides additional documentation for our view of the
Kurdistani pluralism.)

Iran

Fischel, Walter J.
    1950   The Jews of Persia: 1795-1940. Jewish
                Social Studies 12:119-160.
    1953   Isfahan: The Story of a Jewish Community
                in Persia. In The Joshua Starr Memorial
                Volume. Jewish Social Studies Publication,
                Vol. V:111-128.
    1960   Israel in Iran: A Survey of Judeo-
                Persian Literature. In The Jews: Their
                History, Culture and Religion (L. Finkel-
                stein, ed.), Philadelphia: Jewish
                Publication Society of America, pp. 1149-
                1190.

(Fischel was the pioneer in the study of Iranian Jewish history and literature.)

Goldstein, Judith L.
    1980   The Jewish Miracle-Worker in a Muslim
                    Context. In Studies in Jewish Folklore
                    (F. Talmage, ed.). Cambridge, MA.:
                    Association for Jewish Studies, 137-152.

(An Iranian Jewish tale is examined in order to understand Jewish-Muslim relations.)

Loeb, Laurence D.
    1977   Outcaste: Jewish Life in Southern Iran.
                    London: Gordon and Breach.

(A comprehensive, albeit somewhat controversial, ethnography of the Jews of Shiraz during the 1960's.)

Turkey and the Balkans

Angel, Marc D.
    1978   The Jews of Rhodes. New York: Sepher-
                    Herman Press.

(A history with some ethnographic materials.)

Argenti, Philip
    1970   The Religious Minorities of Chios: Jews
                    and Roman Catholics. Cambridge: The
                    University Press.

(Part of a longer history of the Island of Chios.)

Armistead, Samuel G.
    1980   Recent Developments in Judeo-Spanish Ballad
                    Scholarship. In Studies in Jewish Folklore
                    (F. Talmage, ed.). Cambridge, MA.:
                    Association for Jewish Studies, 21-32.

(As two other contributions to the Folklore volume show, the study of the Ladino language and its ballads and tales have the main focus of scholarly attention dealing with this Jewish culture area. This is a good review of the literature.)

Benardete, Mair Jose
   1952   Hispanic Culture and the Character of the
                 Sephardic Jews. New York: Hispanic
                 Institute in the United States.

(An essay of the relationship of Ladino-speaking Sephardim
with their Spanish heritage.)

Friedenreich, Harriet Pass
   1979   The Jews of Yugoslavia: A Quest for
                 Community. Philadelphia: Jewish Publi-
                 cation Society.

(While good as an account of the interwar period, it only
deals sketchily with the Sephardic communities in that
country prior to their incorporation into the Austro-
Hungarian empire, and the new nation states.

ABOUT THE EDITORS

<u>Shlomo Deshen</u> is professor of anthropology at Bar Ilan University. He studied at the Hebrew University in Jerusalem; and received his Ph.D. in anthropology from the University of Manchester (England). He taught for many years at Tel Aviv University. Much of his research was concerned with the integration of North African Jews into Israeli society. He is currently engaged in the historical reconstruction of Jewish communal life in Middle Eastern countries. He is the author of many articles and books in English and Hebrew, beginning with <u>Immigrant Voters in Israel</u> (Manchester University Press). His book, <u>Individuals and the Community: Jewish Societies in 18th-19th Century Morocco</u>, is being published in Hebrew by Tel Aviv University.

<u>Walter P. Zenner</u> is associate professor of anthropology at the State University of New York at Albany. He received his Ph.D. in anthropology from Columbia University. Prior to that he studied at Northwestern University and the Jewish Theological Seminar of America. The theme of his research has been the ramifications of ethnicity. He has done field work with Syrian Jews in New York and Jerusalem, among other studies. He has co-edited <u>Urban Life: Readings in Urban Anthropology</u> (St. Martin's Press) and is currently writing a book comparing Jews with other minorities, as well as articles in professional journals.